Sport Business in the Global Marketplace

Sport Business in the Global Marketplace

Hans Westerbeek
and
Aaron Smith

Foreword by
Kevin Roberts
SportBusiness International

Published 2003 by
PALGRAVE MACMILLAN
Houndmills, Basingstoke, Hampshire RG21 6XS and
175 Fifth Avenue, New York, N.Y. 10010
Companies and representatives throughout the world

PALGRAVE MACMILLAN is the global academic imprint of the Palgrave Macmillan
division of St. Martin's Press, LLC and of Palgrave Macmillan Ltd. Macmillan is a
registered trademark in the United States, United Kingdom and other countries.
Palgrave is a registered trademark in the European Union and other countries.

ISBN 1–4039–0300–X

This book is printed on paper suitable for recycling and made from
fully managed and sustained forest sources.

A catalogue record for this book is available from
the British Library.

Library of Congress Cataloging-in-Publication Data

Westerbeek, Hans
    Sport business in the global marketplace / Hans Westerbeek & Aaron Smith.
        p. cm.
    Includes bibliographical references and index.
    ISBN 1–4039–0300–X (alk. paper)
    1. Sports—Economic aspects. 2. Sports—Marketing. 3. Globalization—
Economic aspects. I. Smith, Aaron. II. Title.
GV716.W46 2002
338.4′3796–dc21   2002075498

Copy-edited and typeset by Povey–Edmondson
Tavistock and Rochdale, England

10   9   8   7   6   5   4   3   2
12 11 10 09 08 07 06 05 04

Printed and bound in Great Britain by
Creative Print & Design (Wales), Ebbw Vale

Contents

Contents

List of Figures and Tables

Figures

Tables

When we launched *SportBusiness International* magazine in 1996 it was warmly welcomed by its intended audience – executives from many different business disciplines who do the deals and deliver the events which make sport the international phenomenon it has unquestionably become.

Outside that group there were quizzical expressions and a certain amount of head-scratching from those who simply hadn't considered the relationship between sport and business.

Of course, in the intervening years we have seen the sector gain acceptance and recognition. The editors of mainstream newspapers are only too delighted to run pictures of sports stars on their business pages if, for no other reason, they make a change from men in suits. There are television programmes devoted to sports and business, and commercial issues are discussed among fans nearly as often as the finer points of sport itself.

Perhaps it's not surprising that it had taken this long for sports business to become recognised as a specific commercial discipline. After all, the relationship between sport and business is never going to be an easy one. Some might even go so far as to suggest that in many respects the two are mutually incompatible.

Sport's attraction lies not simply in the appreciation of athletic excellence but in its essential lack of predictability: in the ability of the underdog to win out, for David to slay Goliath.

Business, on the other hand, is about controlling risk, eliminating uncertainty wherever possible to create the most advantageous environment for turning investment into profit.

Yet the reality is quite different and sports and business share many attributes. Anybody who has ever picked up a business textbook will testify to the common language. Business is competitive, it produces winners and losers and winning requires excellent teamwork and a degree of commitment, talent and unswerving focus which leading athletes commonly share with successful entrepreneurs. There should be no mystery as to why so many leading athletes supplement their not inconsiderable incomes as motivational speakers, using personal experience couched in the language of sport to inspire better performance from their corporate audiences.

And winners in business often want to be associated with sporting success. How many professional sports franchises around the world are owned by individuals who have carved out fortunes from commerce and wear their ownership as a badge of their financial success.

But the critical relationship between sport and business is centred on two things; the passion of fans and the ability of technology to make sport accessible. If one removes either pillar, the entire edifice crumbles.

A fan's passion for their favourite sports, teams and athletes is brand loyalty in a bottle which means that sport – to mangle a phrase coined by a well-known London theatre critic – is pure marketing Viagra.

The business of sport today is centred on the opportunities to leverage that passion. it extends from the promotion and management of events to ensure their widespread exposure via television and other media and selling the promotional and hospitality opportunities which are created.

Sounds simple doesn't it? Rest assured it's not.

It is made more difficult because sport exists in an intensely political environment, in which kindnesses are lavishly repaid and slights and misdeeds not easily forgotten. Outsiders can find it particularly difficult to gain entry.

And those who do can find it extraordinarily difficult to do business with organisations and individuals whose own perspective and experience is coloured by sporting rather than business considerations.

There are, for example, many stories in circulation about the penny-pinching which is common in leading European soccer clubs where the board of directors will smile as they write a cheque for $30 million to buy a new striker but deny the marketing manager $1,000 for some new software. A case of big business bucks coupled to small business attitudes perhaps?

That has to change. The exploitation of sport's commercial potential is undeniably linked to technology: in particular the convergence of broadcast and PCs, the ability to deliver information and pictures to mobile telephones, etc.

Technology has the potential to shift the balance of power in sport away from the major media companies and towards the clubs and athletes. It can make traditional borders and the notion of rights fees based on territories irrelevant. Technology can open up new markets and change the culture of sports consumption.

Yet if sport's commercial potential is to be realised, the sector must become ever more professional in its outlook and begin to understand more fully the forces which drive the sector and its impact on a changing world.

These are the challenges facing sports and the business of sport in the early years of the twenty-first century. In this fresh and insightful volume, Hans Westerbeek and Aaron Smith place the business of sport in context and examine the way it must respond to those challenges and how, in turn, that will impact on the cultural and even political life of hundreds of millions of people around the globe.

One of the authors' most significant achievements is that – despite the range and depth of their observations – they never lose sight of the one rock-solid certainty behind the business of sport – lose the balance of competition, the integrity of the event and you will lose the interest fans and you don't have a business at all. In that respect the business of sport is different from any other: the customer comes first.

KEVIN ROBERTS
Editorial Director
SportBusiness Group
www.sportbusiness.com

ACKNOWLEDGEMENTS

The creation of a book like this is not an easy undertaking. A number of people have, in one way or another, made sacrifices to allow this book to come to realisation. We must affirm our debt to these people for their contributions to what we feel has become an exciting work of 'crystal-ball gazing'.

Inspiration has come to us from academic and practical sources and via organisations and individuals. One such source of inspiration is Berend Rubingh, Manage to Manage founder, co-director and General Manager Europe. Throughout the last 15 years or so, Berend has transformed the way many European sport professionals think about the management and marketing of sport. Working with him as a colleague and as a business partner has been rewarding and enjoyable. We are grateful for his contribution to this book.

In our capacity as consultants and writers we have also enjoyed our partnership with the SportBusiness Group, in particular, through our collaboration with the Editorial Director Kevin Roberts. It was Kevin's initiative to create this unique partnership between a book publisher and a sport information broker. The many late night telephone conversations with Kevin, and working lunches in London which led to passionate discussions about the future directions of the sport business, have greatly benefited this book. As the reader might appreciate, SportBusiness publications have had a revolutionary impact upon the dissemination of information in this industry. Like most people employed in the global sport industry, we can scarcely imagine what life in the business of sport was like without the *SportBusiness International* publication, and the frequent citation of the magazine and special reports throughout this text bears testimony to its usefulness.

Although this book is designed to interest both sport managers and academics, we have ensured that its foundations are based upon empirical evidence wherever possible. We are therefore indebted to our academic colleagues at Deakin University, within the Bowater School of Management and Marketing, the Faculty of Business and Law, and the Centre for Business Research. In particular, we must acknowledge Professor David Shilbury, Head of the Bowater School, as a colleague and pioneer in sport management education and research in Australia, but also as a direct contributor to this book through his supervision of Hans' doctoral work. We would also like to thank John Deane and Paul Turner as long-time colleagues and 'sounding boards'.

Australia, despite its small population base and remoteness, has undoubtedly made its mark in the global sport business. This is largely due to the combined 'intellectual capital' that the Sport Management Association of Australia and New Zealand (SMAANZ) has gathered and cultivated. With its great outdoors, impressive range of hallmark events, vigorous sporting competitions and fervent sport-loving population, Australia has proven to be the perfect feeding ground for the development of sport business knowledge.

A leading scholar on sport and globalisation, Associate Professor Bob Stewart of Victoria University, and Colin Smith, Manage to Manage senior consultant, and one of Australia's foremost consultants on logistics, provided us with insightful and critical comments on the penultimate draft. Their critical feedback proved immensely valuable, and we are grateful for their time, energy and expertise.

Daniel Evans, our colleague with cutting edge expertise in regard to sport and the Internet, supplied us with the insights obtained from his research and consulting experience; Chapter 6 of this book largely reflects Daniel's pioneering work in that area.

We would also like to extend our appreciation to Stephen Rutt at Palgrave Macmillan. We are grateful for his professionalism and responsiveness. With the no-nonsense approach he has shown in bringing this project together, we can only look forward to future collaboration.

Thanks to Loes and Clare, our wives, partners, greatest critics and most ardent supporters.

HANS WESTERBEEK
AARON SMITH

The authors and publishers are grateful to the following for permission to reproduce copyright material: *Sport Management Review* for a diagram from H. M. Westerbeek and D. Shilbury (1999) 'Increasing the focus on "place" in the marketing mix for facility dependent sport services', *Sport Management Review*, 2(1), 1–23; Allen & Unwin for a table from A. Smith and B. Stewart (1999) *Sports Management*, Allen & Unwin, Sydney. Every effort has been made to contact all the copyright-holders but if any have been inadvertently omitted the publishers will bepleased to make the necessary arrangement at the earliest opportunity.

AFL	Australian Football League
AOL	America Online
ASEAN	Australia and South East Asian Nations
CEO	Chief Executive Officer
CONCACAF	Confederacion Norte-Centroamericana y del Caribe de Futbol
ECHL	East Coast Hockey League (USA)
ESPN	Entertainment and Sports Programming Network
FA	Football Association
FC	Football Club
FIFA	Federation of International Football Associations
GDP	Gross Domestic Product
IAAF	International Amateur Athletics Federation
IMF	International Monetary Fund
IMG	International Management Group
IOC	International Olympic Committee
ISP	Internet Service Provider
MCG	Melbourne Cricket Ground
MLB	Major League Baseball (USA)
NBL	National Basketball Association (USA)
NFL	National Football League (USA)
NHL	National Hockey League (USA)
NRL	National Rugby League (Australia)
NSL	National Soccer League (Australia)
OECD	Organisation for Economic Co-operation and Development
OG	Olympic Games
PC	personal computer
PGA	Professional Golf Association
SOCOG	Sydney Organising Committee for the Olympic Games
TQM	Total Quality Management
UEFA	Union Européenne de Football Associations
WAP	Wireless Application Protocol
WTO	World Trade Organisation

CHAPTER 1

S-commerce: Facing the Future of Sport Business

Rejoice, we conquer!
Pheidippides, Greek courier, 490BC
(after running from Marathon to Athens)

When did it all begin? When did sport become a business? For some commentators that moment came in the 1990s along with Michael Jordan, or even with the 1984 'McDonald's' Olympic Games in Los Angeles. For others it began as early as 1975, when International Management Group (IMG) founder Mark McCormack bragged, somewhat presciently that: 'We're by far the most powerful influence on sport in the world. We could turn any individual sport – golf, tennis, skiing – on its ear tomorrow. The position we hold in some of these sports is the ability to reconstruct the whole edifice.' That was two years after Mark Spitz, the US Olympic gold-medal winning swimmer claimed to be a 'commodity', and five years after Ali went toe to toe with 'Smoking' Joe Frazier for US$2.5 million each. It was twelve years after golf professional Doug Sanders mischievously suggested to Arnold Palmer that he 'ought to take a week off, just to count his money'.

Perhaps some of us could trace the beginnings of the sport business back even further. Phillip Wrigley, the legendary baseball club owner, lamented in 1956 that: 'Baseball is too much of a sport to be a business and too much of a business to be a sport.' Dutch football manager, Rinus Michels, was even less ambiguous: 'Football is a business now, and business is business.' In 1950, Sugar Ray Robinson's manager, George Gainsford, summed up the sentiment associated with professional boxing when he announced that, 'We are only interested in money. With us it is strictly a question of finance, not glory or anything silly like that.' Was this the beginning of business and sport's famous collision?

King Henry IV, from Shakespeare's hand, pronounced that: 'If all the year were playing holidays, to sport would be as tedious as work.' Was he right? Is there such a thing as too much sport? The light heavyweight, Harry Greb, asked (as only a boxer can), 'Shakespeare? What weight is he?' The truth is, despite the rampant and vigorous commercialisation of sport common in the new millennium, sport has never been entirely free from the vagaries of business. Even as early as 78BC, Gaius Maecenas warned of the dangers of 'misusing' vast sums of money to provide sporting infrastructure. He counselled: 'Cities should not waste their resources on expenditure for a large number and variety of games, lest they exhaust themselves in futile exertion and quarrel over unreasonable desire for glory.' The pseudo-professionalisation of athletes, the lever-aging of association benefits, the spectacle with 'bums on seats', and the exploitation for money, has been part of sport forever. When did sport become a business? Sport has always been a business and always will be.

Some say that the greatest human inventions were spoken and written language. For others it was the wheel, the printing press, gunpowder, the internal combustion engine, the computer chip or the lift.[1] It is impossible to deny the importance of these inventions. However, the most influential element in the evolution of human civilisation was not an invention, but a discovery: fire. Fire enabled us to discover and define our humanity, it provided us with a warm and safe 'home', it accelerated our progression in the external environment but it also allowed us to discover the fire that is within us. Unlike any other animal on the planet, humans are driven by the need to explore, progress and assess their place in the universe. Humans, to a certain extent, have taken matters into their own hands and have defined the world they live in according to their needs. Some of these needs, for example, are expressed in terms of religion, companion-ship or identity. At the very basis, however, lies our inclination to explore the world and satisfy a range of deep human needs through play, recreation and, ultimately, sport. Sport's importance, as structured and sometimes scripted play in human life, is therefore not adequately captured by the assumption that sport is merely a social invention. As Plato observed: 'What then is the right way of living? Life must be lived as a play, playing certain games, making sacrifices, singing and dancing, and then a man will be able to propitiate the gods, and defend himself against his enemies, and win the contest.' This book is therefore not about sport as an invention,[2] but sport as a discovery that can be used in a variety of ways, to the benefit or detriment of humans all around the world.

If sport's inherent significance is unquestioned, then its economic importance is, at the very least, noteworthy. The magnitude of the present global sports industry has scarcely ever been estimated, but in economic terms must run into the trillions. The truth is, no one knows. Sport, defined broadly to include physical leisure and recreational activities, plays a role in the lives of most of the world's population. There are few barriers to sport's consumption, either personally or vicariously; the need for organised physical activity is human. But where is sport going? Will the forces that are pressuring sport to change transcend its human needs, or will sport simply transform to meet different needs? What will sport bring us in the future? The aim of this book is to explore this future of sport business in the world.

Speculating about the future of sport might seem easy. Dream of the most fanciful technological contraption for bridging the gap between the sporting participant and observer, or increasing the excitement factor, and you are moving in the right direction. After all, is not sport spectating all about vicarious experience and excitement? Can we imagine the technology that allows us to create our own sport teams and play them off against each other? Can we conceive of a technology that allows us to sit in on the holographic sidelines of a World Cup qualifier or next to the starter in the final of the Olympic 100 metres? The truth is, most of us can envisage this level of technology and, for some of us, the leap is anticipated sooner rather than later. The issue is not whether the technology will be available (it undoubtedly will), or whether it will be implemented, but what ramifications it will have on the world of sport as we know it, since that world is already in the grip of a radical transformation from its traditions as independent, compartmentalised, parochial, religious, a folk or a military activity, to the blurred entertainment conglomeration it is today.

For some, the evolution of sport to its present incarnation has not been a happy journey. Sport in its purest sense was never conceived as a revenue raiser, and neither was it ever expected that the movement of an inflated animal skin would command the loyalty and the emotional and financial commitment of millions of otherwise conservative and rational individuals. The location professional sport finds itself in is not the end of the journey either. The question remains then, where will sport ultimately find itself?

Our argument is that sport and entertainment will continue to blur together into indistinguishable commodities where actors and athletes, directors and coaches, will blend in both their activities and their perception, driven by the inexorable progress of technology, and held together by the glue of a changing emotion-based economy. However, we go beyond this trend analysis to present a range of alternative scenarios.

We have encapsulated our approach to this book in Figure 1.1. We begin, later in this chapter, by examining the potential impact of globalisation over the next few decades, and its likely impact upon sport.

In Chapter 2, we explore how it all began by taking a brief look at the history of sport and the factors that have cemented its place in contemporary life, including the motivations and behaviour of that elusive breed, the sports fan. Having considered how sport came to be what we know it as today, we examine the architecture of sport in Chapter 3, and provide the platform for an exploration of the commercial side of sport in Chapter 4. In some cases, we are not presenting anything new or radical in our picture of the future of sport. We believe that trend projections are, all other things being equal, the best methods of foreshadowing the future. At the same time, however, we acknowledge that all things are not always equal, and it is therefore prudent in any futuristic analysis to consider those factors which are both unpredictable and pivotal in shaping world events. We have noted that there are several of these shaping factors at the nexus of alternative futures. The first to be considered is the role of the global economy, particularly the evolution of the service sector. We

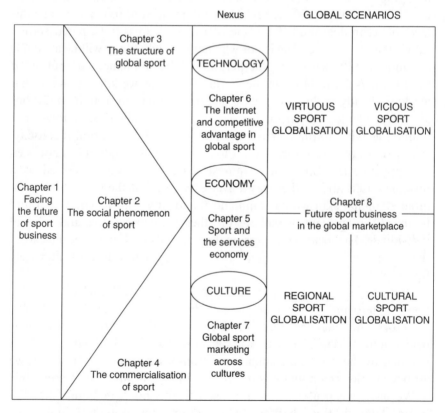

Figure 1.1 Sport business in the global marketplace

consider this in Chapter 5. Technology, especially the Internet, is explored as the second nexus in Chapter 6, followed by an examination of the possible impact of culture in Chapter 7.

We therefore explore the history, current situation and trends that define the sport world today, and present three nexus factors that will determine how these trends ultimately manifest themselves through sport in the future. Thus, after we look at the expansion of globalisation, the raging development of commercialism, the place of technology, the crossover with entertainment, the nature of the economy, the importance of the Internet and the impact of culture, this book concludes with a range of alternative future sport scenarios: virtuous sport globalisation, vicious sport globalisation, regional sport globalisation and cultural sport globalisation. Along with a set of key uncertainties that may help explain the characteristics of 'future sport', the implications of sport-commerce (s-commerce) as a vast industrial sector, economic powerhouse, and arena of political power plays are established.

Given that this book considers the likely future of sport business, it tends towards an analysis of professional (or at least commercialised) sport. That is not to suggest that participation-based sport is any less important. However, we will consistently argue that the humble sport participant is not (yet) deciding the fate of the business side of sport. This book is not just about the rampant spread of Westernised consumer capitalism that always seems to be blamed on McDonald's or Coca-Cola. Naomi Klein wrote a book, which she called *No Logo*, about the ubiquity of consumer capitalism and the series of difficulties and exploitations it brings with it. In some ways this book is all about logos as well, because the future of sport will be full of them and their accoutrements.

Globalisation Trends

It has been said that we are each defined by that which we fear and by that which we desire. In few places only is this more applicable than in the 'new economy'. Judging by the number of mass demonstrations that have taken place in various cities throughout the world over the past few years, we might be forgiven for believing that humankind is divided by both the fear of, and the desire for, the transition from a national to a global economy. Regardless, however, of personal feelings, it appears that (barring some major catastrophe) we are destined to be a part of the seemingly inexorable move to globalisation.

According to the International Monetary Fund (IMF), 'globalisation' refers to the increasing integration of economies around the world, particularly through trade and financial interaction, and includes also the movement of people or labour, and knowledge or technology, across borders. It has occurred as a result of human innovation and technological progress, particularly in the field of communications. In the minds of individuals, though, there are further cultural, political and environmental dimensions that are thrown in with the term.

Globalisation as a concept is neither new nor challenging, and refers only to the increasing degree of cross-border interaction that first began when borders were originally defined. While the word itself is limited in its usefulness, it has become synonymous in the minds of protesters with a new world order. This new order has been greeted with an extraordinary mixture of reactions ranging from exhilaration to terror. These reactions are often embedded in myth, foreshadowing and speculation rather than in fact, trend and probability.

Globalisation has affected more than just economies. Among other things it has affected culture. For example, music, art, literature and language have all crossed borders and have increasingly done so since long before globalisation became a fashionable word. They have not been alone. Sport, too, has crossed borders. Its journey probably began millennia ago as war and conflict spread from village to village, city to city, and nation to nation. Over the past decades sport has probably been the element of culture that has progressed further, fastest. Spurred on by ego, individual and national, sport has crossed virtually every border. Disseminated through radio and television, sport has become universal. As it has become universal, men and women have taken a far keener interest in its progress and viability for they have been quick to notice that the growth of sport held great possibilities for making money. It is to help understand this concept of sport as a business that this book has been written.

To understand sport as a business where should we begin? Since we began this section by suggesting the premise that globalisation was a major forerunner of the growth of sport business this seems a useful starting point.

The Drivers of Globalisation

In December 2000 the United States National Intelligence Council published a report examining global scenarios for the forthcoming decades (*Global Trends 2015*).[3] The report was the result of a study, which commissioned prominent academics and intelligence personnel to provide a detailed review of potential world trends and their implications. The results of the report portray a stark picture of the world and suggest that Western nations may be the principal beneficiaries as the wealth gap between developed and developing nations stretches.

In producing their report the Intelligence Council considered a wide range of factors affecting the global scenario. As many of these factors equally affect the business of sport we would like to pick up on several of them and to add additional factors of our own. These factors are, we believe, the truly important drivers of change. While not the cause of globalisation these drivers of change contain within them many of the elements that have allowed globalisation to spread almost unfettered. Because the topic of globalisation enhances the best of desires yet brings out the worst of fears, we need to ensure that our discussion retains objectivity and cannot be presented as either supporting or rejecting globalisation. To this end, we have chosen to use existing data and the trend that this data suggests as the basis for discussion. The drivers that we have selected to examine are:

- economy
- technology
- social conscience, resources and natural environment
- demography
- governance
- conflict and war
- religion and cultural identity

Underlying all of these drivers is the single concept that humans initiate change, in whatever forms it may take. In many ways, this concept accounts for why we experience our desire or fear. It is the belief that changes have been imposed upon us by the decisions of others that fuels our discomfort. Yet it is important to recognise that few change drivers are uncontrollable. In essence, this means that collectively, we have within us the ability to change the direction in which we proceed. Thus, while the trend data may clearly signify the direction in which we are moving, there is always the opportunity for an additional unknown factor to intervene and to change our direction. This may be a new technological break-through, conflict or war, or simply a desire on enough people's part to move off the designated pathway.

While individual drivers each play a role, none is anticipated to have an exclusive impact on the future. In the context of sport business, some are more influential than others. These more influential factors we have termed 'nexus' factors, and we will discuss these in greater detail later in the book. Our chosen method of discussing change drivers is first to consider them in the general context of globalisation, both now and in the future, and then to discuss them more specifically in relation to the way in which they are likely to affect sport and sport business. This will be done for each of the drivers individually.

Economy

Despite the twin drags of the US recession and the September 11 attacks on New York and Washington, the world economy remains in vibrant condition. The 1990s and the early years of this century brought perhaps the longest period of economic growth since the Second World War. Agreed, that growth is not uniform throughout the world. Japan, for example, still suffers from deflation and it is unlikely that the economy there will grow for several more years. In addition, a number of countries in Europe, particularly Germany and France, have only recently begun to record significant growth figures again, while parts of South America, especially Argentina, are still poised on the precipice of disaster. Nonetheless, the Organisation for Economic Co-operation and Development (OECD) considers that the downturn in world growth will bottom out during the latter part of the year 2002, and from there will slowly, but consistently, move back towards stronger growth.

Despite being patchy, the growth in the overall world economy has been a significant benefit to almost everyone. One of the remarkable reasons for this has to do with a vast increase in the number of free trade agreements between nations. The World Trade Organisation has recently admitted China as a member and in the next few years is likely to admit Russia. The European economic union is on the verge of major expansion, the North American Free Trade Agreement is set to expand, and there is every likelihood of further free trade agreements between Southeast Asian nations. The growth in free trade agreements will not proceed smoothly, but it will proceed. And as it does so, globalisation will become ever more prevalent and visible.

As the globalised economy takes hold, the transmission of ideas, values, products and people will become more evident. The electronic transmission of information will make even the least industrialised countries aware of everything that is going on around them. No country will remain an island. That this may cause some leaders to be fearful and to take every opportunity of rejecting the spread of information. The likelihood is that in general it will increase political stability throughout the world. However, as we shall highlight later, the news is not all good for political certainty and global goodwill. Dependent upon how it is handled, the widespread breakdown in trade barriers may cause some countries or regions to initially respond by seeking illegal or non-acceptable means of protecting their industries. America has done this with its steel industry, and Europe has done it with agriculture. These illegal barriers to free trade will end up being judged by the World Trade Organisation. Unfortunately, many small countries have little sway with the WTO and for some years to come these smaller nations are likely to suffer most from this aspect of globalisation.

Several factors will combine to provide an attractive foundation for the winners of globalisation. On the whole, they will deliver economic dynamism and growth. First, the trend with macroeconomic policy is towards improvement. For example, as a generalisation, inflation rates are currently lower than at any time over the past 40 years. In addition, exchange rates now have more flexibility to move than at almost any time in the past. Increasingly, the euro, and perhaps to lesser extent the yen, are providing opportunities for trade to be undertaken, and paid for, in currencies other than the United States dollar.

Second, trade and investment will continue to increase. For most countries this will mean an improved Gross Domestic Product (GDP) and opportunities to diversify trade partners. For emerging market nations in particular, this should provide an opportunity to expand their export revenues. Venture capital should become more available.

Third, the dissemination of information technology is likely to produce significant advances in economic production for a handful of well-established nations such as the United States, Japan and some countries in Western Europe. Although gains will occur, in some cases at relatively faster rates than in developed nations, integration of cutting-edge technology will improve production, distribution and trade opportunities in leading countries. The prerequisites of effective information technology integration will not be as prevalent in many developing regions. Essential infrastructure and educational opportunities, together with research and development investment, will be limiting factors. In developed nations, the sustained levels of technology utilisation will continue to rise.

Finally, the development of private sectors in emerging market economies points to some opportunities in the globalised economy. Further deregulation and privatisation in Japan and Europe will also add to the growth of the global private sector, and should, through increased competitive pressure, stimulate economic progress and growth.

Regrettably, as we have indicated, not everyone will be a winner. The nations that remain most vulnerable to falling behind from a growth standpoint are those with limited economic diversification. Predominantly, this means that some nations in sub-Saharan Africa, the Middle East, Central Asia and parts of South America may struggle to progress their economies.

As the world economy – the global economy – becomes more integrated, its collective resilience will be bolstered against disruption and collapse. This is not to suggest that the road will be a smooth one for globalisation. Economic crises will occur nevertheless, irrespective of whether they are politically, currency or commodity related, and the more integrated global systems of commerce will cope better than in the past. While there will be an integrated framework, there is little evidence that individual nations will stop using economic growth as the principal determinant of progress and prosperity. Although cosmetically the measure would seem to value the health of an economy by assessing its performance output, the concept makes the invalid assumption that this increased affluence will be equally distributed amongst the citizens of a country. Thus, economic growth, or GDP, does not take into account the gap between the wealthy and the wealth-less, and neither does it distinguish between activities that add value to a national community and those that sacrifice future standards of living. Depleting natural resources, for example, in order to enhance short-term economic progress, no more adds to genuine wealth than does a property owner selling his or her home and living in the street with pockets full of cash.

Sport and the economy

What, then, do these trends suggest in terms of the future and the business of sport? First, and perhaps most important, the breakdown in the economic frontiers between nations will allow sport to become more widespread, to gather more fans, and to present the opportunity for greater business development. Second, more effective and stable macroeconomic policy should contribute positively to the sustainability of sports enterprises by allowing businesses to calculate income and expenditure more readily. This is particularly important in Asian and South American countries where currency fluctuations have challenged domestic professional competitions to attract overseas players or to expand geographically.

Globalisation will also bring with it the availability of larger amounts of venture capital. This is likely to allow more frequent forays into Asian, and to a lesser extent South American sport. Not only will these emerging market nations benefit from greater interest from venture capitalists, businesses and entrepreneurs, but the opportunity should be provided to expand domestic leagues, clubs and events as well as exporting local sporting products.

The spread of information technology will increase not only recognition of new and existing sports but, more importantly, should allow for the widespread use of training programmes and training techniques. No longer will individual sportsmen and women have to travel overseas in order to access the most modern training approaches. They will be available initially through video and shortly thereafter through interactive computer simulation.

Where government-driven sport organisations have been unresponsive and inflexible in the past to consumer needs, opportunities will exist for private enterprise to establish lucrative businesses based on existing models. The Asian market, for example, is capable from a demographic viewpoint of supporting several local equivalents of Manchester United or the Dallas Cowboys.

As economic growth increases GDP, discretionary leisure time and income is likely to increase. In the richer countries improved infrastructure and greater diversity of sports will provide business opportunities. In less wealthy countries the opportunity will exist to develop sporting prowess either in inexpensive, high participation sports such as soccer, or in niche sports such as futbal (beach/indoor soccer) or hockey. Inevitably, some countries will fall further behind in the provision of physical infrastructure and this may limit opportunities to host hallmark events or to sustain professional competitions. The gaps in the standard of sporting performance and levels of professionalism will continue to widen the division between developed nations' leagues, clubs and events, and those in developing countries. To some extent, however, the development of interactive computer simulations will overcome these problems.

Some exciting sporting opportunities may be found in what has become known as 'emerging Asia'. China and India together already contribute one-sixth of the world's GDP and one-third of the world's individual consumers. Naturally, the sporting development necessitated by China's acquisition of the Olympic Games will provide a stimulus for sport in that region. More and more Western firms, including entrepreneurial sporting leagues, clubs, marketers and event managers, will attempt to capitalise upon access to China's extraordinary population. Pepsi, for example, pay around US$6 million to be naming rights sponsors of the China Football Association National Football League. With the stars of the league receiving around US$100,000 for a season, the league will have to be cautious about losing their best players to European or South American leagues.

Similarly, India's democracy and English-language friendly market make it an attractive proposition for Western sport enterprises. Despite horrendous numbers of impoverished citizens, the country is well-placed to capitalise upon its own size and sporting passion. For example, approximately 300 million Indians tune in their radios or watch on television their cricket champion, Sachin Tendulkar, each time he strides to the crease. The several million dollars he receives for the unassuming advertising sticker on his bat is relatively modest given the exposure it receives all around the world.

While the economic performance gap between Western Europe and the United States will diminish, the effect of globalisation will be variable on sporting enterprises. The entrenched, well-distributed, technologically-supported sporting clubs and leagues will flourish, expanding their tentacles to parts of the world that have hitherto never experienced fully-professional marketing and merchandising. Strategic alliances between powerful clubs are likely to drive the shape of sporting leagues, such as those that established an alternative super-league for European basketball (which was perhaps premature and has since returned to uneasy cooperation with the existing competition) and those which are pushing for various forms of European Soccer 'Super' Leagues.

Other, more creative alliances are likely to be established which leverage the participants' entry into otherwise distant markets. The collaboration between the New York Yankees and Manchester United is a good example of this likely trend, although globalisation offers the opportunity for these forms of strategic partnerships to be established with much smaller organisations, which desperately need to expand away from their densely competitive geographical bases.

As Western Europe continues to offer sporting opportunities, especially for well-established organisations, Eastern Europe will clamour to cooperate and integrate. Driven by the promise of European Union membership, Eastern economies will hasten their affiliations with the West at all levels, including facilitating the removal of entry barriers for sport into the West. Genuine European leagues will form and the money that the participating clubs will receive as a consequence of their involvement will provide the opportunity for additional infrastructure development. The prospects for Russia, however, will remain unattractive for quite some time to come since their lack of sporting infrastructure, regulated competitions and security will encourage their best athletes to move West.

Japan, the economic powerhouse of the 1980s and early 1990s has decreased in global importance. The possibilities for Japanese sporting clubs, leagues and events are more promising though, but may peak temporarily after the 2002 soccer World Cup. However, despite its developed economy, Japan will remain as vulnerable as Australia, South America and the rest of Asia to merely providing feeder structures for professional athletes to be headhunted into North American and European professional competitions.

Uneven growth and development can also be expected in the Latin American region. For the more successful countries, such as Mexico, a new generation of entrepreneurial sport activities will be encouraged. Gradually, these countries will become more appealing as locations for international hallmark sporting events and for the provision of more differentiated sport programming by content-starved media giants tired of paying over the odds for established sports and increasingly willing to champion 'new' sport products.

Similarly, the Middle East and North Africa will surge inconsistently towards greater integration of their economies within the globalised context. While sporting infrastructure is likely to improve in many of these nations, they will remain a less-attractive location for the hosting of major events. It will be political stability rather than economic prowess that will determine the sporting fate of this region. From both an economic and a sporting viewpoint, the possibilities for sub-Saharan Africa are significantly limited. Conflicts, famine, lack of educational infrastructure, disease and autocracy will quash economic progress and sporting opportunity. Survival will remain the cornerstone activity.

The economic communities that currently dominate are likely to continue into the globalised future. The axiom that the rich get richer and the poor poorer will hold at both an intra-national and international level. This axiom will also hold true for sport. Nowhere can this trend be seen more clearly than in the exorbitant salaries of players in the most lucrative and popular of sports, including the big four professional leagues in the United States, national soccer leagues in Europe and South America, motor racing, boxing, tennis, basketball and golf.

For example, in 2000, the world's highest-paid athlete was Michael Schumacher, who received US$59 million for driving his Ferrari to a world Formula One Championship. In some ways, the more amazing figure is golf's number one player, Tiger Woods, who had a remarkable season in 2000, winning three out of four majors. The staggering issue was that his Professional Golf Association (PGA) tour prize money accounted for only US$9 million of his US$53 million total salary, which was substantially bolstered by endorsement income. The controversial boxer, Mike Tyson brought in US$48 million ahead of the now reborn, but then still retired, Michael Jordan who received US$37 million for just being 'Michael'.

Some other major earners included: Grant Hill, US$26 million; Dale Earnhardt, US$24.5 million; Shaquille O'Neal, US$24 million; Lennox Lewis and Oscar De La Hoya, US$23 million; Martina Hingis, US$11 million; Anna Kournikova and Venus Williams, US$10 million; Serena Williams, US$7.5 million; and Lindsay Davenport, US$6 million.

In 2001, the average National Football League (NFL) player's salary amounted to US$1.17 million, US$1.48 million in the National Hockey League (NHL), US$2.27 million in Major League Baseball (MLB), and as can already be observed in the list above, the National Basketball Association (NBA) pays the highest average salary with US$4.20 million. In 2002, the heavyweight boxing champion, Lennox Lewis, defended against Mike Tyson for a reported US$25 million each.

Some commentators have even gone so far as to rate the value of athletes on the basis of their performance to salary ratio. *Forbes*, for example, created a list of the top ten highest-paid soccer players in 2000 and evaluated their relative value by calculating the impact they have on the team as measured by action statistics such as passes and shots. While it may be overkill to suggest that statistical weightings are the most effective measures of a player's calibre, the results are at least illuminating. *Forbes* determined that Recoba, whose US$7.2 million salary was the highest in soccer, offered the worst value on the list. Zidane, on the other hand, with a salary of US$4.8 million, represented the most productive player and the one offering the best value. *Forbes* divided each player's productivity score by his salary to determine his value, as reproduced in Table 1.1.

The *Forbes* value list might have proved itself prescient in determining the fate of these players. More recent figures published in *Sport Business International* magazine in July 2001 provided the information shown in Table 1.2.

Perhaps the most illuminating fact about the list in Table 1.2 is that, by the time this book is published, it will be out of date. While the reader might forgive the authors for this, it is illustrative of the economic imperatives of professional football in all its codes around the world. In European football, for example, players are traded like commodities; the revenues generated prop up cash-strapped clubs. Like a new computer, any list concerning salaries and players becomes obsolete shortly after its creation.

Table 1.1 *Forbes* value list

Player (club in April 2001)	Annual salary ($million)	*Forbes* value rating
1 Zinedine Zidane (Juventus)	4.8	323
2 Alessandro Del Piero (Juventus)	4.8	309
3 Luis Figo (Real Madrid)	4.8	272
4 Hernan Crespo (Lazio Roma)	4.8	264
5 Rivaldo (Barcelona)	5.71	234
6 Steve McManaman (Real Madrid)	4.5	198
7 Gabriel Batistuta (Roma)	5.52	186
8 Alen Boksic (Middlesborough)	4.8	174
9 Raul Gonzalez (Real Madrid)	5.76	150
10 Alvaro Recoba (Inter Milan)	7.2	135

Source: Adapted from David Dikcevich (2001), 'Most Soccer Star For The Buck', www.forbes.com, 4 October 2001.

Table 1.2 Soccer's top earners

Player	Club	Annual salary ($ millions)
Zhinedine Zidane	Real Madrid	11.6
Garbiel Batistuta	Roma	8.6
Ronaldo	Inter Milan	7.4
Raul	Real Madrid	7.3
Alessandro Del Piero	Juventus	7.23
Rivaldo	Barcelona	7.12
Christian Vieri	Inter Milan	7.11
Hidetoshi Nakata	Roma	6.72
Luis Figo	Real Madrid	6.44
David Beckham	Manchester United	6.01
Francesco Totti	Roma	4.18

Source: Sport Business International, July 2001.

One interesting study conducted by Matthew Weeks attempted to ascertain the most significant determinants of NBA players' salaries, using a statistical technique known as regression analysis. Basically Weeks was trying to see if players' game statistics were a reflection of economic value. He used statistics such as minutes, points, rebounds and assists per game with a view to getting a feel for whether the salaries were more a measure of popularity or actual talent. Without getting into the limitations of this approach, it is interesting to hypothesise that a player's statistics could have a positive effect on his salary. Certainly, it would be reasonable to expect that such a positive relationship does exist.

More interesting is the fact that the results demonstrated that 'points per game' is the primary statistic that determines a player's salary. However, it only accounted for around 50 per cent of the variance. In other words, a player's popularity, his agent's impact, the additional income he brings to the team through endorsements, defensive capability and other qualitative factors obviously play a significant role in the athlete's salary.

The trend towards greater athlete salaries, and the ongoing divide between the sport 'haves' and 'have nots', is almost certain to continue to widen, although there are examples of well-established leagues (such as Serie A soccer in Italy) where salary differentiation continues despite the ill-health of the overall competition. In fact, European football continues to struggle with the challenges presented by player salaries as a percentage of overall club revenues. According to the United European Football Association (UEFA), the total cost of players as a percentage of turnover is getting dangerously high. In Italy, for example, the costs have risen as high as 125 per cent, while in Scotland, Spain and France the costs are approaching 100 per cent. It is little wonder that clubs are asking for higher player-transfer fees. A study by Deloitte Touche Sport revealed that there is a direct relationship between the average league finishing position and the wages and salaries bill of clubs participating in the English Premier League. The 'richest' club in the world (as measured by total revenue), Manchester United, tops the list in both salaries and position. Nevertheless, in general within countries, already well-established professional sports will flourish and expand, acquiring a greater and greater share of funding sources such as sponsorship. Money will also flow more naturally to elite sports rather than those encouraging participation and health. On an international level, the few national sporting leagues and competitions that have earned genuine international exposure, such as the Olympic Games, the American national basketball, football, ice-hockey and baseball leagues, the European Champions League football, the world cups of soccer, cricket and rugby union, the Grand Slams of tennis and golf, Formula One motor racing and a handful of world championships, will enjoy greater penetration in international markets, and draw the majority of sponsorship revenue. Moreover, the super-clubs and athletes associated with these sports will find themselves with passionate supporters and, more importantly, will bring consumers of merchandise and pay-television viewing from the most distant geographical positions. Where the potential support for the Los Angeles

Lakers NBA club is limited in the United States to the residents of California and expatriate residents now in other states, there is no such geographic limitation in countries such as New Zealand, Japan and the Netherlands. It is not unusual to see Shaquille O'Neal's jersey in the streets of Auckland, Tokyo or Amsterdam. Of the million or so hits received each year by the Lakers' website, the majority have their origins off-shore.

Although globalisation is usually perceived from an economic perspective, few drivers of change have had more impact than the power of information vehicles such as the Internet. These drivers are considered in the following section.

Technology

As the industrial age got under way in the early 1800s, there was only minimal brand-naming of items or advertising. Certainly they existed, but were limited by lack of exposure and the lack of national advertising opportunities. By the mid-1800s, the largest selling national newspaper in Britain, if not the world, was *The Times*, and even that had a daily circulation run of only around 55,000 copies. Most daily newspapers had a circulation of only 2–3,000. The expansion of railway networks throughout the world in the second half of the nineteenth century, together with the growth of the telegraphic system, revolutionised transportation and information systems, just as the motor vehicle, aeroplane and computer did in the twentieth century. The new millennium promises much in terms of technological advancement. The purpose of this section is not to join the list of crystal-ball gazers, but to determine the future of science and technology by extrapolating the known trends and anticipated developments. Naturally, the commentary is skewed to consider those issues that might have the most significant impact on the prosperity of sport business throughout the world.

Several trends must be considered certain to continue into the next few decades, each of which will have a monumental impact on the global community: first, the ongoing integration of scientific developments; second, the continued spread of information technology; third the rapid, vertical development of a range of specialty technologies; and finally, the strong lateral spread of existing technologies.

Integration is a theme that runs through globalisation and the future. The integration of the economy, as we have argued, will not necessarily lead to the social integration of humankind or, indeed, to economic parity between individuals or countries. Similarly, technological integration is unlikely to provide opportunities to bridge the technological gap between individuals and countries. However, the trend for ongoing integration does suggest that increasingly technology will be designed with multi-purpose applications in mind. For example, an entire household might be integrated through an Internet-like computer network that controls access to everything from leisure content to toasters and ovens. This vision of the future has been anticipated for a long time. The question has become less about how and why, and more about when, particularly for Western nations. For the most part, the technological sophistication required for this vision to materialise is available, but has neither been strongly demanded by consumers, nor has yet been adequately supported by the essential infrastructure, such as broadband and cable technologies.

Existing technology tends to be overlooked when addressing the future. It seems we are quick to render working and useful technology obsolete, and seek to move into the newer, sexier products. To assume a radical changeover of technology ignores the firmly established trend data. Rather than radical transformations of technology (although the relative speed of uptake is increasing and, compared with earlier last century is extraordinarily rapid) it is more likely that developments in technology will also be strongly lateral as well as vertical. In other words, established technologies will probably move into new markets and be used in new applications.

Slowly information technology will, of course, penetrate parts of nations and regions that have hitherto been inaccessible or cost ineffective. But, as with the economic prospects associated with globalisation, technology distribution and access will not be an equitable process. Some regions and nations will fail to benefit from the information revolution. Among developing countries, India will pioneer information technology distribution.

Like India, China will lead the developing world in the utilisation of existing, if not cutting-edge, information technology. However the political control of information technology usage and content is inevitably an impossible task given the prodigious numbers of potential users. Other major growth markets will include some countries in South America. Specifically, the countries with strong existing telecommunications infrastructures will profit the most from information technology diffusion. Argentina, Brazil and Mexico are likely to be the greatest beneficiaries. In the developed world, the United States, Japan and Western Europe will continue to lead the invention and introduction of new information technologies.

Perhaps the most daunting impacts of technological innovation are found in those sciences that 'tamper' with nature. Biotechnological advances have placed genetic profiling and engineering firmly into the public domain. It is no longer a subject to be explored in prophetic science fiction films such as *Gattaca*, but an indisputable reality, which is so new that it has caught us all unaware, without moral positions and without legislative protection.

Genomic profiling, the science of decoding genetic structures in order to identify the basis of pathology, is leading the medical establishment to ascertain the genetic antecedents of disease. Without doubt, this science will have a profound effect on the treatment of formerly unconquerable diseases. It has also, of course, led to cloning of animals and the potential for cloning human beings.

Sport and technology

The integration of technology will not necessarily lead to equal opportunities for sporting organisations in different parts of the world, but will provide some, albeit uneven opportunities. For example, the use of the Internet to broadcast live sport is becoming more frequent as cable and broadband technology becomes more commonplace and inexpensive. Small sport organisations have the opportunity to capitalise on these types of technologies which are not exclusive to mega-sport clubs and organisations. We can expect integration to deliver new types of communication channels for sports to distribute their wares. In addition, as existing hardware becomes assimilated into new technologies, the opportunities for sports viewers in some parts of the world will advance.

For example, old, 'mundane' television will continue to spread through Asia and Africa, opening up some areas for the first time to international sporting events and games, some of which will be entirely unfamiliar. In addition, software for analysing sport performance, for instance, will gradually catch up with innovations in computer hardware. Put bluntly, there is still plenty of the world that can be introduced to new sporting experiences without the need for the latest technologies. Whether some countries can afford to acquire the rights to some of sport's biggest events and leagues is another matter.

For example, the NFL has secured the largest television deal in sport. It is an eight-year agreement totalling US$17.6 billion. In fact, it is so large that it can only be realised as a result of four separate contracts with four television networks: Fox, CBS, ESPN and ABC, ESPN's parent company (ESPN stands for Entertainment and Sports Programming Network). For some networks, the financial commitment has proved too much, but the danger for networks is losing out on the phenomenal ratings that the sport seems to produce. As a series, it is the highest rating television aired in the United States. For example, the network holding the coveted rights to the Superbowl receives around US$2.2 million for a 30-second advertisement which is approximately $75,000 for each second of advertising time.

It seems unlikely that any independent network in an emerging country would be able to raise the sort of money required to access mainstream American sport. The most likely scenario (and the present trend) is for one of the multinational media companies such as News Corporation or AOL (America Online) Time Warner, to enter the market and provide access to the programming they already own at no cost.

It also seems unlikely that clubs competing in leagues based in emerging countries will be able to compete with American and European clubs in terms of marketing and promotions. Teams in the NFL, to continue the example, receive an equal split of 95 per cent of the broadcasting revenues, or around US$71 million each per annum. Add to that a share of gate receipts which is divided 66–34 per cent in favour of the home team, sponsorships, revenues from corporate hospitality suites and merchandising, and it can be seen that NFL teams have a substantial operating base from which to conduct business. For most teams, however, up to 75 per cent of that revenue is paid out in salaries to players. In fact, the NFL Players Union industrial agreement ensures that a minimum of 63.5 per cent of a team's gross revenues has to be returned as player salaries.

There is a similar attempt at equitable distribution of broadcasting monies in the English Premier League. Half of the total revenue is divided evenly between all teams in the league, 25 per cent is allocated as a facility fee in payment for the number of matches televised, and the remainder is allocated on merit, reflecting the final positions of the clubs in the league at the conclusion of the season.

Rapid diffusion of information technology through the sporting world will occur largely because hardware costs have dropped radically. National sport federations can link up with their international colleagues via email and Internet. Soon, wireless connectivity to the Internet via handheld devices will become less prohibitive in cost, and more attractive in functionality. It goes without saying that the capacity to watch sport or receive an update on a sport score from anywhere in the world is an appealing prospect to many sport fans. Large numbers of low cost, low altitude satellites are expected to be launched in the next decade, which will improve access and performance, while further diminishing current expensive mobile (cellular) and international telephone charges. The serious beginning of wireless sport applications has arrived. Telecommunications companies are now racing to establish first-mover advantages in the delivery of real time sport scores and delayed replays of important sporting moments, in the form of compressed digital data that can play short bursts of LCD video on the new generation of mobile phones.

In addition to Western nations, a handful of developing countries are well placed to capitalise upon technological opportunities. Their vast numbers of high-tech workers, combined with an increasing penchant for entrepreneurial activity, bodes favourably for the professionalism of Indian sport organisations, for instance. However, they still have a considerable gap to overcome. Despite eclipsing England and Australia in the numbers of cricket participants and spectators, the Indian Cricket Board remains an essentially volunteer organisation. In contrast, the English and Australian cricket authorities employ between 20 and 60 professional administrators each within their national governing bodies.

In addition to India, China and South America offer outstanding, if uncertain, markets for sporting organisations to introduce strategically crafted penetration strategies. In many cases, these strategies are so well supported by technology that they may require little more than a customised, language-specific website. Certainly, technological diffusion offers opportunities for expansion that have never before been contemplated. The question remains, however, whether sport organisations that fail even to generate a following in domestic markets have the potential to interest other markets.

Among the greatest challenges for sport in the future is the overcoming of the bottleneck of distribution that has been created by new forms of communication such as the Internet, as well as the availability of sport content via free-to-air and pay-television. Historically, innovations in distribution, production and communication have brought additional, cheaper products to the market and retail distribution systems have become increasingly jammed, forcing new ways of managing the flow of products. The log-jam of traditional production and distribution has largely been overcome, but the introduction of the Internet has created the next generation of this familiar problem. The impact of the Internet is so significant that Chapter 6 has been devoted to investigating its role in sport fully. In particular, the chapter tackles the subject with a strong consideration of the strategic usage of the technology in sporting organisations.

The possibility of engineering super-human athletes for sporting contests – another commonly imagined possibility – is almost certainly upon us. As the consequences of a group of super-humans in sport are perhaps more of a sociological question than a technological trend, we shall leave this discussion for more qualified commentators. However, the developments in genomic profiling and biomedical engineering have some other practical impacts upon sport. The treatment of sport-related injuries is a pivotal element in sport clubs' activities. At the most interventionist, biotechnology in medicine is likely to lead to the 'growth' of replacement human limbs and organs, the engineering of cells designed to replace dysfunctional constituents in the body such as in blindness or hearing loss, and will ultimately provide mechanisms for overcoming spinal injury and paralysis. While perhaps not of direct consequence to the twisted ankle or wrenched knee common in sport, the flow of knowledge from these cutting-edge sciences will have a profound effect on injury management in elite and participation sport. We are not far away from surgery one day and playing the next. Who knows, perhaps it will be easier to amputate a leg with a ruptured anterior cruciate knee ligament and replace it with a new limb, grown in a bio-chamber from the athlete's own DNA.

Developments in what is known as nanotechnology (what we may understand in lay terms as the science of the building blocks of matter), are also set to provide some interesting opportunities for sports, and professional sports in particular. Nanotechnology can provide quantum-sized computer chips that can diagnose ailments, identify specific athletes amongst groups, determine their nutritional and training requirements, specify their genetic structures and even confirm their drug-free status.

In addition to genetic manipulation, bioengineering and the range of barely imaginable developments probable in the next few decades, the existing dilemma of drugs in sport will probably only worsen. While it is reasonable to anticipate that drugs will be employed for genuine therapeutic reasons, it is also likely they will continue to be utilised in order to gain performance advantages. It is also reasonable to suspect that more resources – through some of the largest and most powerful companies in the world, those in the pharmaceutical industry – will be devoted to designing drugs than to detecting them. We can be assured that drugs in sport will continue to remain a significant issue until genetic manipulation can produce athletes who do not need such advantages. Genetic engineering of food products may provide superior nutritional supplements for athletes as well, although the precise effects of these modified foods on the human body is still a source of contention. Interestingly, the degree to which these technologies might be employed in society in general, and sport in particular, may well be subject more to the social conscience of communities rather than their availability.

Social conscience, resources and natural environment

The social perception of the environment will have a significant impact upon the way sport is delivered, as well as the resources it can manage to acquire in an increasingly competitive marketplace. Before we discuss the impact that a growing international social conscience is manifesting, it may be worth spending some time exploring exactly where we stand now in terms of world resources and the environment. First, however, we need to be certain that we do not examine this driver of change in an emotional way. The following commentary is therefore designed to set the boundaries in which a debate upon the role of sport may be considered rationally.

Despite popular concerns, food production and food stocks are quite sufficient to satisfy world demand well into the early part of this century. The unfortunate fact, however, is that distribution problems and economic inequalities will ensure that much food is wasted while famine stalks millions of people throughout the developing world. In fact, the severity of this problem is increasing. In sub-Saharan Africa, for example, the number of people suffering from chronic malnourishment is predicted to expand by a further 20 per cent over the next two decades.[4] Political instability will also act as a deterrent for the North Atlantic Treaty Organisation (NATO), United Nations and other aid interventions. Ironically, the social outcry from concerned Western Europeans and Americans about the appropriateness of genetically modified crops has stalled the introduction of one of the few potential solutions for meeting the needs of the poor in developing countries.

Within two decades, nearly half of the world's population will live in water-stressed regions.[5] A combination of factors exacerbates the shortages, such as salination, overpumping of groundwater into agricultural areas and declining water tables. Water shortages will undoubtedly be a cause of international conflict in the future. The possibility of conflict is sharpened when considering the fact that approximately 30 nations receive more than one-third of their water from outside their borders.

The global economy will become more energy-efficient during the forthcoming decades. This is partly a consequence of genuine improvements in traditionally energy-demanding sectors such as manufacturing, and partly because the manufacturing industry in the global economy is gradually being supplanted by service and knowledge industries. Nevertheless, despite a relative efficiency increase, economic growth will precipitate a 50 per cent increase in oil consumption over the next two decades. The demand for natural gas will increase by 100 per cent.[6]

However, despite these alarming statistics, the increase in energy demand is neither a supply challenge nor, at least theoretically, the stimulus for major price hikes. Somewhere around 80 per cent of the world's available oil and 95 per cent of natural gas is still in the ground. In addition, many nations possess vast supplies. At current rates of usage, the United States has enough reserves to last a decade, while Iraq, in comparison, has enough for around 260 years. While it appears that there is no desperate shortage of oil, at least in the world generally, the popularity of fossil fuels is certainly not improving. The damage to the environment that their use has caused is undeniable from a scientific viewpoint.

As we have noted, global economic prospects are relatively buoyant, particularly for developed nations and a handful of emerging regions. The downside of these promising economic projections is continued stresses on the environment including the ongoing erosion of arable land and forests, amplified greenhouse gas emissions and pollution, and rampant desertification. These demands are unlikely to constrain present living and health standards in developed nations, but will prove challenging for developing nations, especially those with massive cities. Although evidence is scanty, there is some speculation that the post-communist era will not address the chronically mismanaged nuclear facilities in Eastern Europe, either. Some of these countries may slowly begin to address their pollution and other environmental problems as they strive for membership of the European Union and the World Trade Organisation (WTO).

Perhaps the greatest issue concerning the environment is that there is little evidence upon which to hope that serious change will come about. Although there are some existing agreements such as the Montreal Protocol, which is designed to address damage to the ozone layer, the damage is done and cannot be reversed other than through natural regeneration.

Over the next two decades, the pressures on the environment will continue, ironically as a result of achieving most countries' main objectives; economic growth. Global warming will present some major environmental hurdles, along with some international political tensions. Even if the Kyoto Protocol on Climate Change is ever universally implemented, the improvements will only be incremental.

A cosmetic look at these natural resource and environmental issues does not necessarily lead to direct implications for sport organisations. However, when these issues are placed within the context of a burgeoning social conscience and the perceived negative impact of globalisation, the links become clearer. The availability of food, water and energy, along with the status of the environment and the negative impact of globalisation, plays a role in establishing the social conscience that can either support sport as an essential cultural element, or reject it as a waste of public monies that would be better spent on some kind of community support or international aid.

We have noted the obvious trends associated with the depletion and disintegration of the earth's natural resources. The most noteworthy change has been in perception, for while the environmental lobby has consolidated its numbers and political status, the Western world has embraced a new form of resources that can be mined and exploited in much the same way as fossil fuels and minerals: the 'brand'.

The birth, development and maturity of brands in the Western world are as much a focus of effort and economic activity as any natural resource on the planet. In fact, the most dominant existing brands in the world must be responsible for billions of dollars of economic activity. In some ways, places such as the 'Coca-Cola' United States and 'BP' Britain are right to covet, bolster and protect the brands that have been born in their lands and exported so successfully. The truth is, there are few nations that can claim to possess more than a handful of brands which may be rightfully considered serious resources perfect for economic exploitation.

Sport, the social conscience, resources and natural environment

Damage to the environment is likely to have a direct effect on sport. For example, global warming in concert with water shortages may discourage sport participation and infrastructure in arid, desertified regions, particularly for sports requiring grass for training and competition. Countries such as Saudi Arabia will continue to divert increasingly large resources into sustaining and developing massive de-salination plants. However, not all desertified nations are fortunate enough to have other natural resources, such as oil, to subsidise these activities. In addition, the degradation of the earth's ozone layer will place the inhabitants of countries such as Australia and Argentina at an even greater risk of skin cancer, a possibility that does not bode well for outdoor sport participation. Moreover, the impact of environmental pollutants may restrict outdoor sport participation in large, urbanised cities.

The social conscience, as we have named the political movement encouraging greater environmental management, has not yet significantly harmed professional sports, but it is likely that confrontations will occur in the next decade. The removal of corporate sport sponsorship sectors, such as the tobacco industry, demonstrates the growing social conscience

that is being heard by legislators in some regions. Other corporate entities, intrinsically linked to sport, have been the targets of hostility and protest. Nike has been plagued, for example, with negative press concerning its manufacturing operations in south-east Asia. Nike's critics argue that the company exploits its Asian employees by severely underpaying them and coercing them to work in poor conditions. In response, the company has repeatedly pointed out that their remuneration policies are consistent with the labour markets of the countries they operate within, and are generous in contrast to comparable work. The company further notes that the only real censure of its employment practices has come from Western nations where the labour market is vastly different. In some ways the labour issues that Nike has faced, particularly during the late 1990s, are indicative of the company's controversial status in the community. Nike is unlikely, even now, to make superannuation companies' lists of 'sustainable' investments, which have become so popular in the last few years. While Nike has gone from strength to strength in terms of sales and profits, it has not been without its critics. In addition to the debate surrounding its labour policies, the company has received negative press from sources such as the International Olympic Committee (IOC) for its use of ambush marketing. Nike has recently returned to the IOC's good books as official Olympic sponsors in 2000.

Increasingly, the brand name is being mined and exploited in a way similar to that of natural resources. The value of brands is not lost on sporting enterprises. The IOC commissioned research that ultimately reported that their rings were the most recognised non-written symbol in the world. Other highly recognised brand logos included those of Shell, McDonald's, Mercedes and the Red Cross.

FutureBrand, the brand consultancy division of global advertising group Interpublic, recently released a report specifying the most valuable sports brands.[7] They examined the financial performance of each contending sport enterprise, undertook surveys with fans and supporters, and considered loyalty, stability and retention. The results are reproduced in Table 1.3.

According to the report, exploitation of each club's brand through effective marketing is pivotal. It is the ability to leverage the associations made with the brand that sets apart the teams on the list in terms of revenues. Deloitte & Touche's *Sport/FourFourTwo* magazine survey identified the 20 richest football clubs in the world. England's Premier League held eight of the top 20 places, with Manchester United heading the list. The remaining places were filled with six Serie A (Italy), two Bundesliga (Germany), two Primera Liga (Spain) and two Scottish

Table 1.3 FutureBrand's top 10 most valuable team brands

Placing	Brand
1	Dallas Cowboys (American Football)
2	Manchester United (Soccer)
3	Washington Redskins (American Football)
4	New York Yankees (Baseball)
5	New York Knicks (Basketball)
6	Real Madrid (Soccer)
7	Bayern Munich (Soccer)
8	San Francisco 49ers (American Football)
9	Los Angeles Lakers (Basketball)
10	New York Rangers (Ice Hockey)

Table 1.4 Comparing the top five (US$ million turnover) soccer and American football clubs

Soccer team	Turnover ($million)	American football team	Turnover ($million)
Manchester United	177	Washington Redskins	149
Real Madrid	157	Dallas Cowboys	142
Bayern Munich	139	Cleveland Browns	132
AC Milan	136	Tennessee Titans	125
Juventus	134	Tampa Bay Buccaneers	122
Total	**743**		**670**
Average	**148.6**		**134**

Source: Football Business International, December 2001, pp. 3–11.

Premier League clubs. To complete the comparative picture, Table 1.4 lists the top five soccer teams (US$ million turnover) and the top five American football teams.

Demography

Given the limited threat of a global nuclear conflict, population growth is arguably the gravest issue facing humanity, with the possible exception of the HIV–AIDS epidemic that is wiping out an entire generation of Africans. Although this problem is far removed from the citizens of many Western nations, it is ultimately one that affects all people. Naturally the most direct consequences of overpopulation are localised. However, the indirect effects are causing some severe environmental strains such as salination, overgrazing, desertification, the overpumping of scarce waterways for irrigation, topsoil erosion, and the burning of fossil fuels.

We can be quite unambiguous about demographic changes in the world over the next few decades. There are going to be more people around; lots more. Approximately 6.1 billion people currently inhabit the earth. Alarmingly, this will grow to 7.2 billion by 2015.[8] The good news is that the number of children per female is dropping. The bad news is that while this net reproduction rate is declining, there are significantly more women on the planet than ever before, many of whom are part of a massive population bulge in Asia and the Middle East. Nevertheless, the population growth rate is diminishing: 1.7 per cent in 1985, 1.3 per cent today and 1 per cent predicted in 2015.

The essential issue is that the majority of the increase in world population – some 95 per cent – will occur in the expanding urban areas of emerging nations. Developed nations will not grow much. For example, Japan's current population of 130 million is likely to fall to around 100 million by 2030. Instead the developed world's population will become older on average, which will in turn place significant pressure on its social services, welfare, pension and health systems. The decreasing ratio of working population to retirees will force governments to delay pension opportunities, enforce higher superannuation contributions and encourage increases in migrant workers. In contrast, rapidly expanding youth populations will persist in regions such as sub-Saharan Africa and the Middle East, where unemployment and political tension may prove destabilising.

Urbanisation will prove the most significant population challenge for most nations. According to the United States Bureau of Census, by 2015 more than half of the world's population will be urban. The more frightening prediction is that the number of people living in 'mega-cities' of more than 10 million inhabitants, will double to around 400 million. These cities will probably include Mumbai, Karachi, Calcutta, Jakarta, Shanghai, Beijing, Tokyo, Cairo, Lagos, São Paulo, Buenos Aires, New York, Mexico City and Los Angeles.

This urbanisation is the key to understanding the impact of the population challenges facing the world over the next few decades. The real issue that arises out of drastic urbanisation is not population density but resource sustainability. For example, Hong Kong supports 320,000 people per square mile, which is around 20 times more than New York City.[9] The problem is not the proximity, but the limited self-sufficiency of such extraordinary populations. The requirements of such cities for external resources are prodigious and shortly will be too great for the rest of the world to provide. Unfortunately, the answer to this diabolical problem will not be found in one sweeping political or technological solution.

Sport and demography

With people living longer and the average age increasing markedly, the ramifications for sport are substantial. Fewer people are likely to engage in the most popular traditional and, incidentally, most athletic sports, such as soccer, other forms of football and basketball. These sports will need to market their products differently in order to satisfy the requirements of the older spectator or supporter. This may mean far more comfortable sport areas with greater and better access to car parks, bars and restaurants. It may mean showing top sports during the day or much earlier in the evening, with far less television coverage on Fridays and Saturdays when older viewers prefer to visit friends, go to restaurants or have a beer at the local pub or club. The 'ageing viewer' syndrome, for such it may well be, will probably herald a realisation that new sponsors will be required for sport. Colas and sport shoes may be fine for the under-35s, but the older generation may prefer a good red wine and comfortable slippers. It will be the sporting organisations and sponsors who can create the idea of youth combined with the comfort of older age which will be most successful in the next half century.

As the age structure changes, the emphasis on particular sports may change. As suggested, participation and possibly spectatorship of athletic sports may decline. Tennis, golf, lawn bowls and swimming – and, indeed, any sporting activity that may be continued into senior years – will be undertaken, and with participation comes following. We doubt that the Manchester United Lawn Bowls team will ever be more ardently supported than its namesake's soccer team, but expect it to be highly visible, nevertheless. Thus, there will be a gamut of opportunities to provide sport, leisure and related entertainment products and services to this wealthy, retired group, which will be looking for recreational experiences to spend their money on.

The impact of urbanisation will be mixed for sport. Urbanisation will offer the opportunity for larger markets within confined geographical regions to be tapped. A sports club participating in a regional or international competition representing cities such as Tokyo or Mumbai, which will shortly contain more than 20 million inhabitants, would need only a fraction of local support in order to be viable. The difficulties are already prominent in cities like Mumbai, however, for popular sports such as cricket. Such cities have little hope of providing sufficient infrastructure to allow popular sport, leisure and recreation activities to be accessed by all willing participants. The explosive growth of cities, particularly in developing countries, will challenge governments to generate the investment levels required in order to sustain sport employment and develop infrastructure at the local level as well as for major events.

Urbanisation is also likely to facilitate the adoption of information technology and other technological advances. Where inhabitants have little chance of actually attending a sporting event, they will have greater opportunities of enjoying the event via television, the Internet, pay-television or alternate broadcasting platforms. The theme of increasing gaps between the wealthy and the poor holds true here as well though: more will be available to fewer.

Shifting demographic trends, immigration and urbanisation will add to the diversity of sporting experiences on offer. While the majority of new (or at least underexposed) sports will struggle to gain prominence and funding, the size of the market and the alternative broadcasting possibilities will open doors for innovative and opportunistic sport organisations.

Governance

Instituting change to combat problems such as overpopulation necessitates altering the shape of global society. To a large extent, the effectiveness of our individual actions upon population growth is determined by how we influence public institutions and policy. Thus, traditionally, motivating and facilitating government intervention have effected change. This will continue to be the natural approach throughout the next few decades, but the by-products of globalisation will compromise both the capacity and willingness of governments to intervene.

Globalisation, as we have already highlighted, has brought with it a greater flow of information, products and people, along with a diffusion of power and authority. Power has steadily moved from governments to non-state, private-sector organisations which have accumulated influence by virtue of their size, wealth and politically entrenched representatives. The first major challenge for governments globally will be to maintain legislative authority and control over the mega-conglomerates that wield extraordinary wealth and make significant contributions to national economies.

Globalisation has also encouraged a trend towards greater democratisation. Although the precise constituents of a democracy may still be debatable, approximately half of the world's nation states loosely fit into that category. As this trend continues, the popular demands for participation in politics and transparency of decision-making will also increase.

The opportunities for multinational companies have improved as a result of the growth of globalisation. Indeed, the numbers of multinationals are growing with incredible rapidity as well, particularly as the Internet has allowed resource-limited companies fo expand into geographically diverse markets that ordinarily present formidable entry barriers. Large, commercial companies will enjoy involvement in products and services that have traditionally been discharged by governments. The deregulation of economies, privatisation of state-owned enterprises and the liberalisation of financial markets and trade opportunities will ensure that the commercial sector has more influence than ever before. It is likely, however, that state and national sport associations will be undersupported by governments.

The news is better for smaller, locally-based enterprises. Shifts away from government regulation and the broadening of financial and banking services will encourage the linkage of small firms to create broader, global networks that can compete with multinationals in flexibility and responsiveness to market trends. Similarly, the opportunities afforded by globalisation for regional sport organisations to network and leverage their activities and market power is significant, particularly as they are forced by governments to seek self-sufficiency.

Sport and governance

As we demonstrate in some detail later in this book, sport organisations have acquired influence that is not commensurate with their size and economic contribution. While the economic impact of hosting the Olympic Games is indisputable, it is hard to believe that a city would throw a public party to celebrate a pharmaceutical company's decision to relocate its manufacturing operations in the same way that winning an Olympics bid is hailed. Despite the social and tourist benefits of hosting a hallmark event like the Olympics, the presence of a major manufacturing operation may have just as much economic impact for a prolonged and sustained period, without the massive local capital expenditure.

Professional sports clubs are undoubtedly getting larger and larger, but even the largest, publicly-listed clubs (worth several billion dollars) do not come close in market capitalisation to the super-corporations in industries such as oil, mining, pharmaceuticals, software and telecommunications, which are valued in the hundreds of billions. However, as we highlight later, an increasing number of publicly-listed and franchised sports clubs are being purchased by media companies seeking lucrative content. In the future, sports clubs will increasingly move from private ownership to corporate structures where shares are freely available for any individual or institution to purchase.

However, some sports clubs are so deeply entrenched in their local and national contexts that they will never be treated with the same imperatives that govern the behaviour of commercial enterprises. There are a handful of professional soccer clubs in Europe, for example, that are so heavily in debt as a result of borrowing money in order to finance the acquisition of star players that they would be immediately sent into receivership were they commercial organisations.

It is likely that governments will be forced to work closely with the private sector in both commercial and altruistic endeavours, such as attracting hallmark sport events to their shores. Organisations such as the Victorian Major Events Company in Melbourne, Australia, and Rotterdam TopSport in the Netherlands exemplify this approach. These government bodies work to attract major sports and tourist events and integrate them into their respective cities. This cooperation between the private sector and government will prove critical to successful sport tourism in the future.

The fierce economic and industrial independence some sports leagues have demonstrated is indicative of the growing power some sport enterprises are exercising in their governance. For example, the NFL has evolved radically since its inception in 1920 when the franchise fees were set at US$100. The most recent movements in ownership of franchises within the four major US professional leagues are staggering. Some in the NFL have changed hands at more than half a billion US dollars, such as US$530 million for the Cleveland Browns (1998) and US$800 million for the Washington Redskins (1999). The value of high-profile sports clubs in developed economies will increase even further in the near future.

The importance of the ownership models propagated in the United States is tremendously significant for the global world of sport business. One of the themes in this book is the growth in centralised ownership of the world's resources, including sporting organisations. A United States Development Report,[10] in 1996 noted that a total of 358 people own as much wealth as the poorest 2.5 billion people on the planet own collectively. Similarly, the wealthiest 20 per cent of nations receive

84.7 per cent of the world's combined GDP.[11] This trend has not by-passed the professional sports industry where, as we have variously observed, the ownership of teams is a privilege reserved for a handful of immensely wealthy individuals and organisations, notwithstanding the public shares that the average fan can purchase to own a modest stake in those clubs with corporate structures. It is worth a brief review of changes in ownership across the 'big' four professional leagues in the United States over the past year or so to substantiate this point.

Let us begin with major league baseball: Larry Dolan purchased the Cleveland Indians at the end of 1999 for US$323 million. Dolan is most noteworthy because he is the brother of Cablevision chairman Charles Dolan, and apparently earned his wealth through ownership of Cablevision stock. The former Chief Executive Officer (CEO) of Wal-Mart, David Glass, purchased the Kansas City Royals for US$96 million; an art dealer paid US$50 million for a 35 per cent controlling stake of the Montreal Expos; and Canada's largest cable company, Roger's Communications, secured an 80 per cent controlling interest in the Toronto Blue Jays. In January 2002, the Boston Red Sox were sold for US$660 million to a group led by Florida Marlins owner, John Henry.

In early 2000, Robert Wood Johnson, heir to the pharmaceutical giant Johnson & Johnson, grabbed the New York Jets for US$635 million, outbidding the aforementioned Cablevision founder, Charles Dolan. The deal was at the time the highest price ever paid for an NFL team that excluded a stadium. In February 2002, the Home Depot business magnate, Arthur Blank, bought the Atlanta Falcons for US$545 million.

Internet benefactor Mark Cuban, founder of Broadcast.com (which he sold to Yahoo Inc. in 1999), purchased a majority share of the Dallas Mavericks from Ross Perot Junior for US$280 million. Unlike the Jets deal in NFL, Cuban's arrangement ensures him a stake in the American Airlines Centre. Another recent NBA ownership change was Wal-Mart heir Stan Kroenke's escalation from minority owner of the Denver Nuggets to majority owner for US$450 million. The deal also included the NHL's Colorado Avalanche. Michael Heisley, the CEO of Heico Companies, bought the Vancouver Grizzlies for US$160 million.

In the NHL, the New Jersey Devils were partially sold to Puck Holdings LLC, an affiliate of YankeeNets, for US$175 million. Yankee-Net now effectively controls 50 per cent of the franchise in addition to their ownership of the MLB team, the New York Yankees, and the NBA team, the New Jersey Nets. Computer Associates executives Charles Wang and Sanjay Kumar purchased the New York Islanders for around

US$190 million, and the Phoenix Coyotes were sold to Los Arcos Sports for an estimated US$87 million.

As the largest and wealthiest sports enterprises have developed greater independence in their governance, they have also shown increased willingness to expand their spread of influence in the global marketplace, just as their media overlords have. When media giants Time Warner and Internet powerbrokers America Online merged, it also provided an insight into the direction that sport will take in the near future. Not only did they create the fourth largest company in the United States with a stock market valuation of around US$342 billion, but they also signalled their vision of moulding the company into an integrated entertainment empire. However, the longevity of this corporate giant might be limited to their ability to wield their newfound size effectively.

In a sense, the future of sport business might be better understood by looking at the history of human cooperation. It might be argued that clubs are like countries. History demonstrates that villages joined or were incorporated by stronger villages to become towns, then city-states. In turn these joined to become small countries, and the stronger countries forced the smaller countries into unions. For example, England subsumed Wales, then Scotland and Northern Ireland, America joined its states to become a single entity and Australia federated separate states to become a nation. In time, nations have united, economically and politically, such as in the European Union and NAFTA. Businesses have done the same. However, increasingly, while this continues, people are physically demonstrating a desire to de-amalgamate and to break into smaller entities, such as the Basques and Catalonians in Spain, the break-up of Yugoslavia and the Soviet Union, Scotland and Wales seeking devolved government and the potential division of Canada. In addition, more large companies are decentralising as they become too large to be responsive to fickle consumers. The question is whether 'mega' sport companies will become similarly bloated, expensive and inflexible, and will eventually follow suit. There is a strong likelihood that in the next few decades sport organisations will become too large to operate as single entities. However, the evidence suggests that they are still entrenched in the expansion, amalgamation and alliance stage in order to acquire greater market leverage.

For example, the New York Yankees recently announced a marketing alliance with English Premier League glamour club, Manchester United. As we will observe on several occasions in this book, in the near future, the ownership and governance of large and influential sport enterprises will increasingly fall under the control of fewer and fewer. In other words, those few companies will seek to acquire the sporting clubs that can be profitably leveraged within their range of media and entertainment products. Just as with the Manchester United–New York Yankees marketing alliance, it also appears likely that more clubs will cooperate across leagues and nations to maximise penetration into new markets in order to allow themselves to exist in the 'global' arena, particularly when they are effectively governed by the same puppet-masters. Thus the Manchester/New York alliance will continue for a while until a formal partnership is achieved and will last only until it gets too big for one board to handle, or until the sport business world acknowledges, as have their larger corporate counterparts, that the sum value of the parts is sometimes worth more than value of the whole. This may subsequently lead to the break-up of the major entity into self-supporting divisions. Before this happens, we will see the 'mega-merged' companies operating in the media/ entertainment segment of the sport industry, such as AOL Time Warner and News Corporation, begin to fragment in order to preserve their competitive advantages. Alliances will remain, but the trend towards physical mergers and acquisitions will eventually cease as the process comes full-circle.

The United–Yankees deal is not limited to copromotion in theory, although at present it seems more like a mechanism for distributing information and merchandise over the Internet, as well as to facilitate the sale of broadcasts to overseas media outlets. However, the revenue-generating capacity of this cross-promotional strategy may be restricted as both teams are limited in their rights to sell broadcasts to their games. One of the most interesting sticking points for the future of professional leagues will be the interaction between the broadcast rights owners – in some cases, also the owners of the teams participating in the league – and the league itself. However, the alliance is likely to allow the teams to construct sports programming that will be suitable for re-packaging, particularly for the Internet or other underexplored 'new' media. Of course, the Yankees also hope that they can expand their brand recognition beyond the United States, just as Manchester United has acquired a strong awareness in Australasia.

The ownership and governance model exercised by Manchester United and the New York Yankees stands in vibrant contrast to the arrangements held by NFL club, the Green Bay Packers. Although a rarity in the company of extraordinarily valuable NFL franchises, the Packers are a non-profit organisation that is also one of the most successful teams in the league. There are few other examples of such ownership in high-profile and powerful sports clubs with international brands. Barcelona Football Club's fan ownership structure and the membership-based clubs in the

Australian Football League provide interesting counterpoints to the massive private franchises and PLCs in American professional leagues and European soccer.

Increasingly, the future of sport is in the hands of the private sector, where economic opportunity will prove the driving focus of investors and broadcasters, and government involvement, intervention and funding will move further to the periphery. Thus, the original owners of sports and clubs – the fans – will become further marginalised, left to watch powerlessly as media empires seek and gain control and ownership of sport institutions. Decisions will be made according to the special interests of these owners. Accountability and transparency will not be hallmarks of their business operations. The fans will rarely have an insight behind the veil of decision-making in their own clubs and, in some sports, will become further out-priced when it comes to acquiring a ticket to their club's matches. Although some of the clubs in the English Premier League have embarked upon customer retention pricing strategies, effectively acknowledging the importance of grassroots support for their club, one thing remains certain: great sporting experiences will be available to anyone providing they are prepared to pay for the privilege.

The biggest obstacles in the path of sport businesses' evolution will not only be tackled by sport owners and mega-corporations fighting over lucrative media content, but will be faced by governments in the way they handle changing communal identities and networks. By leveraging the opportunities provided by globalisation and decreased government authority, communal groups, both religious and ethnic, will be better placed to act on perceived discrimination and political dissatisfaction. The internal tensions will largely remain political in most Western nations, but in some regions the dissonance between ethnic or religious groups will be sufficient to incite physical conflict, war and terrorism.

Conflict and war

It is not difficult to appreciate the negative impact conflict and war has on all things. One of the frightening realities that accompanies globalisation is that with increased accessibility to information comes the likelihood that dangerous materials may fall into the hands of groups that wish to use it for destructive purposes. This problem may be exacerbated with the deterioration of national border control, export regulation and sanctions. Simply put, arms and weapons technology transfer will become even more difficult to control. The possibility that weapons of mass destruction will be used against developed nations, especially the United States, will increase, but principally from rogue states or terrorist factions. Many commentators have soberly noted that the nature of life in the Western world was irrevocably changed as a result of the terrorist attacks on the United States in September 2001. Strategic weapons of mass destruction 'threats' will potentially exist from Russia, China, North Korea, Iran, Iraq and several other nations. However, the chance of conflict between developed nations will remain low.

Scuffles and conflicts between developing nations will remain frequent, but generally not on a large scale. The greatest danger zones include Asia, where India and Pakistan, China and Taiwan, and North and South Korea may extend their existing rivalries, the Middle East, where the Israeli–Palestinian tensions are likely to continue until a Palestinian state is negotiated, and sub-Saharan Africa, where internal skirmishes between power-seeking groups have caused millions of deaths over the last few decades. More and more, the United Nations and other independent organisations will be required to intervene, pressured by the major stakeholders – developed nations – to restore stability to the fighting regions and ensure that the fallout does not reach their shores or impose upon their access to resources. The greatest concern for most developed nations will remain the cultural, religious and ethnic affiliations that are manifest in the Middle East.

Sport, conflict and war

Naturally, global conflict would have a devastating effect on sport. Even the threat of terrorism in the United States following 11 September, culminating in the Salt Lake City Winter Olympics, was sufficient to cause substantial security chaos and, for a short time, the cancellation of sport events. The threat of terrorism in Western nations, and localised conflict in other regions of the world, such as the Middle East and Africa, will be enough to curtail the globalising forces of sport in the near future, which have traditionally been amongst the most 'borderless' activities in the world. However, not all conflict that will forge the future of sport business will be physical, or fought outside the boundaries of Western nations. The conflicts that will decide the future of the sport business will be contested in the boardrooms of some of the world's most powerful media companies.

Some of the more interesting conflicts in the world of the 'new economy' will occur between the media multinationals who are fighting for control over the ownership of the most recognised brands. Mike

Marqusee noted that contemporary sport is being used to 'brand' larger and larger amounts of public space, be it material, televisual or cyber. He believes, as do many sport commentators, that the single most powerful individual within what he calls the corporate–media–sport nexus must be Rupert Murdoch. Murdoch's empire is alarmingly widespread and all-consuming. There are few areas of professional sport that remain untouched by his hand, and even fewer that have escaped his attention. He has also shown a particular preparedness to enter new markets and capture a first mover's advantage that only a handful of others would have the resources and infrastructure to contemplate.

Murdoch's empire is founded upon three levels of sport entertainment. First, his Fox, Sky and Star television networks broadcast major sporting events across North America, Europe, Australasia and South America. This base level of his sport entertainment empire is solidly built upon event coverage and exclusive ownership of broadcasting rights. The second level leverages this coverage magnificently by using the events to provide inexpensive and almost inexhaustive content for Murdoch's newspapers in Britain, the United States, Australia and Asia. Quite clearly the opportunities for repeatedly selling the same overlapping content have not gone unnoticed or unexploited.

The final tier of Murdoch's sport entertainment empire comprises a number of prime sport enterprises that are either directly owned or controlled by his companies. They include British and German football clubs, major league baseball teams in the United States and rugby league clubs in Australia's National Rugby League (NRL) competition. It is worth conducting a further stock-take of a few other pivotal stakeholders in the global sport entertainment battlefield, since these are the largest and most powerful factions fighting for control of the future of sport.

We have already mentioned Rupert Murdoch. Murdoch has recently started to direct some of his cash into the Internet, although his son Lachlan has been benched after a disappointing run with One-Tel in the telecommunications industry in Australia, which collapsed in 2001 and took with it a billion of Rupert Murdoch and Kerry Packer's money. Murdoch has agreements with Yahoo, and Star is collaborating with the powerful sport broadcaster ESPN and their 20 television networks that cover almost 200 countries. Importantly, ESPN also operate the most 'hit' sport website in the United States. They are proving an essential portal to sport information and viewing. ESPN is only a flank of the army, however, which is anchored by ESPN's owners, the Disney Corporation. On the other flank, Disney's network (ABC) holds the rights to a range of US sports. Like Murdoch's News Corporation, Disney has also ventured into purchasing sport content by owning the factors of production, including MLB and NHL teams. Despite the magnitude of News Corporation and Disney, the newly formed AOL Time Warner, under Chairman Steve Case, may be the best placed company to determine the future of the sport business in North America. With 34 million Internet subscribers, television stations, film studios, cable television and sport franchises, the company has the opportunity to become the first to make the distribution of sport through the Internet a practical reality. The successful accomplishment of this will be the first decisive battle of the new millennium on the sport business field. However, a cautionary note is required. Big may ultimately prove too big. AOL Time Warner reported a massive loss in the year 2001, either a sign of the need for investment patience or, indeed, a sign of faltering progress. Profit margins on narrowband are great but these margins will dramatically decrease when consumers switch to broadband technology, given the fact that large investments are required to upgrade the distribution infrastructure. Massive adoption of broadband technology will also lead to an increase in downloading (pirating) music and film products that are still too big for narrowband, reducing the advantage of having a wide range of content products. Placing an early bet on the future, the colossal vertically-integrated companies of today may fracture into myriad relatively independent entertainment cluster specialists in a decade or so.

Like capricious warlords, a number of the companies competing for the future of sport have formed alliances to manage some products, while fighting fiercely over others. For example, Murdoch and Packer are notorious enemies, having nearly destroyed Australia's national rugby competition between them, but have collaborated on a number of projects to their mutual benefit. The future of sport business promises similar levels of bitter competition, uncertainty and uneasy collaboration.

Other major factions include the Italian President and television magnate, Silvio Berlusconi, who is the principal owner of AC Milan and a significant stakeholder in the recently collapsed Internet company Sportal. Although struggling under the burden of an estimated £5 billion debt, the German media group Kirch have been, up until recently at least, significant players in international sport broadcasting. One of the problems has been Premiere, Kirch's pay-television platform, which has been losing around £1 million a day. Worse, News Corporation is one of Kirch's largest creditors and is expecting a £1 billion refund of the capital it invested in the platform. However, in an attempt to avert bankruptcy, Kirch have placed their 58 per cent of SLEC, the company that controls the broadcasting and media rights to Formula One on the market.

Ironically, the former master of Formula One, Bernie Ecclestone, might be one of the potential buyers. It was Ecclestone who transformed Formula One into a global sport phenomenon that entices 350 million viewers in 150 countries to tune in to watch the world's most over-engineered cars race and crash. In fact, Formula One has grown to such an extraordinary size that only the Olympic Games deliver higher global television sports ratings. Ecclestone is also the promoter of his own tracks in Belgium (Spa), Germany (Hockenheim) and France (Magny-Cours). These revenues have been variously estimated to generate Ecclestone an additional US$200 million in a total revenue approaching US$500 million per year. However, Ecclestone's grip on Formula One had loosened with the Kirch Group's control of Formula One holding company SLEC, which had in turn stimulated car manufacturers to get itchy feet and threaten to start their own series when the existing agreement expires in 2008. Other noteworthy factions include Canal Plus, the French pay-television station that also owns Paris St-Germain football club, while Fiat owns the Juventus football club and the Ferrari Formula One motor-racing team. Few other cultural icons with nationalistic origins have incited a more fanatic following than Ferrari and its Italian tifosi.

Religion and cultural identity

For the moment, we are concerned with the impact of globalisation on the future of the world and upon the nature of future sport business. To that end, we shall confine our commentary in this section to a macro overview of the issues as they arise from globalisation. Nevertheless, like the Internet, we believe that cultural issues will play such a significant role in shaping the future of sport that we have dedicated a chapter to detailing it from a micro perspective later in this book.

From a macro viewpoint, the impact of religion promises to have a significant impact on the way in which the world unfolds this century. Presently, the two major world religions are Christianity and Islam, which command approximately 1.9 billion and 1.1 billion adherents respectively. Around 900 million people reserve judgment, while Hindus, Chinese folk religionists and Buddhists comprise 760, 380 and 350 million advocates worldwide.[12]

Christianity and Islam are widely dispersed over several continents and already capitalise on the opportunities for propagation afforded by technology, such as television and the Internet. Most of the world's states are ethnically and religiously heterogeneous. In other words, most countries in the world house people adhering to more than one religion and ethnic background. Globalisation would suggest that religious heterogeneity amidst nations would grow. However, this view tends to assume that the power of globalisation is superior to that driving religious affiliation. While this may hold true for some parts of the developed world and, in particular, Western nations, this may not hold true for regions such as the Middle East.

Samuel Huntington's book, *The Clash of Civilizations and the Remaking of World Order*, may turn out to be prescient in its consideration of the role of religion in the future. Huntington argues that a number of factors increased the conflict between Islam and the West in the late twentieth century, and this conflict marks the growing religious congregation of Islamic communities across the globe. To extrapolate, instead of developing affiliations on the basis of geography (EU, NAFTA, ASEAN) or even mutual need, the civilisations of the future may be characterised by religious homogeneity.

First, Huntington notes that the Muslim population has grown significantly. In fact, he predicts that in somewhere between 25 and 50 years from now, Islam will become the most followed religion in the world, and the numbers following Christianity will fall considerably. Population growth, especially what we noted as the youth bulge, has created growing numbers of unemployed and disaffected young people who have migrated to Islamic causes. Second, the Islamic resurgence has provided a renewed sense of worth and importance in the world order, also helped along by oil resources. Third, the West's continued distribution of values and unwelcome intervention in Middle Eastern conflicts has fostered significant resentment. Fourth, the degeneration of communism removed a common enemy of the West and Islamic states. Finally, globalisation has increased interaction between Westerners and Muslims and has had the effect of reinforcing the differences between the two.

The essential issue that Huntington raises is whether future civilisations will be constructed on the basis of diversity and multiculturalism or on the foundation of cultural commonality. Certainly, the forces of globalisation, as we have noted, are pushing the world towards greater universalism and integration. It remains unclear whether the power of globalisation will be adequate to dilute religious affiliation in the Middle East, or whether religious grouping has the strength to overcome pressures to globalise. This constitutes one of the key uncertainties for the future that we shall tackle at the conclusion of this book.

Sport, religion and cultural identity

The possibility of homogeneous groupings rather than geographic or national boundaries may be a revealing concept for the sport business. Part of the difficulty facing professional sport organisations is their assumptions concerning the rest of the world. In essence, professional sport has been propagated in the West, and other professional sport enterprises around the world have followed this model. It has been argued, for example, that the international trends emerging in sport are examples of 'Americanisation' rather than genuine globalisation. This trend might be interpreted as an outcome of the explosion of sports on television, particularly on pay and cable platforms such as Fox in the United States, Star TV in Asia, BSkyB in Britain and Foxtel in Australia. From these vast warehouses of sport entertainment comes the not so subtle reinforcement of the consumption experiences that have become commonplace in the United States.

The problem is cultural compatibility. The professional Western sport model is not the only method of delivering sport. The Western world seems to want to reinvent sport in the rest of the world in its own image, but this universal approach does not necessarily stand up in areas that hold fundamentally different value systems to the West. For the moment, it is incomprehensible to imagine professional sport prospering in the Middle East, for example, simply because the values of professional sport are incompatible with the wider culture. Sport will never make significant inroads into the Middle East and other Islamic nations until sport managers abandon the need to inculcate it in Western values. Is the prosperity that globalisation promises worth a dilution of a nation's distinctive national, ethnic and religious cultures?

Negative Impacts of Globalisation for Sport

While on balance the news for professional sport in the future is good, there are a number of negative impacts of globalisation that should be considered. Peter Ellyard[13] in his book, *Ideas for the New Millennium*, highlights eight factors that have already disadvantaged many nations and interest groups. We have picked up on some of Ellyard's prognostications and discuss them within the sport context below. Given the picture we have just painted concerning the globalised future, it is likely that these factors will become even more damaging, and will severely curtail the success of some sport organisations.

First, as we have already highlighted, the economic futures of some developing nations are likely to develop under the shadow of a new generation of economic imperialists enforced by the globalisation winners. As the economic opportunities diminish in developing nations, so too will their sporting possibilities. The potential for genuine, balanced international sporting competition will continue to be an elusive target, although there will always be a handful of nations that perform well above our expectations in certain sports, despite a lack of resources. We might, for example, anticipate that countries such as Kenya and Cameroon will continue to produce world-beating distance athletes and football sides, respectively. Developed countries may remain reluctant to accept imported sports and will react by erecting rigid barriers to entry in order to protect their own domestic sports' popularity. Similarly, at a micro level, even within developed nations, the gap between the wealthy and the deprived will expand. This economic divide will create an entire class of people relegated to extremely limited sporting spectatorship and participation options. For a tiny minority of these people, sporting prowess will be their liberation from poverty but, for the majority, an unhealthy lack of involvement in sport participation may restrict their opportunities for financial independence through education and training.

Second, globalisation has exacerbated the negative aspects of corporate restructuring which has included the relocation of manufacturing industry from developed to developing countries. While these domestic job losses do not largely influence the sport industry in developed nations, save for the manufacturing side of sport products, the subsequent unemployment increases have an unfavourable effect on sport spectatorship. In addition, with higher unemployment comes a more restricted flow of discretionary leisure income, as other workers fear the possibility of retrenchment.

Third, globalisation is encouraging the migration of people from rural communities to urban regions all around the world. While this is great news for large, city-based sporting competitions – professional sport – it disadvantages rural districts in personnel, participants, infrastructure and opportunity. The very locations that have the greatest geographical and environmental prospects for sport are also the most marginalised.

Fourth, with globalisation comes the opportunity for taking advantage of the increasingly networked global financial system. Powerful currency traders who almost single-handedly destroy the value of some countries' trade circumstances are examples of these 'cowboys' of capitalism. Increasingly we shall see sport cowboys who will be quite prepared to exploit players, spectators and governments in their desire to acquire wealth. There are plentiful examples of sport agents and entrepreneurs who have devalued sport by offering shoddy products, and of respected sporting officials accepting bribes to sway their political affiliations. There are also numerous opportunities for politicians to use sport and hallmark sport events to manipulate their own popularity irrespective of the price that their public has to pay. The celebrated debt left from the Montreal Olympics did not dissuade Nagano from jumping into the same deep waters.

Allied to this is the alarming growth of global, organised crime. As crime syndicates have globalised more effectively than law enforcement agencies, we shall see more examples of sporting franchises that are owned by criminal groups as money-laundering vehicles. The use of sport events as venues for terrorism and other extreme political activity will also increase.

Fifth, as we noted, the divisions between dominant and subjugated cultures within both developed and developing nations are likely to continue, probably with an increased gap. The benefits of globalisation enjoyed by the majority groups are not necessarily being passed on to minority populations. The outcome will be that the dominant cultural activities, especially sporting ones, are subsidised and popularised, while the activities associated with minority cultures are comparatively ignored and marginalised. An example might include lacrosse in North America.

Finally, the separation between educated and less educated parts of the world is being stretched by globalisation. Ironically, educational opportunities are growing constantly and have risen to an all-time high. The problem is accessibility. Selected countries have more opportunity than ever before, while opportunities for others still remain sparse. Technological advancements, instead of bridging this gap by providing inexpensive distance education, are more likely to provide ever-greater options for those countries already heavily educated. This lack of education again underscores the potential that the next few decades may have on sport for many emerging nations. Lack of infrastructure, resources and trained personnel will not facilitate the development of any local sporting success.

George Wright also noted some tendencies of globalisation as they directly affect the conduct of sport.[14] The interesting element of globalisation is that while it can obviously be observed as a global trend, it is manifested at the local level. Thus, for example, we have seen a proliferation of involvement in professional sport by what Wright considers global telecommunication oligopolies, including News Corporation, Disney and Time Warner. Their involvement is rarely limited to silent ownership. They demand significant control of the timing, production, marketing, merchandising, licensing and viewing of sport. Wright points to Disney as an example, which owns the following sports-related subsidiaries: ABC Sports, ABC Sports International, ABC Sports Video, ESPN, Eurosport (along with TF 1 and Canal Plus), the Anaheim Angels (MLB), and the Mighty Ducks (NHL). Indeed, Disney, AOL Time Warner and News Corporation are embroiled in a war to own some of the most valuable global sporting assets. News Corporation's infamous attempt to purchase Manchester United after securing the Los Angeles Dodgers has become the archetypal example.

The impact of global corporations on sport is probably best evidenced by Rupert Murdoch's News Corporation activities, which cranked up a notch some years ago on the back of the existing NFL rights. He later purchased the LA Dodgers for 25 times its earnings. It has been widely speculated that the team's multinational line-up, including players from Mexico, Korea and Japan, were a strong element in the club's attractiveness. The subsequent signing of pitcher Kevin Brown on a seven-year US$105 million contract (roughly US$400,000 per game) has been seen by some commentators as a further step blurring the distinction between sport and show-business. Smaller clubs complained about the deal and its implication (that they would no longer be competitive whilst media-owned companies could sell their own clubs as the only worthy attractions).

Murdoch also ventured unconditionally into the world of rugby. Perhaps most memorable was his Super League adventure in Australia. Interestingly, Super League was based not on the traditional, member-based model of club ownership traditional in Australian sports, but instead upon privately-owned, profit-seeking franchises with few teams, each of which had been granted exclusive catchment zones. The league also established pooled merchandising and advertisement revenues through joint marketing deals. However, the attraction of the new Super League was only enough to splinter the fans between the existing Australian Rugby League competition and the breakaway group. The two merged to form the National Rugby League. Not long afterwards, a new governing body for rugby union was established across South Africa, New Zealand and Australia, known as SANZAR. Six weeks later Murdoch agreed to pay US$50 million over 10 years for exclusive world rights to all rugby in those countries.

The impact of the media, in particular television, cannot be underestimated in the escalation of the value of professional sport leagues. We mentioned earlier the television rights deal in the NFL is indicative of the financial magnitude that the largest professional sports can command. Table 1.5 summarises the sport broadcasting television deals that have been struck by American networks up to 2000.

Table 1.5 United States sport broadcasting rights deals

League	Network	Years (Ends)	Amount (US$)
NFL	ESPN	8 (2006)	4.8 billion
	Fox	8 (2006)	4.4 billion
	ABC	8 (2006)	4.4 billion
	CBS	8 (2006)	4.0 billion
NBA	NBC	4 (2002)	1.75 billion
	Turner	4 (2002)	890 million
MLB	FOX	5 (2000)	575 million
	NBC	5 (2000)	400 million
	ESPN	6 (2005)	850 million
NHL	ESPN/ABC	5 (2004)	600 million
NCAA Hoops Tournament	CBS	11 (2003–2013)	6.0 billion
NCAA Football BCS	ABC	8 (2006)	930 million
NASCAR	NBC/Turner	6 (2006)	1.2 billion
	Fox	8 (2008)	1.6 billion
Olympics	NBC	13 (2008)	3.5 billion
PGA Tour	ABC/CBS/NBC/ESPN/USA and the Golf Channel	4 (2006)	850 million

Wright also observes the use, and perhaps abuse, of manufacturing sporting goods in developing countries. For some companies, he claims, the outsourcing of manufacturing has created a sort of third class of personnel. Without leaping to any moral conclusions, the trend is clear: in a global economy labour is not confined to national boundaries.

Third, Wright believes that international sport federations are assuming new responsibilities. While international sports federations (ISFs) such as the IOC, the Federation of International Football Associations (FIFA) and the International Amateur Athletics Federation (IAAF) have enjoyed tremendous revenues as a result of selling television rights and sponsorships, they have paved the way for smaller ISFs to acquire the financial support they need to expand globally. This trend dovetails with Wright's fourth trend, that of substantial, long-term sponsorships of leagues and clubs by multinational corporations. This can be evidenced all over the world from the big four leagues in the United States – football (NFL), basketball (NBA), baseball (MLB), ice hockey (NHL) – to European soccer, world rugby league and union, cricket, tennis, golf, motor sport and sailing, to name a few. All offer fundamentally the same sponsorship association opportunity to sell an extraordinarily diverse range of products and services, only some of which are directly relevant to sport itself.

Fifth, the control of events and influential athletes has migrated from sport associations to independent and entrepreneurial international sports management firms, such as IMG, Octagon and SFX. These companies control athletes, the events that their athletes compete in, the associated television rights, sponsorships, endorsements and publicity.

Globalisation has also, according to Wright, magnified the numbers of foreign athletes on professional teams. While this remains the exception rather than the rule in the United States, it has become an intricate part of professional sport in Europe, Asia and, to a lesser extent, South America. Although in the English Premier League Chelsea has become famous recently for fielding a side without a single Englishman, the trend seems to have gained virtually universal, if reluctant, acceptance.

Professionalisation of formerly amateur sports, such as athletics, is Wright's final global sport trend. This professionalisation has emerged out of the immense sums of money associated with the Olympics and the disintegration of the amateur Olympic ideal. The linkage between sport's professionalisation and globalisation is simultaneously obvious and complex.

Summarising Globalisation Trends in Sport Business

We have employed trend analysis to present a great deal of information in this chapter, both about the general trends we anticipate throughout the world and the trends that will emerge in sport business. We have also made clear that the sport industry is significant in magnitude from economic and social perspectives. In fact, the sport, leisure, recreation and entertainment industry is economically the third largest legal industry in the world behind oil and automobiles (drugs and guns are the largest).

Despite the many popular opinions, we concur with the definition provided by Theodore Cohn in his expansive book, *Global Political Economy*,[15] which explains globalisation as the broadening and deepening of interdependence amongst (sport) organisations and (sport) activities across the world. Broadening refers to the geographical extension of linkages, while deepening refers to an increase in frequency and intensity.

A leading scholar on sport globalisation, Bob Stewart, provides us with a useful, practical set of trends associated with the concept:

- growth of the global economy
- dominance of the transnational corporation and transnational brands
- explosion of international trade in cultural goods
- growth of international finance markets
- expansion of international telecommunication and media
- increasing international travel
- acceleration of global migration
- growth of international tourism
- expansion of global governance and regulation

Building on Stewart's points, we can summarise the trends associated with sport globalisation as shown below:

1. Proliferation of sports on television and other media/entertainment mechanisms (radio, print, Internet, pay-television).
2. Ongoing increase in value of genuinely global sport properties, including athletes.
3. Blurring of what is sport and what is entertainment.
4. Vertical and horizontal integration of sport enterprises by entertainment and media companies.
5. Integration and consolidation of sport, leisure, recreation, television, film and tourism industries into elements of the entertainment industry.
6. Growth in the economic effects and impacts of sport.
7. Increase in venture capital and investment in transnational sports and sport properties.
8. De-fragmentation of sport governance.
9. Simultaneous professionalisation and marginalisation of smaller sports and leagues. (They will professionalise their management and marketing, but the gap between the sport enterprises that are globally successful and those which remain only domestically viable, will grow.)
10. Convergence of economic power in sport ownership. Fewer and fewer will own more and more of sport.
11. Development and utilisation of technologies which enhance the entertainment value and radically improve the diffusion and distribution of sport to new markets.

12. Increase in world acceptance of capitalism as the pre-eminent economic philosophy and of sport as an effective vehicle for achieving wealth.
13. Increase in 'Americanisation' and 'Westernisation' of sport.

Final Comments

This chapter was about the drivers of world change, the trends they are presently manifesting, the likely circumstances if they persist and the ultimate implications upon the business of sport. Thus, we have painted a portrait of the world of sport business if today's trends continue into the future. In summarising, we must immediately acknowledge that the impact of these trends varies considerably depending upon the site in which sport is played. It is useful, therefore, to divide the world on the basis of this geography. Four categories of sport business development in nations can be identified: Hyperdeveloped, Developed, Developing and Underdeveloped.

The United States stands in a league of its own in terms of the evolution of its sport business industry. It is therefore the only nation that might be considered to possess a Hyperdeveloped sport business system. Developed sport business systems include countries such as Canada, those in Western Europe, Australia and Japan. Developing sport business systems include a number of South American countries, as well as China, India, South Africa and some in Eastern Europe. Underdeveloped sport business systems encompass the remainder (and majority) of the world, including most of Africa and many countries in Asia. This segregation is not designed to serve as a formal typology of sport business development, but rather is used here as a reminder that only small parts of the world have embraced the sport business in significant ways. To that end, when we talk about sport globalisation and commercialisation, we are usually talking about developed nations and the United States. We will return to this division of sport business systems in Chapter 3.

We do not know whether the trends we have identified in this chapter will continue. There are factors, which we have named 'nexus factors' (the economy, technology and culture), which we believe can potentially play a 'switching' role in the development of sport business's future. We will explore these variables in Chapters 5, 6 and 7, respectively. Nevertheless, the future of sport is still unwritten, and this book culminates in a set of future scenarios that encapsulate the alternatives, taking into account the directions in which the nexus factors might take sport business. We also acknowledge that, whatever the future holds, it is likely to lack parity.

As a final note in this chapter, we would add a caution about getting too carried away about the position of sport business as a major global entity. There are really only a handful of genuinely global sporting properties: Nike, Manchester United, the Olympics, the World Cup, Formula One, the Dallas Cowboys, the New York Yankees, and Ferrari are examples. Most of the rest are not genuinely global. Even those that we may consider to have a genuine claim as a global sport brand are relatively small players in the larger pond of media/entertainment companies such as AOL Time Warner.

We must therefore add a tone of reservation to offset the hyperbole and hubris presented by some sport commentators who tend towards hyper-globalisation scenarios. Although we note the magnitude of the sport industry, we must also recognise the fact that its size is not necessarily evidence of a blistering global economy so much as a reflection of sport's importance in many individual societies. It therefore remains of importance for us to define the range and classification of the industry, and to further clarify its role in the 'new' world order. We shall shortly therefore determine the constituents of the global sports industry in Chapter 3.

As highlighted earlier, the industry consists of multiple constituents that have overlapping, sometimes ambiguous relationships with increasing centralisation tendencies, at least in the near future. In Chapter 4, we will consider conglomerate oligopolies that own a range of subsidiaries, including sport enterprises, as well as other companies that feed from the sport industry: sports teams and clubs, some participatory in nature, others mass entertainment in orientation, still others focused upon manufacturing; national sports leagues that promote their teams and athletes and have developed sponsorship and merchandising relations with global companies; international sports organisations and federations and national sports governing bodies; businesses that fit into the sport value chain, including suppliers of food and beverages, raw material suppliers for sports apparel and footwear, advertising groups, lawyers, and doctors; and gambling, a perennial associate of sport.

However, before we venture into the current form of professional, commercial sport, we will cast our investigation back to the beginnings of it all, and attempt to determine how sport came to be what it is today, and why it is that people might be motivated to become sports watchers and consumers.

Notes and references

1   The lift may be the critical factor in the development of cities since it enabled people to build up as well as out.

2   In no way do we imply that sport equates to 'play', which is why we have attempted to summarise extensive academic research into defining sport. In the context of this book we argue sport to be structured and sometimes scripted play. This definition does not do justice to the elaborate academic discussion that has taken place in regard to the proper definition of the collection of activities that are understood to be sport. However, this book is not the place to enter into such discussions. Rather, we aim to set the scene for sport as an increasingly ubiquitous development in modern society with significant influence on how society further develops. In order for us to develop our arguments, we have chosen to position sport as something that is a core element of human nature (and hence had to be discovered) which, through societal transformation, has increasingly been commodified. Excellent insights into the definition of sport are provided by: A. Guttmann (1988) *Games and Empires: Modern Sports and Cultural Imperialism*, Columbia University Press, Chapel Hill; J. Bale (1989), *Sportgeography*, E. & F.N. Spon, London; M. Bottenburg (1994), *Verborgen competitie, over de uiteenlopende populariteit van sporten*. Uitgeverij Bert Bakker, Amsterdam; C. Gratton and P. Taylor (2000), *Economics of Sport and Recreation*, E. & F.N. Spon, London; T. Dejonghe (2001), *Sport in de wereld: Ontstaan, evolutie en verspreiding*. Academia Press, Gent.

3   National Intelligence Council (2000), *Global Trends 2015: A dialogue about the future with nongovernment experts*, National Foreign Intelligence Board, Washington DC.

4   M. Rosegrant, S. Meijer, J. Witcover (2001), *Global Food Projections to 2020: Emerging Trends and Alternative Future*, International Food Policy Research Institute, Washington, DC.

5   Stockholm Environmental Institute. (1997), *Comprehensive assessment of the freshwater resources of the world*, Stockholm.

6   International Energy Outlook (1998), US Department of Energy, Washington, DC.

7   Reuters (19 February 2001), *Futurebrand*, www.reuters.com.

8   United States Bureau of Census (2000) *2000 Population Estimates*, Washington, DC.

9   *The World Almanac and Book of Facts*, (2000), ed. M. Hoffman, Pharos, New York.

10   UNDP (1996), *Human Development Report*, New York, July.

11   *The Economist*, 3 February 1996.

12   Encyclopaedia Britannica *World Book*, 2000, Encyclopedia Britannica, Chicago.

13   P. Ellyard (2001), *Ideas for the New Millennium*. Melbourne University Press, Melbourne.

14   G. Wright (1999), 'Sport and Globalisation', *New Political Economy*, Spring.

15   T. Cohn (1999), *Global Political Economy: Theories and Trends*. Addison-Wesley, Reading, MA.

CHAPTER 2

Bums on Seats: The Social Phenomenon of Sport

Two things only the people anxiously desire: bread and circuses.
Juvenal, Roman poet, c. 100, The Satires

The purpose of this chapter is to trace the origins of sport and, in so doing, begin to appreciate why it has become so important in modern life. Despite popular opinion, the most successful sport organisations in the world are not the ones that understand sport (their products and services) the best. The most successful sport enterprises are those that understand sports' consumers the best. To that end, the second part of this chapter is concerned with the sports fan and the variables that influence their motivations and behaviour.

We all know what sport is. It permeates modern life with such penetrating intensity that even for those who loathe sport there is little chance of escape. Beyond describing sport as a simple 'physical contest' or 'game', there are six ingredients that paint a more complete picture of sport today.[1] First, it has set and defined rules: in other words a player must behave within certain boundaries to (questionably) enhance 'fairness'. Second, modern sport is highly organised with fixed structures and often substantial systems of infrastructure. Third, sport remains a physical pursuit that includes an element of 'playlike' activity. Fourth, equipment and facilities are essential features of contemporary sport. Fifth, at the heart of all sport lies an intrinsic uncertainty of outcome: there can be no sport unless there is a chance of either victory or defeat. Finally, modern sport requires (ironically) both cooperation and conflict, within the framework of a competition.

These six characteristics of modern sport seem so obvious that we barely question how we have come to understand sport in the same way as individuals thousands of miles across the globe and yet, today, sport does exist in a generically consumable format. Irrespective of your location in the world, if you are familiar with a particular sport you can play it.[2]

However, this has not always been the case. In the days of the ancient Olympiad, sport games and rules were unique to the culture in which they were played.

'In the beginning', sport emerged from the religious and combat rituals of primitive societies. The worship of great hunters, soldiers, leaders and later, great athletes, was common throughout the ancient world. In Europe, Asia and the Americas, people organised funeral feasts, music and games to celebrate the achievements of heroes, keeping both their memories and teachings alive. The ancient Aztecs 'played' a ball game that was actually a 1000-year-old ritual symbolising the struggle of light against darkness, life against death. Similar ball games are known to have emerged from the Indians of North America, and developed over time into what we know today as lacrosse.

The early Greeks (1000BC to 100BC) organised games, athletic events and festivals to honour their gods. Events such as the Olympic Games were hosted in honour of the most powerful of all gods, Zeus. Athletics, in particular, had a huge impact upon Greek society, and reflected the social structure of that civilisation. The abilities of young, wealthy males were praised and valued, whilst the participation of women, older people and those without resources was limited.[3]

Sport-like activities in Roman society (100BC to 500AD) were principally used by leaders to prepare men for warfare. In the interest of the expansion of the Roman Empire, physical activities were deemed useful only if they were also practical from a military viewpoint. Spectacles reminiscent of warfare, such as gladiator fights and chariot races, were organised in massive arenas. These events also served to provide distractions in the form of 'bread and circuses' for the ever-increasing masses, and to dispose of the undesirable (thieves, rapists, murderers and later, Christians). In both Greek and Roman societies, athletic excellence was acknowledged. Victory in the Olympic Games meant athletes could 'sell' their talents in further competition at the Pythian, Isthmian and Nemean Games.[4] Roman 'athletes' were less generously rewarded. Victory in the gladiatorial contests or chariot races often meant that their lives were spared until the next fight or race.

During the Middle Ages (500–1400AD) the nationwide spectacles of the Greeks and Romans were replaced by local games and tournaments. The sport-like activities played reflected a society divided between the masters and masses. The dominant institution of the time, the Catholic Church, adapted various 'pagan' rituals for worship. Many of these ceremonies featured a symbolic tossing of a ball back and forth to represent the struggle between good and evil. These playful dramatisations soon leapt the boundaries of their religious origins. As the Church provided seasonal holidays and areas for play, ball games flourished. By the twelfth century peasants enjoyed numerous types of handball, football and stick-and-ball games. No written rules existed; each game evolved differently from one place to another according to local custom and whim. But in the play of medieval peasants lay the roots of virtually every ball game known in the modern world.[5] The sport of the aristocracy developed quite differently. Since they had won their high standing and fortunes through warfare, they were obliged to fight in order to retain their positions. The dominant play-like activities of nobility were war games known as tournaments. Two different forms of combat dominated the tournaments: jousts and melées. In a melée, 'any number of men fought on each side, wielding dull-edged swords in hand-to-hand combat. In the joust, only two men competed against each other, charging on horseback, with lances raised, down either side of a barrier in an attempt to unseat each other'.[6] Severe injuries and deaths were more the rule than the exception.

In the early 1400s the Renaissance movement (1400–1600) dramatically changed the social, political and spiritual face of Europe. During the Renaissance, which began in Italy, scholars and artists cut themselves free from the ties of the medieval Church and the nobility. The Italian Renaissance man embraced the ancient Greek ideal of a united 'body and soul', and became a 'jack of all trades' including social, intellectual, artistic and sporting activities.[7] For the whole man, physical as well as mental development was important. During this period of renewed appreciation of the human body, the masses continued to practise their localised games, no longer constrained by the strong arm of the Catholic Church. Ruling nobility and monarchs during the Renaissance did not see too much harm in peasants exercising and playing in their own parochial ways.

However, for northern Europe the Renaissance arrived later and with less impact. The northern European Renaissance merged with the Pro-testant Reformation, resulting in a much less colourful and open-minded humanism compared to the Italian Renaissance. Art, literature and education were based in religion and the pursuit of 'godliness', which became the basis of protest against sports in northern Europe. Protestant reformer John Calvin, for instance, claimed that engaging in 'trivial' activities such as sport could infect a person with the poison of sin. The outcome was a fanatic condemnation of amusement and games. Yet, although Calvin and his followers were enormously influential in England for a short period of time, they remained a minority and their extreme views were not accepted and practised by the common people. The forbidden public pastimes proved remarkably resilient and, by the end of the seventeenth century, local, social activities and popular sports thrived as never before in England. This trend continued during the Enlightenment period (1700–1800) during which competitors from different social backgrounds increasingly practised sport-like activities. The colonisation of North America saw some of the popular English games being introduced to groups of immigrants and indigenous people, resulting in a movement away from religious ritual and ceremony. The emphasis was beginning to shift away from ceremony and military preparation towards finding interesting and challenging ways to pass free time.

It was not until the second half of the nineteenth century that sport really began to find a foothold beyond its religious and military roots, in a process historians describe as 'sportification'.[8] Sportification occurred when local sport-like activities evolved into standardised, internationally recognised sports. A handful of sports were modernised in the early 1800s before the Industrial Revolution, the by-product of a small group of the elite and wealthy who travelled liberally and insisted upon standardised rules wherever they played. The formation and development of the prominent sports of the time are summarised in Table 2.1.

The origins of popular sport and regulated sport forms lie in England where the initial development of 'modern' sport was a function of wider social developments, such as government and infrastructure. In other words, the civilising processes that occur in the development of modern nation states can partly explain sportification, or the development of modern sport.[9]

Table 2.1   Periods of sport development

Period	Type of sport
Before 1800	Horse racing, golf, cricket, boxing, rowing, fencing
1820–30	Shooting, sailing
1840–60	Baseball, soccer, rugby, swimming
1860–70	Athletics, skiing, polo, cycling, canoeing
1870–80	American football, lawn tennis, badminton, hockey, bandy
1880–1900	Ice-hockey, gymnastics, basketball, volleyball, judo, table tennis, bowling, weightlifting, speed skating
After 1900	Korfball, handball, orienteering, squash, netball, karate, aikido, tae kwon do

Source: Adapted from M. Bottenburg (1994), *Verborgen competitie, over de uiteenlopende populariteit van sporten.* Amsterdam: Uitgeverij Bert Bakker, p. 17.

The medieval folk activities in Britain were based on local customs and had limited or no rules. Local communities played against each other and, in the context of the game, communal identity was more important than individual identity.[10] In eighteenth-century British society, which was increasingly pacified (internally) and subject to governmental (parliamentary) rule, the first modern sport forms emerged. These sports were more restrained and standardised and developed the first written rules. The 'civilising spurt' that took place at the level of the ruling group in British society extended to groups lower in the class hierarchy, leading to a simultaneous transformation of their approach to politics and leisure. As Elias observed, 'The "parliamentarisation" of the landed classes of England had its counterpart in the "sportisation" of their pastimes'.[11]

Further justification for the theory that modern sports are an exemplification of a civilising process can be observed in the movement towards involving 'independent' match officials in sports such as boxing, rugby and soccer, by using sanctions rather than physical chastisements; these were what we would understand as the first 'penalties, fouls and free-kicks', which were obviously designed to disadvantage the erring participants.[12] As a result of this civilising process – which remains one of the central issues associated with the globalisation of sport – folk activities became further culturally marginalised. Circumstances for the masses began to change dramatically with the Industrial Revolution in England. Trains, cars, telegraphs and telephones created opportunities for inter-regional and (inter)national communication. Magazines, papers and radio provided insights into the lives and activities of people (relatively) far away. Increased opportunities to travel rapidly beyond the borders of one's township or city enabled organisers of local games to play with and against people in other regions. In order to regulate these first inter-regional games, basic rules acceptable to both teams had to be formulated. In other words, sport and society modernised simultaneously: for example, the spread of soccer clubs in the Netherlands was closely related to the development of the Dutch railway system. Increased travel remained the key determinant of sportification.

Throughout history, sport-like games have had meaning beyond the simple activity of tossing a ball between teams. Whether it is to symbolise the fight of good versus evil, or to practise warfare skills, the reasons for participating in sport have been shaped by the societies of the times. Similarly, the evolution of sport spectatorship has developed with those societies to the point where the humble sport watcher, rather than the sport participant, has become the driving power behind the success of global sports. But why do otherwise rational human beings become sport fans, and how might we explain their fanaticism and fickleness?

Before we devote some specific attention to the sports fan, it is appropriate to briefly look ahead to the influence culture can have on sport consumption. If sport is considered a suitable means to express oneself, then cultural orientation to a large extent determines what are and what are not appropriate means of communication in the context of particular sports. Research into the differential popularity of sports led to the recognition that the popularity of a sport is largely determined by the social circumstances and relationships between different societies, rather than as a result of the inherent characteristics of the sport.[13] In other words, if a sport is able to express a (sub)culture's dominant value orientation, it is more likely this sport will become popular in a society than other sports that do not have an equal expressive ability. This is closely related to the evolving of a 'body conscious culture' as a direct result of sportification. Because sportification offered a rational and scientific approach to playing sport, the increasing specialisation of athletes in order to achieve peak performance also led to the establishment of sport as an expression of important (sport-related) cultural values. Sport became a new expression and upholder of community conscience when local communities and folk culture became increasingly marginalised elements of the social fabric. Along the same lines of how local sports became popular nationally (football will be discussed as an example in Chapter 4), national sports became popular internationally. Maarten van Bottenburg argued that individual sports spread from their country of genesis (centre country) to neighbouring countries with close cultural links (semi-peripheral countries), and then on to countries (peripheral) that have cultural similarity with semi-peripheral countries. It goes without saying that those sports that have an extended international history have a first mover advantage in the popularity polls of today. Based on the principle of sports spreading from a centre country to peripheral countries, Trudo Dejonghe[14] proposed a typology that explains the make-up of the global sport system based on cultural affinity of peripheral countries with the sports' country of origin. In principle he argues that when a peripheral country is *passive* in its acceptance of imported sport, it either embraces the external culture, or is not in a position to fight it. This form of 'cultural imperialism' took and takes place in countries such as sub-Saharan Africa, Latin America and the Caribbean, where hegemonic countries such as Britain and the USA introduced their sports. When imported sport is critically assessed, and considered in the context of a host culture as beneficial, neutral or threatening, the peripheral country's attitude can be termed *participative*. Former British colonies, such as South Africa, Canada, New Zealand and Australia, have embraced those sports that help them define themselves as independent nations in their own right and have rejected sports that did not fit their newly found national identity. Canada in particular has developed a range of 'new' or hybrid sports (lacrosse, ice hockey and Canadian football) that serve as identifiers of identity and nationality. Along the same lines, Australians have developed their own unique brand of Australian football. A peripheral country's *conflictuous* response to imported sport is the result of significant cultural difference and incompatibility with the centre country's orientation.

Leading up to the development of the Cold War, the former Soviet Union and its satellite states initially rejected all forms of sport that were direct expressions of Western capitalism. However, when they realised that the truly international sports could be used as tools of cultural and political warfare, mainly to express superiority, they embraced most 'capitalistic' sports, and further re-focused on developing minor sports that were represented at international competitions such as the Olympic Games in order to boost their medal tally.

In his typology, Dejonghe discusses situations in which countries further nurture their locally important sports (such as darts, speed skating, sepak takrow) in concert with the development and (non-) acceptance of global sports. However, in regard to understanding the differential popularity of sport globally, an appreciation of the passive, participative and conflictuous typology is sufficient. From the popularity of sports across nations it is now time to take a closer look at the all-important base in the sport food chain: the sports fan.

The Sports Fan

The fan is an integral part of the contemporary sport landscape, but what are the key influences that affect the behaviour of sports fans? To be certain, understanding the motivations and drivers of fan behaviour is, arguably, the most important element of success for sport enterprises. In this section, we shall highlight the 'harder' elements that have always been associated with fan behaviour, including economic factors such as admission prices, income levels and the degree of 'competitive balance', as well as the less discussed, but equally important, 'softer' factors such as entertainment value, promotional campaigns, venue quality, the game aesthetics, and fan involvement and identification. An array of economic, social, and cultural factors are combined to construct a typology of sport spectatorship which identifies a number of distinct behavioural features that can be used to better understand the sport watching market.

Sport spectator behaviour

The one area that sport's governing bodies, government authorities and the commercial sector have not been able to neatly regulate or manipulate is the values, habits and behaviours of sport spectators. Sporting attendances are more volatile than gross attendance and viewing figures would have us believe. While fluctuations and shifts in attendances and television ratings for sporting events have been documented, and some specific economic influences have been examined, little consideration has been given to the more general cultural and commercial forces that may explain these fluctuations. Neither have there been many attempts to construct a model of sports spectatorship that considers questions such as the following:

1 Under what conditions will sports fans choose to attend a sporting event, watch it on television, or allocate their time to an alternative activity?
2 What factors influence fans to attend games and events on a regular basis or, alternatively, to attend spasmodically? That is, what makes a fan committed, and under what circumstances might that commitment be broken?
3 Why do some fans attach themselves to a single team or player, while others have no special attachment, but still attend games regularly?

The attraction of sports for some is higher than it is for others. Some explain this attraction in terms of fan identification,[15] and the personal commitment and emotional involvement that spectators associate with a sporting team. At one level there are people who have no interest in sports watching, and who go to great lengths to avoid contact with spectator sports. At another level there are people who show strong interest, but attend only occasionally: 'social' fans. At a third level there are regular attendees or watchers who enjoy the spectacle, but forget it quickly. At the fourth level are the fans whose interest is so intense that part of every day is devoted to reflecting on either a team or the sports competition of which it is part.

The frequency with which fans attend sport events tells only part of the spectator story. Every sport has its own special features and public image. Some sports cater for the general public, while others focus on a narrow band of supporters. Games such as bocce and polo do not pretend to embrace a wide cross-section of the community, but both satisfy specific needs in different ways. In one case ethnic identity is important, while in the other exclusivity is dominant. Basketball, on the other hand, has broad appeal, with a particular attraction to adolescent males. Tennis is a game for the middle class, but does not have the gender bias of games like rugby and soccer, while golf is for the rich. At least, these are the popular perceptions. Therefore, while some sports are perceived as 'niche' market, and 'boutique' activities, others attract enormously broad support. A Formula One Grand Prix can generate an international television audience of up to 500 million, while worldwide spectacles such as the World Cup and the Olympic Games consistently attract television audiences in excess of two billion. However, these impressive figures hide the weekly and seasonal variations that occur in most sports competitions, and usually do not explain why some sports always attract more fans than other sports.

The fact of the matter is that a variety of factors impinge upon sports fans' decisions to attend sporting events. Most of the detailed research into sporting attendances has been viewed through the prism of economic models that highlight admission prices, the size of the surrounding sport market, income levels, and team win:loss ratios.[16] These factors are not unimportant, but there are many cultural and social forces that can also have a dramatic influence on the behaviour of fans. Sport watching cannot be reduced to an exercise in cost benefit analysis, and does not often conform to a rational use of scarce time and resources. Sport watching is a social experience, but it is also highly personal. It is often bound up with identity and self-image, and is influenced by the behaviour of others. In other words the faddish and fashionable can mould decisions on how to spend one's spare time. Sports watching can induce responses of such intensity that it resembles some sort of deep spiritual experience.[17] Sport policy-makers and planners are usually mindful of the fans' intense emotional commitment to their teams, but the sport policy maker's drive for structural efficiency, relocation and rationalisation often clashes with the fan's need for continuity and traditional practices. So, what is it that makes sport watching such a passionate pastime for so many people in so many different countries and cultures?

Catharsis and escape

People have always watched others play and, more often than not, paid for the privilege. Sport has never had any difficulty in generating passionate interest. For most fans it provides excitement and arousal in contrast to the routine ordinariness of every day life, and elicits a pleasant level of stimulation, which is essential for the maintenance of mental health.[18] It constitutes the quest for 'excitement in an unexciting society'.[19] Collision sports, such as rugby and American football, and person-on-person sports, such as soccer, netball and basketball, therefore have a strong attraction to fans who need to escape from their tightly controlled work and social environments. In these situations fans are encouraged to take the role of the 'shouting, screaming, arm waving spectator' before returning to their 'more restrained roles of parent, employee and civilised citizen'.[20] For many fans, sport watching is the ultimate escape experience.

Social integration and community

Watching others play sport not only provides an escape from a mechanistic work environment into a world of uncertainty and spontaneity in which sublimated and pent-up emotions can be dissipated: it also supplies a feeling of continuity and familiarity that comes from participating in a seasonal ritual. The weekly cycles of the dramatic match, the match day stimulation, the mid-week review and pre-match media analysis are repeated within a cultural framework insulated from the dirty politics and economics of the 'real' world. For a short time, at least, it takes the fan away from the stress and rampant change in society and the economy. The sport fan is therefore seeking simultaneously opposite experiences. On one hand there is a need to enter a world of high emotion and spontaneity, but on the other there is a strong desire to feel part of a tightly bound community celebrating an event which has its roots, as we have shown, in the distant past.[21] Accordingly, these attitudes are reinforced when the athletes themselves demonstrate 'reciprocity' by pronouncing their loyalty to the club, and their connection to the fans.[22] Community, a sense of belonging, and national pride are frequently associated with athletic success and, as far as most countries are concerned, nothing binds them together more than victory against an old foe.

Ritual and ceremony

The communal experience of sport also works in other ways. It can range from the desire to emulate the hunting patterns of primitive societies,[23] to the need to bring meaning into an increasingly secular society.[24] To this end, 'mythical images', symbols and icons are very important parts of a fan's sporting experience.[25] The Olympic Games exemplify this need by the importance attached to the Olympic torch relay, the lighting of the flame, the Olympic oath, the closing ceremony, and its capacity to generate prodigious symbolic images. For sporting clubs, the theme song, club colours, insignia and mottos fulfil the same function by providing powerful images that signify a common affiliation.

Personal identification

Attending a sporting event also meets the need for social connection, which it does very well by allowing fans to share a common interest in the game, or to express one's shared allegiance to a club or player. Moreover, the connections that fans make with teams and athletes are an important source of 'tribal' identification and self-esteem.[26] Fans who associate with a successful player or team are able to use that success to pretend that they too are successes. In other words, they can bask in the reflected glory of a premiership, pennant or major player award.[27] The supporters of the Arizona Diamondbacks had little to do with the training regimes or team tactics that helped the club win the 2001 US baseball World Series, but their joyous celebrations revealed an intimate emotional affiliation with the team. Such vicarious pleasure may even transform into feelings of competitive success. Research[28] on the area is beginning to confirm what sport marketers have suspected for some time: even though spectators are not actively involved in the game, their exposure to the sport leads to feelings of personal competence and mastery, thus further enhancing their enjoyment of the game. And the more mastery experienced, the more money is spent on ensuring that exposure to the event (and, by association, to self-esteem bolstering experiences) are uninterrupted.

Aesthetic pleasure

Sports watching also gives aesthetic pleasure to fans. While winning gives a strong sense of personal worth, fans are also prepared to pay good money to experience excellence. For many fans the great attraction of sport is its ability to constantly provide memorable incidents that stay in the collective memory. They are the 'great moments' of sport in which drama, virtuosity, and sheer beauty are realised.[29] These great moments were repeated many times over at the 2000 Olympic Games, and included the exceptional diving talents of the Chinese, the raw speed of Marion Jones, the elegant gait of Michael Johnson, and the flawless stroke of Ian Thorpe.

Entertainment and spectacle

Sports watching can be as simple as entertainment and 'instant drama'.[30] Through watching an engaging contest, fans are able to embrace a pleasurable sensory experience. According to Bob Stewart, it may not reveal any mystical force, provide any great spiritual insight, confirm any political or social injustice, or reinforce the fan's place in the world, but merely provide intense enjoyment.[31] At its best, sports entertainment also provides spectacular events and images that 'appeal to the eye by their mass proportions, colour and other dramatic qualities'.[32] Some researchers[33] have found that aspects of game attractiveness, which included special events and record-breaking feats, were positively related to attendance numbers in American Major League Baseball (MLB). Similarly, an FA (Football Association) Cup Final, the NASCAR motor racing event and the Kentucky Derby all provide an appealing blend of high performance, carnival, theatre, emblems and noise which bombard the senses and excite the emotions.

Economics and the Sports Spectator

The above factors help us to understand the general interest and involvement of people in spectator sports and why different social groups respond more positively to some sports, and not others. However, they do not easily explain trends and fluctuations in attendances, or why the popularity of one sport falls while support for another increases. It is therefore useful to consider some specific game-related issues, and some broader cultural and economic forces that are likely to influence levels of sports spectating.

One of the difficulties in investigating changing attendance patterns is to distinguish between those factors affecting long-term trends, and those affecting short-term fluctuations. Changes in cultural practices and patterns of consumer expenditure can partly explain long-term shifts in the numbers of people attending major sporting events, while fad and fashion, saturation marketing, the weather, and the quality and balance of competition help explain weekly and seasonal fluctuations. While it is also difficult to establish precisely the relative strength of specific factors, economists have used mathematical models to explain the impact of quantifiable variables such as price, income, seating capacity, win:loss ratios, and level of competitive balance of the league.[34] These pivotal influences on the demand for team sports can assist sports policy-makers and planners in repositioning events, restructuring leagues, and rescheduling fixtures. As result, they can more effectively deliver the benefits and satisfactions that fans want from their sport experiences.

The balance of the competition

There is general agreement that match attendance will be influenced by the closeness of the pennant or championship race. As more teams have a chance of reaching the finals or play-offs, fans will expect a close contest, and anticipate high quality play. This anticipation will be reflected in a higher level of fan enjoyment and consumer utility, and a boost to crowd size. The term 'parity' is frequently used to describe a situation where, at the beginning of each sports season, most teams are expected to have an equal chance of reaching the play-offs, and where the teams in the play-offs will vary from season to season. In Australia's major team sports leagues during the late 1970s and early 1980s, the level of parity was frequently low, and this coincided with falling attendances. Between 1975 and 1985 only six clubs out of a total of twelve participated in the Australian football grand final. Over the same period, the Sydney Swans (previously South Melbourne), St Kilda, Geelong, Melbourne, Footscray and Fitzroy clubs, the worst performing six, collectively played in only eleven final series. In Sydney rugby league, Penrith, Western Suburbs, North Sydney and St George were also infrequent participants in the finals. However, during the 1990s, a combination of player drafts and salary caps created more balanced competitions in both rugby league and Australian football, resulting in a sharp increase in attendance levels.

Uncertainty of game outcome

Generally, the closer the expected result of the match, the more attractive a game will be to fans.[35] On the other hand, fans will be less enthusiastic about a game in which the outcome is seen as a foregone conclusion. An examination of the premier Scottish Soccer League showed – somewhat unsurprisingly – that games which were expected to be close, and which had a bearing on the championship, attracted the largest crowds.[36] Similarly, a study[37] on a leading French soccer club discovered that the single most important variable affecting fan attendance was the possibility of seeing an exciting match where neither team was expected to dominate. Consistent results were found with premier Australian football leagues, where a close seasonal competition was associated with larger crowds.[38]

The quality of visiting teams

The effect of the visiting or opposing team on home match attendances can be significant. Games between clubs with low win:loss ratios will not attract fans, even if they are expected to be close contests. Moreover, when a good team is playing a poor team, a good home team will attract substantially more spectators than a poor home team. Naturally, fans would rather identify with a winning team than a losing team, and will pay for the opportunity. When a team is doing well, attendances will be high regardless of which opponent it is matched against. On the other hand, when a team is doing poorly, fans need an additional incentive to attend, such as comfortable seating, an opposing team with a good win:loss record, star players, or some other attraction. A study of Major League Baseball in the USA has shown that promotional campaigns and special discounts are effective in building crowds in these cases.[39]

Identification with a winning team

As indicated in the previous section, supporters achieve satisfaction from identifying with a winning team. It is no surprise that clubs such as the New York Yankees, Manchester United and the Los Angeles Lakers also have the largest supporter base. A team that consistently loses will have difficulty attracting large crowds. The attraction of a winning team will also often extend beyond the season in which the title was won, or relative success achieved. This expectation of success might explain the large crowds that follow unsuccessful teams. At the start of each season, officials and fans build up each other's expectations until there is serious agreement that a championship victory is imminent. It has been noted that home team spectators require more than a 60 per cent chance of winning before attending a Major League Baseball game.[40] One explanation for this blatant demand for a winning team was that it costs too much to attend a Major League Baseball game to chance witnessing a loss.

Prices

This factor is not important within a season since prices are usually fixed, and will be the same for nearly all venues. Between seasons, however, price changes may influence match attendance. In the past, some anecdotal evidence indicated that increased prices were associated with falling attendances, but analysis of longer time series data on some sports have suggested that total attendances have been only marginally influenced by admission prices.[41] The demand for spectator sport is therefore generally price 'inelastic', that is, an increase in admission prices and the cost of attending is not likely to diminish attendances to a marked degree. In some ways this is surprising given the costs of attending professional sport, particularly in the USA. For the National Basketball Association (NBA), National Hockey League (NHL) and National Football League (NFL), the average ticket is priced over US$50. Major League Baseball (MLB) is more reasonable at around US$20. However, as we will argue later, professional sport is being played less for the benefit of the live fan, and more for the benefit of television spectators.

Income levels

All the evidence shows that the relationship between income levels and match attendances is an inverse one. As real personal disposable income increases, there will, all other things being equal, be a fall in match attendances. Longitudinal studies in Britain showed that for every 1 per cent increase in consumer expenditure between the 1950s and the 1980s, the demand for football (soccer) fell by 1 per cent.[42] Since soccer was traditionally a working-class game (that is, it was more popular amongst those on lower incomes), improvements in living standards provided these people with the income to indulge in alternative leisure activities. As more people obtained access to cars and television sets, they devoted more of their leisure time to these products. Weekends could be used to visit relatives, go on picnics or relax in front of the television. Many spectator sports are therefore seen as 'inferior goods', which means that as people become wealthier and more exposed to other leisure activities they develop more exotic patterns of consumption and spend less on traditional sport activities. Sport marketers have been a little slow to pick up on this fact, which for some seems counter-intuitive. Nevertheless, the better sport enterprises have worked hard to give their products a more sophisticated twist. In part, successfully selling the sport product to the corporate market via hospitality packages has addressed this issue.

Catchment population and location of clubs

The location of clubs and competitions also impacts upon attendance and interest levels. Even though fans are attracted to successful clubs, an equally important factor influencing the crowd size is the size of the market that surrounds the club's home base. In other words, the positioning of teams in high population regions will increase the potential spectator base and lead to larger crowds.[43]

The venue

The stadium or arena in which a team plays can also affect interest. A facility will attract fans if it is able to provide an attractive setting, a convenient layout, good directional signage, a visually appealing and watchable scoreboard, comfort, a better and proximate view of the contest, or easy accessibility. More recently, studies have made significant advances regarding the relationship between venue management and attendance.[45] It has been revealed that the standards of stadium design, food and drink, ticketing, child facilities, access and other auxiliary entertainment options have an effect on attendance levels. Not only are these quality factors a drawcard for fans, but they are also a negative influence on attendance when seen to be inadequate or below expectations.

The special experience

Special experiences will vary with the subjective responses of fans. They may involve the participation of a star player or personality, the likelihood of a record-breaking performance, the probability of a dramatic or even violent encounter, the expectation of highly skilled and aesthetically pleasing play, or indeed anything that may give pleasure to fans. There is some evidence that the appearance of a 'personality player' and a belief that fans are obtaining value for money are increasingly important triggers for people to attend sporting events.[46] Whereas, in the past, most of the stadium seats were filled by loyal supporters of one or the other competing teams, more spectators are now there to enjoy the experience, rather than to see their favourite team win. To an increasing number of fans, the entertainment value comprises more than just the contest between the competing teams. The value can result from the availability of reserved seating, access to a private box, and the opportunity to meet a celebrity or even a politician. Other value-adding experiences include the expectation of a special occurrence, a pairing of special players, the presence of a glamour player, a complementary display or event, and attractive drinking and eating facilities. The contest is just part of the total package or experience.

Promotional factors

Promotional strategies, particularly when accompanied by admission concessions, sales vouchers and merchandising discounts are important influences on attendances. An American study of basketball indicated that advertising, direct mail outs, giveaway prizes, the promotion of upcoming games and the provision of premium seating can increase crowd sizes.[47] A similar study of baseball showed that promotional campaigns were effective in bringing fans to games, particularly where the probability of the home team losing was high.[48] It has also been demonstrated that the promotional effect of viewing home games on commercial or pay television, as well as listening on the radio are positively associated with subsequent attendance at a game.[49]

Weather conditions

The weather can affect match attendances by influencing both the conditions under which spectators watch the game, and the quality of the game itself. A waterlogged, or rain-affected ground will not only inconvenience many fans, but may also produce restricted, slow-moving games in which elements of spectacle are eliminated. If very poor weather keeps people away then so too might very good weather. Studies of American football in the Great Lakes area showed that a sunny day enabled people to engage in substitute leisure activities.[50] In Australia, Sydney's temperate climate, in combination with the close proximity of a variety of water-based activities, may partly explain its inability to draw fans to major sporting events in the way that Melbourne does. Conversely, Melbourne's frequent dull and overcast days may be ideal for attracting fans to games since it discourages other forms of outdoor activities. The relationship between the state of the weather and crowd size is usually framed within an intuitive logic that says that rain and wind will stop people from attending games, but much of the discussion is still speculative.

Alternative activities

The availability of alternative activities will also influence match attendances. While this factor is not usually significant in influencing the variations in weekly attendance figures, it can be used to explain a decline in long-term per capita attendances. The cinema, Internet, video games and the development of other 'minor' sports has cut into the market for traditional national sports. People have become increasingly mobile and are able to choose between an increasing number of leisure and entertainment alternatives. This trend is continuing as many more major events and festivals in the arts and sports are conducted. The choice between competing leisure activities has never been more demanding.

Social change, fashion and fad

A combination of changing family and inter-gender relations, and the increasing participation of women in the workforce, has also influenced attendance levels at major sporting events. It has been speculated that the loosening-up of gender roles has forced men to take on additional family responsibilities. As a result, sports watching is given a lower weekend priority. On the other hand, the increasing divorce rate and the 'weekend father' phenomenon have led to the need for additional 'single parent' weekend activities such as spectator sport. The net impact of these opposing forces has probably been initially to reduce match attendance, but it is still highly speculative.[51] Changing social relationships can work in other ways as well. The halo effect, where the attitudes of friends, colleagues and reference groups influence the behaviour of individuals, can affect decisions to attend sports events. An American study of minor league baseball competition showed that the positive views of friends about the game, as well as its potential to provide exciting entertainment, is important in drawing crowds to games.[52] Community views on violence in sport have produced some ambiguous outcomes. On one hand, the brutality that surrounds boxing has created a poor public image and falling attendance; on the other hand, rugby union, which promotes itself as a collision sport, is enormously popular, particularly at an international level.

Fractured traditions

The letters to the editor section of the most national newspapers inevitably include someone's lament that the rampant commercialisation of sport has caused fans to lose interest in professional team sports. Fans frequently mourn the loss of player loyalty to clubs, and growing influences of business and businessmen over sport. However, the impact of fractured traditions is more complex than the critics would have us believe. The commercial entrenchment of sport has also created a level of public awareness and interest that would not have been possible in the quasi-amateur days of the 1960s. It has brought with it more attractive venues, created strong intercity rivalries, and established a colourful variety of images and icons that links fans even more closely to the collective personality of the club and its players. It is clear that the hypercommercialism of professional sport has squeezed much of the romance out of the game, destroyed the myth that sport can be separated from business, and undermined the paternalistic claim that real sport is only played by amateurs. It has also created 'in your face' spectacles and intercity rivalries where sensory stimulation is a central source of spectator pleasure. The contemporary sporting experience offers a massive array of benefits and delights, and sports fans are increasingly customising these benefits to meet their own idiosyncratic needs. With so many influences on spectator behaviour, it is difficult to establish clearly the relative strength of each factor, their interdependencies, and how they may be grouped around common themes and behavioural categories.

Modelling Spectator Behaviour

It has been our contention that understanding the factors that affect spectator behaviour is critical to understanding sport's future. While many of the previously discussed factors are outside the control of sporting policy-makers and planners, the key factors of game quality, competitive balance, venue quality, some of the special experiences, promotion, and 'traditional practices' are clearly in their domain. We have also demonstrated that there are many influences on sporting attendances, and a strategy that addresses the varied needs of fans is essential if sports are to maintain their loyalty. While innovative fixturing and promotion are essential, it is also important that appropriate recognition be given to history and tradition, and the passionate fan identification that goes with it. Sports fans are driven by a complex array of personal needs and fantasies, collective affiliations and material incentives.

A model of spectator behaviour

We have gone to some lengths to demonstrate that there are many dimensions to the sports fan, and that understanding these dimensions will ultimately prove fruitful in clarifying global sport and its future. We have also shown that not all sports fans share the same characteristics or hold the same views about their favourite pastimes. They have different motives for watching, different patterns of attendance, different levels of affiliation and identification, and different beliefs and attitudes about the place of tradition and nostalgia in their sports. They have different ideas about the importance of peripheral services at the venue, and different behaviours when it comes to reflecting and commenting upon the game. That is to say, there are many different ways of understanding, viewing and consuming sport. For some fans, identification with the team is so strong that attendance is habitual. For others, the only significant factor in determining their attendance is the likelihood of a favoured team winning. On the other hand, some fans, while wanting to experience a high-quality game, will see it not in terms of winning or losing, but rather in terms of the game's entertainment value. Another group of supporters may want a rewarding sensory experience, while some others may be primarily interested in the appearance of a star player. In short, we can no longer talk about the average sports fan, or notions of mass spectator appeal, since there now exists a broad spectrum of fan beliefs and behaviours.

Bob Stewart and Aaron Smith outlined a model that has proved useful in understanding and even segmenting fans.[53] The primary distinction is that some fans regularly attend games, whilst others are irregular. For example, in Europe it has been established that around 56 per cent of total football spectators attend less than one-third of all matches.[54] Similarly, an Australian football survey found that those who attended fewer than ten games over a 22-week season accounted for nearly 60 per cent of total attendance.[55] It was also established that those who attended matches irregularly had been consistently irregular in their attendance over the previous three years. Conversely, those who frequently attended matches had been consistent in their attendance patterns over the same time period. It was concluded that the key to increasing attendances was to ensure not only that there be an increase in the total number of 'irregulars', but that there also be an increase in their attendance pattern.

The second distinction to make is that fans have different motives for attending games. Some fans go ostensibly to see their favourite team contest the game. These *passionate partisans* are loyal to their team and get despondent when their team loses and elated when it wins. They are prepared to incur inconvenience in the form of a wet day, or a long, slow trip to the stadium. They form the core support base of the competition, and their moods and identity are bound up with the successes and failures of the favourite team. They are heavy purchasers of memorabilia and club merchandise, and are great defenders of club history and traditions. They have a significant personal investment in the club and its season-to-season performance.

There are also many sport fans who are more interested in supporting a winning team than blindly following their team through ups and downs. These *champ followers* share some of the emotional highs and lows of the passionate partisan, but are more flighty and less fanatical. The champ follower's allegiance will change according to whatever team happens to be the top performer. Alternatively, champ followers often remain hidden from public view until their favourite team starts winning a few games. They become vocal and active supporters until such time as their team begins to lose again.

A third category is the *reclusive partisan*, whose interest in the 'game' and commitment to the team is strong, but who attends infrequently. Reclusive partisans are opinionated, and apparently loyal to their team. They are susceptible to the influence of others, and may attend in response to reference group advice, politically correct signals, a change in fashion, or media saturation coverage of the event.

The common motive shared by each of the above categories is the desire to see their team win. Their dominant concern is not whether it is likely to be a close contest, whether it will be skilful and stimulating to watch, or whether fireworks, ethnic dance activities and a 'rock and roll' band accompanies the game, but the likelihood of success. They are attracted to team performance or team quality. They are parochial.

There are, at the same time many fans who, while notionally committed to a particular team, are more interested in the 'game' and attend more frequently than the reclusive partisan but less frequently than the passionate partisan. They are called *theatregoers*. The theatregoer is motivated to seek entertainment through having a pleasurable experience. However, the entertainment involves more than cheerleaders, sky-divers, giveaways and brass bands: it also includes comfortable and proximate viewing conditions, easy access, the availability of complimentary services, a close contest and the participation of star performers. The theatregoer is attracted to comfort, enjoyment, excitement, sensory stimulation and uncertainty of outcome. Since their team and game loyalty is initially low, most theatregoers will attend less frequently than passionate partisans unless the likelihood of exciting and pleasurable contests continues throughout the season. At the same time, a few theatregoers will put such high value on their sporting experiences that they will become regular patrons. In other words, theatregoers may be described as either *casual* or *committed*.

The final spectator category is the *aficionado*. Like the theatregoer, the *aficionado* will be attracted to games which are expected to be exciting, and which contain star performers. However, unlike most theatregoers, aficionados attend frequently because of their strong attachment to the structure of the game and its athletic practices. They value games that provide high skill levels, tactical complexity and aesthetic pleasure, even if they are likely to be one-sided or unexciting. They are purists, and will be at their match of the day, which may or may not include the top-performing teams. The aficionado will also be attracted to a quality venue since it will accentuate a quality performance. Both the aficionado and the theatregoer show only moderate concern about who wins or loses. Their dominant concern is game performance or game quality, and not the likely success or failure of a particular team.

While each of the above categories contains fans with an interest in the game or competition, there are significant differences in the ways in which their interest is expressed. Different incentives will activate different segments. A change to the structure or conduct of a competition that attracts more of one type, or segment, may be resisted by another type or segment. On one hand, theatregoers are likely to attend more games where the stadiums are comfortable, games are expected to be close and competitive, and where complimentary entertainment is provided. On the other hand, passionate partisans and champ followers may think that such changes undermine the essential nature and traditions of the game, and lessen the expectation of success. Theatregoers will be excited about

the sensory delights that they see arising from new rules designed to speed up the game, an expanded league or the relocation of one team to another city; but passionate and reclusive partisans will view such adjustments as treachery, and may in extreme cases sever their relationship with their club. Table 2.2 summarises the different categories of spectators, their motivations and behaviour.

Figure 2.1 illustrates Stewart and Smith's model of sports spectatorship. It clarifies some of the motivational and behavioural characteristics of spectators, and gives sports policy-makers and planners a useful tool for determining future strategic directions for their competitions. The model's aim is to identify different categories of spectators, and for each category establish their preference for particular types of games. One type of game emphasises team quality in which the focus is on the winning team, and fan identity with that team. The other type of game emphasises game quality in which the focus is on the close, exciting, entertaining, skilful or significant contest. At the same time, the model looks at the

Table 2.2 Spectator categories and motivations

Type of Spectator	Motivation	Behaviour
Aficionado	Seeks quality performance	Loyal to 'game' rather than team, although may usually have a 'preferred' team; attends on regular basis – puts emphasis on aesthetic or skill dimension.
Theatregoer [casual and committed]	Seeks entertainment, close contest	Only moderate loyalty to team; frequent losses create disinterest only in team; but may attend other games.
Passionate partisan	Wants team to win	Loyal to team; in short term loyalty undiminished by frequent losses; strongly identifies with, and responds to teams success and failure.
Champ follower	Wants team to win	Short term loyalty; loyalty a function of team success; expects individual or team to dominate otherwise supports another team or spends time elsewhere.
Reclusive partisan	Wants team to win	Loyalty not always translated into attendance; strong identification but provides latent support only

Source: Reproduced from A. Smith and B. Stewart (1999), *Sports Management: A Guide to Professional Practice*, Allen & Unwin, Sydney.

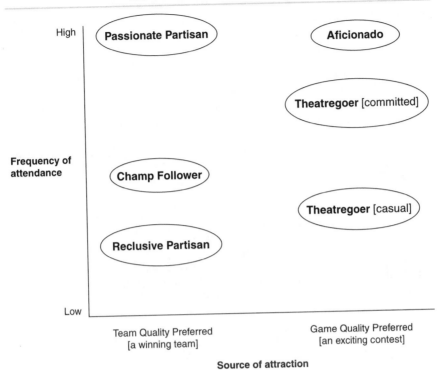

Figure 2.1 Stewart–Smith model of sports fans

frequency with which each spectator attends games, with infrequent at one end of the scale and habitual attendance at the other. The model therefore classifies sport fans on the basis of two criteria. The first centres on the sources and dimensions of the attraction: it can be the team or the game; the skill or the entertainment; and expecting to win or expecting to watch a close contest. The second centres on the frequency of attendance, which can range from infrequent to habitual.

In this world of customised production, the segmented market, multiple identities and shifting loyalties, the successful sport organisations will be those which can identify the different needs of fans and deliver a variety of benefit packages. The age of the mass sport spectator market has passed. Why people play sport today and purchase tickets to watch games can only be understood when we understand the modern social setting. Sport remains as important to today's society as play-like games were to ancient societies. However, today the face of sport has been transformed by technology, and the economic benefits of sport have been exploited ruthlessly. Sport business is a complex set of structures and activities.

Notes and references

1   D. Shilbury and J. Deane (2001), *Sport management in Australia*, Strategic Sport Management, Melbourne; J. W. Loy (1968), 'The nature of sport: A definitional effort', *Quest*, 10, 1–15; H. J. VanderZwaag and T. J. Sheehan (1978), *Introduction to Sport Studies: From the Classroom to the Ballpark*, William C. Brown, Dubuque, Iowa.
2   M. Bottenburg (1994), *Verborgen competitie, over de uiteenlopende populariteit van sporten*, Uitgeverij Bert Bakker, Amsterdam.
3   J. J. Coakley (1990), *Sport in Society, Issues and Controversies* (4th edn), Times Mirror/Mosby, St. Louis, Missouri.
4   W. J. Baker (1988), *Sports in the Western World* (rev. edn), University of Illinois Press, Urbana, p. 22.
5   W. J. Baker (1988), *Sports in the Western World*, p. 40.
6   W. J. Baker (1988), *Sports in the Western World*, p. 50.
7   W. J. Baker (1988), *Sports in the Western World*, p. 59.
8   M. Bottenburg (1994), *Verborgen competitie*.
9   N. Elias (1994), *The Civilizing Process: The History of Manner and State-Formation and Civilisation*. Blackwell, Oxford; N. Elias and E. Dunning (1986), *Quest for Excitement: Sport and Leisure in the Civilizing Process*, Blackwell, Oxford.
10 E. Dunning (1999), *Sport Matters: Sociological Studies of Sport, Violence and Civilisation*, Routledge, London, p. 89.
11 N. Elias (1986), 'The genesis of sport as a sociological problem', in N. Elias and E. Dunning (eds), *Quest for Excitement*, p. 34.
12 E. Dunning (1999), *Sport Matters*, p. 64.
13 M. Bottenburg (1994), *Verborgen competitie*.
14 T. Dejonghe (2001), *Sport in de wereld: Ontstaan, evolutie en verspreiding*, Academia Press, Gent. p. 117.
15 W. A. Sutton, M. A. McDonald, G. R. Milne and A. J. Cimperman (1997), 'Creating and fostering fan identification in professional sport', *Sports Marketing Quarterly*, Vol. 6, No. 1, 15–29.
16 S. E. Bramvold, D. W. Pan and T. E. Gabert (1997), 'Effects of winning percentage and market size on attendance in Major League baseball', *Sports Marketing Quarterly*, Vol. 6, No. 4, 35–42; L. M. Kochman (1995), 'Major League Baseball: What really puts fans in the stands', *Sports Marketing Quarterly*, Vol. 4, No. 1, 9–21; J. A. Schofield (1983), 'Performance and Attendance at Professional Team Sports', *Journal of Sports Behavior*, Vol. 6, 196–206.
17 M. Novak (1976), *The Joy of Sports*, Basic Books, New York.
18 C. Gratton and P. Taylor (1985), *Sport and Recreation: An Economic Analysis*, E. & F.N. Spon, London.
19 N. Elias and E. Dunning (1971) 'The Quest for Excitement in Unexciting Societies', in E. Dunning (ed.), *The Sociology of Sport: A Selection of Readings*, Routledge, London.
20 A. Guttmann (1986), *Sports Spectators*, Columbia University Press, New York, p. 156.
21 A. Cooke (1994), *The Economics of Leisure and Sport*, Routledge, London; G. A. Smith (1982), 'Profile of the Deeply Committed Sports Fan', *Arena Review*, March, 60–72.
22 T. Crossett (1995), 'Toward an Understanding of On Site Fan-Athletic Relations: A Case Study of the LPGA', *Sport Marketing Quarterly*, Vol. 4 No. 2, 31–8.
23 D. Morris (1981), *The Soccer Tribe*, Jonathan Cape, London.
24 A. Guttmann (1986), *Sports Spectators*.

25 J. Segrave and D. Chu (1996), 'The Modern Olympic Games: An Access to Ontology', *Quest*, No. 48, 57–66.

26 L. Sandercock and I. Turner (1981), *Up Where Cazaly? The Great Australian Game*, Granada, Sydney.

27 J. McKay (1991), *No. Pain, No. Gain? Sport and Australian Culture*, Prentice Hall Australia, Sydney.

28 D. L. Kerstetter and G. M. Kovich (1997), 'An Involvement Profile of Division I Women's Basketball Spectators', *Journal of Sport Management*, Vol. 11, 234–49.

29 J. Kupfer (1988), 'Sport: "The Body Electric"', in W. J. Morgan and K. Meier, *Philosophic Inquiry in Sport*, Human Kinetics, Champaign, pp. 467–8.

30 N. Wilson (1990), *The Sports Business: The Men and the Money*, Mandarin, London, p. 181.

31 R. Stewart (1990), 'Sport as Big Business', in G. Lawrence and D. Rowe (eds), *Powerplay: The Commercialism of Australian Sport*, Hale & Iremonger, Sydney.

32 J. MacAloon (1981), *This Great Symbol: Pierre de Coubertin and the Origins of the Modern Olympic Games*, The University of Chicago Press, Chicago, p. 243.

33 R. A. Baade and L. J. Tichen (1990), 'An Analysis of Major League Baseball Attendance, 1969–1987, *Journal of Sport and Social Issues*, Vol. 14, No. 1, 14–32.

34 J. Cairns, N. Jennett and P. J. Sloane (1986), 'The Economics of Professional Team Sports', *Journal of Economic Studies*, Vol. 13. No. 1, 3–80.

35 J. Marcum and T. Greenstein (1985), 'Factors affecting attendance of Major League Baseball', *Sociology of Sport Journal*, March, 3–30.

36 N. Jennett (1984), 'Attendances, Uncertainty of Outcome and Policy in the Scottish Football League', *Scottish Journal of Political Economy*, Vol. 31 No. 2., 3–30.

37 A. Ferrand and M. Pages (1996), 'Football Supporter Involvement: Explaining football match loyalty, *European Journal for Sport Management*, Vol. 3, No. 1, 7–20.

38 P. Fuller and M. Stewart (1993), 'Attendance Patterns at Victorian and South Australian Football Games', *Working Papers Series in Economics and Finance*, RMIT, Melbourne, April.

39 J. Marcum and T. Greenstein (1985), 'Factors affecting attendance of Major League Baseball'.

40 L. M. Kochman, 'Major League Baseball'.

41 C. Morley and K. Wilson (1986), 'Fluctuating VFL Attendances: Some insights from an Economic Analysis', *Sporting Traditions*, Vol. 3, No. 1 (November), 69–81.

42 A. Cooke (1994), *The Economics of Leisure and Sport*, Routledge, London.

43 M. Rosentraub (1997), *Major League Losers: The Real Cost of Sport and Who is Paying for It*, Basic Books, New York.

44 K. Wakefield and H. Sloan (1995), 'The Effects of Team Loyalty and Selected Stadium Factors on Spectator Attendance', *Journal of Sport Management*, 9, 153–172; K. Wakefield, J. Blodgett and H. Sloan (1996), 'Measurement and Management of the Sportscape', *Journal of Sport Management*, 15–31.

45 D. Robertson and N. Pope (1999), 'The Causes of Attendance and Non-attendance in Live Professional Sport: A case study of the Brisbane Broncos and the Brisbane Lions', *The Cyber Journal of Sport Marketing*, Vol. 3, 1–13.

46 J. Zhang, D. Pease, S. Hui and T. Michaud (1995), 'Variables Affecting the Spectator Decision to Attend NBA Games', *Sport Marketing Quarterly*, Vol. IV, No. 4, 29–39.

47 J. Zhang, O. Pease, S. Hui and T. Michaud, 'Variables Affecting the Spectator Decision to Attend NBA Games'.

48 J. Marcum and T. Greenstein, 'Factors affecting attendance of Major League Baseball'.

49 J. J. Zhang, D. G. Pease and D. W. Smith (1998), 'Relationship Between Broadcasting Media and Minor League Hockey Game Attendance', *Journal of Sport Management*, Vol. 12, 103–22.

50 R. Noll (1974), 'Attendances and Price Setting', in R. Noll (ed.), *Government and the Sports Business*, Brookings Institution, Washington, DC.

51 It may be noted that about 65 per cent of females aged 65 years and over are widows. With the ageing of the population, the gap between the life expectancy of the sexes closes due to women working and smoking more. The gender composition of the growing group of retired people will therefore increasingly balance out and this may have significant effects on sport participation; on support activities (partners accompanying their counterparts to the stadium if indeed the necessary comfort and safety is provided); on sport viewing (for example, older people have different sleeping patterns than young people which may impact sports programming); and finally, sport sponsorship (for example, global wine brands replacing global soft drink brands).

52 K. Wakefield and H. Sloan, 'The Effects of Team Loyalty'.

53 A. Smith and B. Stewart (1999), *Sport Management: A Guide to Professional Practice*, Allen & Unwin, Sydney.

54 A. Ferrand and M. Pages, 'Football Supporter Involvement'.

55 Victorian Football League (1985), *VFL Football: Establishing the Basis for Future Success*, Melbourne.

CHAPTER 3

Putting Sport on the Map:
The Structure of Global Sport

I did everything from leading the band to running races with horses.
I had baseball teams, basketball teams and candy bars named after me,
sold soda pop and danced in dance marathons. None of these ventures
turned out to be profitable.
Jesse Owens, 1951 (on his career after his Olympic triumph in 1936)

As the previous chapter outlined, the beginnings of sport were deeply rooted in ritual pastimes, military service and political distraction, and formed an indistinguishable interrelationship with the social constructions of the communities in which the sport was played. The economic benefits of sport were quickly pursued, as the emotional attachments people made with some sports grew, until they were themselves an indispensable element in the socio-sport alloy. The inevitable outcome was the development of a sport-based industry. Table 3.1 summarises the development from local sport to global sport, along the lines of the civilising process discussed in the previous chapter, and with consideration of the dominant means of international communication and relationships.

The road to global sport marks the changing role of sport in society, and it provides the building blocks of the sport industry as we know it today. An industry can be defined as a group of organisations that produce products or classes of products that are close substitutes for each other.[1] The sport industry therefore consists of those organisations producing sport-related products that may be substitutable. Within the sport industry, however, there are different groupings of organisations that produce similar sport products.

Given the rapid growth that the sport industry has enjoyed, and the increasingly blurred distinctions between sport, recreation, leisure, entertainment and business, it is helpful to consider some models of how the industry is grouped and classified. Packianathan Chelladurai[2] provided one of the first useful definitions of the industry, arguing that a product-

Table 3.1   The road to popular modern sport

Period	1850–1914	1918–1980	1980–now
Principal objective	Morality, education, values	Spectacle	Commerce and communication
Institutional and legal framework	Non-profit independent clubs	National and international federations	Commercial corporations
Driver of progress in sport	Muscles	Sophisticated sporting equipment	Science
Scope of competition	National	International	Global
Number of participants at the Olympic Games (OG)	13 (1896)	59 (1948)	197 (1996)
Principal media	Written media	Radio	Television
Number of OG television spectators	–	200,000 (OG 1936)	33.4 billion (World Cup 1998)
Number of international competitions	20 (1912)	315 (1977)	700 (1996)
Principal financing	Participants	Spectators	Television, corporations and shareholders

Source: Adapted from T. Dejonghe (2001), *Sport in de wereld: Ontstaan, evolutie en verspreiding.* Academia Press, Gent; J. F. Bourg and J. J. Gouget (1998), *Analyse economique du sport*, PUF, Paris.

based classification is appropriate. He used six main categories of sport products to describe the sport industry, including sporting goods, participant services, spectator services, sponsorship services, psychic benefits and social ideas. It is worth exploring these divisions in order to better understand the nature of the sport product.[3]

Sporting goods include all the equipment needed to engage in various kinds of sports. A *participant service* distinguishes between consumer services and human services. Consumer services are routine services and involve little information or expertise (for example, renting equipment) whereas human services use information and knowledge to make an impact upon the client. But it is in relation to *spectator services* that the model hits upon the entertainment element of contemporary sport. Entertainment is the core product of exchange, consisting of three significant components. These components are the contest (including a certain level of excellence in competition), the spectacle (including different forms of entertainment around the sporting contest), and the 'third' place (the sporting venue as an opportunity for casual sociability). We shall return to these three elements of entertainment later as we consider the linkages between traditional entertainment and sport.

Within *sponsorship services*, the sport organisation provides the sponsor with access to communication with a specific market: the fans and spectators. In addition, opportunities for the sponsors to associate themselves with the sport organisation are exchanged. When fundraising or seeking a donation, altruistic and/or *psychic benefits* are exchanged, and when sport organisations are involved in promoting health, fitness or non-smoking behaviour, they are operating in the business of exchanging *social ideas*. Management of the sport organisation is all about organising and producing the different products that are being exchanged. This typology is presented in Figure 3.1.

Hans Westerbeek and David Shilbury[4] have taken this product approach slightly further by identifying four main categories of sport products. They pick up on the pivotal dimension that the sport facility plays in the production process of sport products, and list sporting goods, sport activity services, sport facility services and sport consultation services as the main categories. They feel that sport activity services and sport facility services would best be combined as facility dependent sport services. Both product groupings are highly dependent on the sport facility when producing and distributing the sport product. Another characteristic of facility dependent sport services is that the sporting activity is the core element of the total service experience. Without sporting activity there is no sport product. Their typology is presented in Table 3.2.

Facility Dependent Sport Services

As we have already observed, sport as an industry is increasingly prominent in terms of its economic importance on a global scale. Economic importance is of course, expressed in financial terms (in this case, how much an industry contributes to overall economic activity). Nearly five years ago, the General Association of International Sports

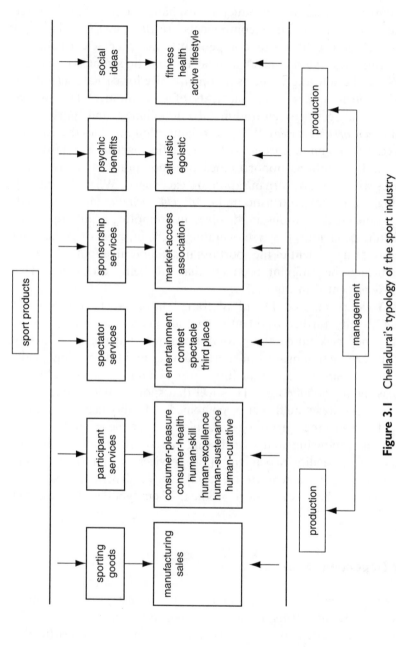

Figure 3.1 Chelladurai's typology of the sport industry

Source: P. Chelladurai (1994), 'Sport management: defining the field', *European Journal for Sport Management*, 1(1), 7–21.

Table 3.2 Westerbeek and Shilbury's classification of the sport industry

Sporting goods	Sport activity services	Sport facility services	Sport consultation services
• apparel • shoes • equipment • team and/or league merchandise • 'sport' licensed products	• PE lessons • sport specific instruction • event organising • community based programmes • coaching	• government owned and operated • government owned, privately operated • privately owned and operated	• programming • management and marketing advice • medical advice • design, building and maintenance advice

$$\Downarrow \qquad \Downarrow$$

Facility Dependent Sport Services

Source: H. M. Westerbeek and D. Shilbury (1999), 'Increasing the focus on "place" in the marketing mix for facility dependent sport services', Sport Management Review, 2(1), 1–24.

Federations (GAISF) estimated that the turnover of the global sport industry was approximately US$80 billion, contributing about 3 per cent to total global trade.[5] However, this figure calculates the size of the sport industry based only upon revenue figures from gate receipts, television rights and sponsorships; sport services that have become part of the industry sector defined as 'corporate sport'.

Corporate sport

According to David Shilbury and John Deane,[6] sport management scholars at Deakin University in Australia, there are six primary characteristics of corporate sport:

- the sport possesses a significant administrative structure
- the sport pays athletes to play (it employs professionals)
- the sport has the ability to generate substantial income (this implies income through three sources: gate receipts, television rights and sponsorship)
- the sport's management adopts both internal and external perspectives
- there is uncertainty of outcome (of the sporting contest)
- the sport provides entertainment.

Of all these elements, the ability for sport to generate substantial revenues has become the most prominent feature of corporate sport. In some countries such as Spain, gate receipts remain the chief source of income (in Spanish football, match day income represents 45 per cent of total revenue, against 38 per cent as a result of television income) for corporate sport organisations. However, average income from television rights and commercial activities such as sponsorship are steadily increasing in relative importance. For example, in the Italian and French soccer leagues, television revenues represent 56 per cent of the total revenue picture. In other words, the majority of income for international sports federations and large domestic sport organisations is generated by selling spectators services, sponsorship (commercial) services and broadcast rights.

In the United States in particular, a fourth category has emerged as a major source of revenue: licensing rights. Sport organisations sell off the right to use their trademark on a broad range of merchandise. In the four leading sporting leagues in the United States (NFL, NBA, NHL, MLB) the relative importance of the sources of income differs in each league. For example, in regard to the total income picture, gate receipts are far more important in the NHL compared to the other three leagues. Television rights are most important for the NFL franchises while, in the NHL, more money is made through selling licensing rights when compared with the other leagues.

Participant sport

A second category of facility dependent sport services may be defined as participant sport (Chelladurai's participant services). Participant sport includes all sporting activity that is not corporate sport. The main distinction is that professionals do not undertake participant sport. Amateurs play participant sport for a myriad of personal reasons, but not for a living. Participant sport organisations primarily offer opportunities for people to engage in sporting activities, either on one-off occasions or in organised competitive settings. Local football or basketball clubs are examples of participant sport organisations. The higher the level these sport organisations are competing at, the more likely it is they become hybrid sport organisations, the third category of facility dependent sport services.

Hybrid sport

Hybrid sport organisations offer a mix of corporate and participant sport. Their elite teams perform at a high or the highest level(s) of competition, and the organisational structures supporting these teams are likely to have developed corporate sport characteristics. On the other hand, in the same sport organisation, a number of teams might be singularly devoted to offering participant services, although some (junior) teams might act as 'feeder' or developmental squads for the elite. Hybrid sport organisations have evolved from the traditional (participation oriented) sporting clubs (in Europe and Australia) or college-based sport organisations (in the USA). Governing bodies of sport are also likely to be hybrid sport organisations. They are charged with developing a mass participation base for the sport with the ambition of securing its longevity, while encouraging and promoting the few outstanding athletes that can perform at the corporate level. This provides the sport with the exposure so essential to its popularity but, more importantly, develops the basis for corporate sports' revenue streams. Sports that have proved to be extremely successful corporate sport entities, such as soccer in Europe and South America, basketball, baseball and American football in North America and Australian Rules football and cricket in Australia, have turned themselves from hybrid sport organisations into corporate sport organisations. Although they understand the importance of developing new elite performers through mass participation, they concentrate on producing corporate sport. Put another way, they focus on a 'pull' rather than 'push' approach. Other (affiliated) organisations strive to provide more balance. Corporate sport enterprises often support mass participation organisations through funding or professional services.

The Global Sport Industry

The central thrust of this book is the expansion of sport into the global marketplace. As we have noted, it is critical to map out the global marketplace before a full exploration of the future of sport business can be realistically considered. In short, we need to crystallise the sport industry into a digestible form that allows us to discuss its nuances later.

Conceptualising sport's complex structure and delivery on a global level can be best accomplished through the integration of some of the typologies just described. To that end, by synthesising the work of Chelladurai and Westerbeek and Shilbury with the three categories of facility dependent sport services just discussed, a more comprehensive model can be created. This typology of the global sport industry is presented in Figure 3.2. The typology is divided into four levels. At the highest level, level 1, Westerbeek and Shilbury's general groupings of sport products are used, which allows for the inclusion of all sport products but, more importantly, makes a clear distinction between those products that directly involve sporting activity (facility dependent sport services) and those products that merely contribute to the sporting activities (sporting goods and sport consultation services). The model distinguishes between three categories of facility dependent sport services at level 2. At this stage it may be noted that both sporting goods and sport consultation services incorporate massive and complex subindustries in their own right. Because they do not directly involve sporting activity, Westerbeek excluded them from the discussion in his original work. Examples in the model presented in this book are organisations such as Nike and Adidas as major operators in the sporting goods industry, and organisations such as the International Management Group (IMG) and Octagon as operators in the sport consultation services industry. Level 3 distinguishes between corporate-related products and participant-related products. Corporate-related products, because of their transparent economic importance, include product categories that supply corporate and hybrid sport organisations with their main sources of revenue. Finally, level 4 product groups replicate Chelladurai's psychic benefits and social ideas; products are exchanged in relation to both corporate-related and participant-related sport. It may be argued that benefits delivered through these products are derived from buying the products at level 3. By associating with the sport organisation through purchasing sponsorship opportunities, for example, altruistic emotions can be packaged as part of the sponsorship service. For sport consumers, it simply feels good to do something for your favourite club or sport. Purchasing a licence to manufacture Sydney Olympic merchandise may be associated with a healthy environment given the fact that the Sydney Games were co-branded as the Green Games.

Towards the end of Chapter 1 we grouped nations in four categories of sport business development: hyperdeveloped, developed, developing and underdeveloped. It needs to be stated here that those categories, in the context of the global sport industry model presented in this chapter, only relate to corporate sport. For example, if we were to compare the United States and Australia on 'participation sport development', Australia would be categorised as 'hyperdeveloped' and the United States as 'developing' or 'developed' at the most. Australia's community based

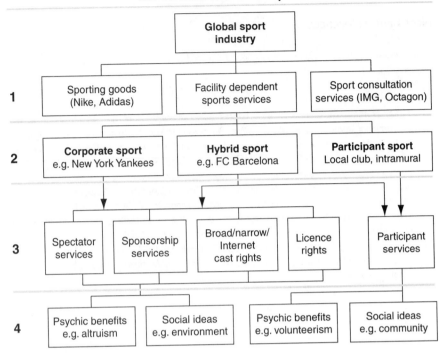

Figure 3.2 Westerbeek's product-based typology of the global sport industry

club system provides a much better and more comprehensive system of 'sport for all' participation than does the college-based broad participation structure in the USA. However, as noted earlier, this book focuses on sport business.

In conclusion, the purpose of this chapter was to briefly outline the development of a global sport industry model that captures the essences of the industry from a structural point of view. The model presented in Figure 3.2 provides a structural description of the core constituents of the industry. The establishment of a number of product-based main industry segments has led us to appreciate that their impact on the sporting contest may be either direct or indirect, leading to further consideration of the specific category of facility dependent services. Within that category the drivers of modern sport business success can be categorised. They are the products delivered to participants, spectators, commercial partners, media outlets and licence holders. Finally, the industry may consider a range of intangible spin-off products that increasingly are commodified in order to become more suitable for commercial exploitation. It is this industry structure that will form the basis for our discussion of the commercialisation of sport in the next chapter.

Notes and references

1   P. Kotler (1994), *Marketing Management* (8th edn), Prentice Hall, Englewood Cliffs, NJ, p. 225.

2   P. Chelladurai (1994), 'Sport management: defining the field', *European Journal for Sport Management*, 1(1), 7–21.

3   Much of the next section of this chapter was previously published as an article in the *International Journal of Sport Management*. Permission to use the material was kindly granted by the publishers of the *Journal*, American Press, and the *Journal* editor, Dr W. Stier. See also H. M. Westerbeek (2000), 'Sport in the global village: A product-based typology of the international sport industry', *International Journal of Sport Management*, 1(2), 103–20.

4   Table 3.2 reprinted with kind permission of the Sport Management Association of Australia and New Zealand, publishers of the *Sport Management Review*. See also H. M. Westerbeek and D. Shilbury (1999), 'Increasing the focus on "place" in the marketing mix for facility dependent sport services', *Sport Management Review*, 2(1), 1–24.

5   *Telegraaf* (1998), 'Sportbranche goed voor f213 miljard', *De Telegraaf*, 11 March, p. 1.

6   D. Shilbury and J. Deane (2001), *Sport Management in Australia*, Strategic Sport Management, Melbourne.

CHAPTER 4

Business or Pleasure:
The Commercialisation of Sport

*The curse of commercialism is the ruin of sport, and the degeneracy of
motor racing as a sport is due to the financial issues now involved in
every race ... the charm disappears, and I can see in the near future,
and before the racing of cars dies the death that is yearly predicted, the
sporting element obliterated altogether by the all-devouring monster of
commercialism – the curse of the Twentieth Century.*
Charles Jarrot, racing driver, 1905.

This book reflects upon the interaction and integration of sport,
globalisation and commercialisation. Having previously identified the
essential elements of the global sport industry, this section focuses upon
the processes through which sport has evolved into an economic entity,
and begins to develop the unique configurations of the global,
commericalised sport triumvirate.

Commerce may be defined as 'the activities and procedures involved in
buying and selling things'; a commercial activity 'involves producing
goods [and services] in large quantities in order to make a profit'; and
commercialisation is 'mainly concerned with making money'.[1] When
applying these definitions to sport it seems logical that the commercialisation of sport involves producing sport products in order to make a profit.
Naturally, it is corporate sport that has the highest potential to be
commercialised.

Corporate sport lends itself to commercialisation for three principal
reasons. First, corporate sport has mass spectator appeal. Put simply,
companies support sports that command respectable popular interest.
Second, because of this appeal, the sport has the ability to generate
substantial income, mainly in the form of revenue from gate receipts,
television and Internet rights, sponsorships, merchandise and licensing
rights. Finally, because of substantial sources of revenue, the sport can

employ highly skilled and experienced professional managers and marketers, who further capitalise upon the commercial opportunities sport offers. Money and corporate sport are therefore inseparable.

While total gate receipts have remained relatively steady in magnitude, income from sponsorship (worldwide) has more than quadrupled since 1989.[2] The same trend can be observed when looking at income from television rights for the two biggest sporting events in the world, the Olympics and the World Cup. Values of television rights are presented in Figure 4.1 and Figure 4.2.

Arguably the world's most powerful media 'mogul', Rupert Murdoch believes that sport 'absolutely overpowers all other programming as an incentive for viewers to subscribe to cable and satellite TV'. When addressing his BSkyB shareholders in 1996 he commented: 'we intend to use sports as a battering ram and a lead-offering in all our pay-television operations'.[3] Since this shareholder meeting, Murdoch's News Corporation has purchased the Los Angeles Dodgers baseball franchise, and ended up owning large stakes in the Los Angeles Lakers and the New York Knicks (National Basketball Association – NBA – basketball franchises), as well as the New York Rangers (National Hockey League – NHL – ice hockey franchise), the latter two as a consequence of investing in Rainbow Media, the sports programming arm of Cablevision systems. Although we now know that even Murdoch believes that prices paid for sports rights have spiralled out of control, and should lead to a rationalisation of the sports marketing and sports rights industry, sport remains king when it comes to the list of most attractive media entertainment properties. The terrorist attacks of September 11 and the consequent downturn in the global economy has led to a drop in advertising revenues linked to major sporting events, partly explaining why sport rights are 'suddenly' beyond a level of economic sustainability. However, they are only relatively minor hiccups in the process of achieving a balance between the 'real' value of sport rights and the number of organisations bidding for the privilege to commercialise them. While there will be a change in value, it will be a correction rather than a long-term downward trend.

The attractiveness of sport to media investors is why some media commentators believe near-total corporate ownership of professional sport is inevitable. They argue that despite the ability of sporting leagues to regulate against it, ultimately the nature of the sport-entertainment matrix is likely to demand it.[4] Demanded or not, when Murdoch's BSkyB proposed to buy Manchester United, the world's most famous soccer club, for a staggering US$950 million[5] (some US$200 million more than

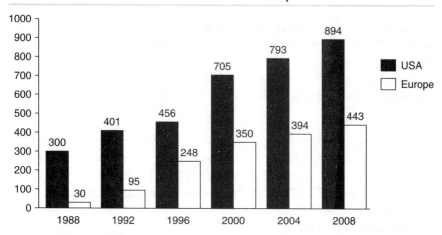

Figure 4.1 Value (US$ million) of summer Olympic Games television rights

Source: Adapted from International Olympic Committee (1996). *Marketing Matters: The Olympic Marketing Newsletter,* 8 (Spring), Lausanne.

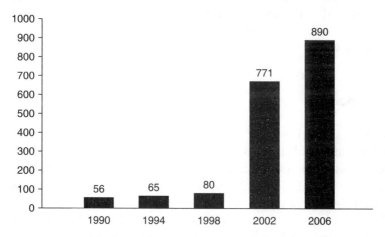

Figure 4.2 Value (US$ million) of worldwide (excluding USA) World cup television rights

Source: Adapted from *TV-rights revenue,* factsheet at http://www.fifa.com (2002).

the capitalised stock market value), it became quite obvious it was not at all about the value of the actual club. Communication conglomerates are, unsurprisingly seeking communication instruments: in this case, world-wide sporting properties with established bases of 'fandom' through which a whole range of entertainment and other products can be sold on. Enormous profits lie in the application of the communication instrument when developing untapped or even previously unidentified markets. Sport organisations are established brands and brand loyalty is high in the sport industry. People are emotionally attached to their teams, especially when the team has a long and proud history which both gently and forcefully converts new generations into loyal fans. It is the powerful mix of potential strategic alliances that attracts communications companies to sport:

> [there is] a growing need for live-event programming in a zillion-channel broadcast, cable and satellite universe; the emergence of sports franchises as solid brands that can be exploited in numerous ways; and the opportunity to blend sports with the company's entertainment properties in stadium and arena complexes where the game is only one of the many attractions.[6]

Why develop a brand when you can buy an established one? This is the main reason why a sporting organisation has an entirely different kind of value for the old-fashioned, gate-receipts oriented sport manager compared with the new corporate owners. That is why Murdoch, if permitted, would have bought Manchester United for an 'inflated' US$950 million.

Global Sport

Most sport spectators in the new millennium will watch a sporting contest from the comfort of their own homes. During the weekend of 10/11 April 1999, across eight television channels in England (both terrestrial and satellite), sport fans could choose from Five Nations rugby, the English and Scottish Cup football semi-finals, the Brazilian Grand Prix (Formula One), the Grand National horse race, a one-day cricket international between England and India, the US Masters golf tournament, a WBO World Featherweight title fight (boxing), curling from Canada, tennis from Portugal and snowboarding from Switzerland.[7] Without attending spectators cheering on the athletes, would these events have the same value as a television spectacle? Have live sport fans developed their own place in the total spectacle? In reality, their involvement ranges from passive observers to highly involved and fanatical contributors. Concerning the latter, it has been noted that:

> on the periphery of [German] *Bundesliga* football a youthful subculture has developed. Self-organised and not controlled by society's institutions, it has its own norms, symbols, designations, and rituals.

As it represents and defends its territory within the curves of the stadium, it generally, collectively, and demonstratively represents and defends itself against the world outside.[8]

Throughout history, sport or 'sport-like' rituals and activities have attracted those who participate in the event vicariously. Evidence of sport spectators dates as far back as the ancient Egyptians, where the spectators of wrestling and stick fighting addressed Rameses II in hieroglyphics praising him like a god of war.[9] Youths who had formerly faced each other in combat congregated in the local stadium with broadly similar ends in view.[10] Modern sporting arena architecture mirrors the first sporting stadia in ancient Greece (athletics) and Rome (horse racing and gladiatorial fights). The organisers of opera performances and *calcio*, an Italian ancestral version of contemporary soccer, competed for the favour of 'customers' in ways similar to how contemporary 'live' sport events around the world compete with the performing arts, movie theatres, theme parks and even home entertainment products (such as video games, video movies) for a share of the consumer dollar.

However, sport is not just another entertainment option for the majority of sport watchers. As a matter of fact, 'far from being merely play or marginal unserious activities, [sports] are key, multifaceted components in the complex constitution of most societies (certainly all modern ones) and a central aspect of the globalisation of culture, and of the local resistances to it'.[11] The development of mass spectator sports such as soccer and other football codes, with specific attention devoted to the 'live' stadium experience of sport spectators will be highlighted in the coming section, leading into a discussion of a number of trends impacting on the development of global, commercial sport.

The Development of Global, Commercial Sport: A Case Study of the World Game

The development of global, commercial sport has been touched upon in previous sections. This section intends to explore the relationships between sport, commercialism and globalisation further by comprehensively examining the case of football (soccer), arguably the most globalised of all sports. As we shall discover, an investigation of the development of football uncovers the essential ingredients that are at play in the cultivation of any global, commercial sport.

It has been suggested by historical researchers[12] that the beginnings of the modern day version of soccer can be found in late medieval Italy where a game of kicking (*gioco del calcio*) was developed and played in the city of Florence. However, it can be argued[13] that there is insufficient evidence to confidently claim that the development of the modern game of soccer was in any way instigated by the game of kicking that originated in Florence. Eric Dunning acknowledges the existence of games (in China, Japan, Greece, Italy, ancient Rome, France) that could have been an ancestral form of soccer but argued that there is no doubt that modern day versions of soccer and rugby originate from England. He agrees with Johan Huizinga,[14] who described England as 'the cradle and focus of modern sporting life'. Dunning suggests that the process of developing more restrained and regulated sport forms in England was more a function of wider social developments, such as government and infrastructure than it was of the properties of the emerging sport forms.[15] In other words, the civilising processes that occur in the development of modern nation states can partly explain sportisation[16] or the development of modern sport.[17]

The medieval versions of folk football in Britain were based on local customs and had limited or no rules. Local communities played against each other and, in the context of the game, communal identity was more important than individual identity.[18] In an eighteenth-century British society that was increasingly pacified (internally) and subject to governmental (parliamentary) rule, the first modern sport forms emerged. These sports were more restrained and standardised, and were the first to develop written rules. The 'civilising spurt' that took place at the level of the ruling group in British society extended to groups lower in the class hierarchy, leading to a coinciding transformation of their approach to politics and leisure. As Norbert Elias[19] observed, there was a relationship between the sophistication of civilisation and the modernisation of sport.

Soccer and rugby are two examples of global modern team sports, both evolving from one 'football game' invented at public schools in eighteenth-century England. The first surviving written rules of football date from 1845 and were produced at Rugby, a public school in the English Midlands. School authorities decided to let the game of football be guided by stricter rules to ensure greater control over the levels of 'unacceptable violence' taking place on the field. This on-field attempt at regulation and control coincided with the public school system being usurped by members of the aristocracy and gentry to cater for the educational requirements of the upper and middle classes. Thus the development of soccer and rugby was part of a concentrated civilising spurt of English society. It had been the status rivalry between Etonians and Rugbeians – former students from the public schools of Eton and Rugby – that was the

main reason for the incipient bifurcation of football into the association
and rugby forms:

> The FA [Football Association] emerged from a series of meetings held
> in London in 1863 and attended mainly by public school 'old boys'
> (former pupils) and other 'gentlemen'. At first, those in attendance
> attempted to form a unified football code. A majority favoured a
> mainly kicking game from which hacking had been eliminated, but
> proponents of versions of football modelled on the form played at
> Rugby preferred a rougher, mainly carrying and throwing game in
> which the violent practice of hacking retained a central place. Hence
> they withdrew themselves banding together in 1871 to form the RFU
> [Rugby Football Union].[20]

As we noted in Chapter 2, the use of sanctions rather than physical
chastisements might be considered further evidence of this civilising
process.[21] Although no conclusive evidence exists demonstrating that
soccer had a ritual (religious) origin, it can be safely stated that soccer
was (and is still) used as an accepted means for expressing conflict between
rival groups with the intention of demonstrating their relative superiority
and group identity.[22]

As a result of this civilising process, which remains one of the central
issues associated with the globalisation of sport, folk football became
culturally marginalised. This process was enhanced by the development of
soccer and rugby in the public school system in England. Six critical
developments contributed to the new forms of football games (soccer and
rugby). These included the documentation of the rules, a stricter demarcation of the size and shape of the playing area, the imposition of stricter
limitations on the duration of matches, a reduction in the numbers taking
part, an equalisation in the size of competing teams and the imposition of
stricter regulations on the kinds of physical force that were considered
legitimate to employ.

Within the public school system, soccer and rugby were quickly taken
up as the new status-enhancing activities for gentleman. Coinciding with
the industrialisation and urbanisation of Britain, this ironically led to the
rapid increase in popularity of soccer in particular. The first written rules
of the game of soccer were drawn up in 1863, originating at Cambridge
University,[23] and these rules (stipulating that the handling of the ball was
to be forbidden) were to have a lasting influence on the development of
the modern game. The rules formed the basis for the Football Association
(FA), founded in 1863, and made the schools favouring the 'rugby rules'

break away from the schools forming the FA. In 1871 the first FA Cup competition was organised, allowing the game to spread geographically and attract interest from spectators, but more importantly to gain popularity amongst the lower social classes. This involvement of the lower social classes was one of the essential ingredients for the ultimate commercialisation and geographical expansion of the sport. The increase in spectators consequently led to some of the clubs charging admissions. This income was used to pay players, and hence the FA ratified professionalism as early as 1885, leading to a professional 'Football League' of twelve teams in 1888. As early as 1901 FA Cup games drew crowds in excess of 100,000, with 110,820 witnessing the final between Tottenham Hotspur and Sheffield United. The first 'international' games between Scotland and England drew crowds in excess of 50,000 through-out the 1890s.[24] In 1893 a second division to the professional soccer competition was created which led to the promotion and relegation system that has become a common characteristic of many professional soccer leagues in Europe. The buying and selling of players – the so-called transfer system – emerged almost as soon as the FA adopted profession-alism. In 1905, Alf Common was transferred for £1,000 from Sunderland to Middlesborough, which forced the FA to impose a £350 maximum transfer fee. However, even in the early days of the transfer system the imposition of maximum transfer fees was doomed to failure.

With industrial development in the late nineteenth century offering increased opportunities for travel (to and from mainland Europe) the game of soccer spread rapidly to the other side of the Channel. In most cases it was Englishmen abroad (such as sailors, soldiers, physical education teachers, and expatriates) who introduced the game, either on their travels or as part of their (semi-permanent) residence. In 1878 the first German club was founded; the Netherlands followed in 1879, Sweden in 1887, Italy in 1890 and France in 1892.[25] Outside Britain the first continental Football Associations were formed in 1889 (Denmark and the Netherlands), 1895 (Belgium and Switzerland), 1900 (Germany) and 1906 (Portugal). Delegates from Belgium, Denmark, France, the Netherlands, Spain, Sweden and Switzerland founded *La Fédération Internationale de Football Associations* (FIFA) in Paris in 1904.[26] During the same period other games of football evolved in countries closely associated with the British Empire. In the 1860s the rules for American football were drawn up and in 1866 Melbourne hosted the codification of Australian Rules football.[27] Both Australia and the United States, as former British 'colonies', created their own codes, partly as a means of creating a distinct identity. Contrary to the spread of soccer in non-British countries, their national codes have proved more popular than soccer. Soccer leagues in the USA were either organised by people with no real interest in the game (often they were baseball team owners who sought more capital-intensive use of their sports grounds), or by 'foreigners' who were recent immigrants from Europe.

The American Football (soccer) Association was founded in 1884, a short-lived professional league in 1894, a greater Los Angeles Soccer league in 1902, and two years later a similar league in San Francisco. However, to be a 'normal American kid' meant that you either played baseball or American football. Although visiting European teams often drew sizeable crowds, they remained exceptions to the rule.[28] The same popularity problems for soccer were present in Australia. The main competitor to Australian Rules football for national dominance was (and remains) rugby (league). Soccer languishes as the second most popular football code in most Australian states behind either rugby league (Queensland and New South Wales) or Australian Rules football (Western Australia, South Australia, Victoria). In some ways, those parts of the world that had been touched by British Imperialism were also left with soccer as part of the colonial baggage. For example, India was the jewel in the British imperial crown where soccer was played with enormous passion by clerks in the Indian public services as much as soldiers in the British army.[29]

In a similar fashion soccer was introduced in China where in 1886 the Hong Kong Football Club was founded, and in 1887 John Prentice from Glasgow set up the Shanghai Football Club. The Singapore football association was founded in 1892. However, the spread of the game into Asia and Africa was not as smooth, coinciding with the end of colonialism. In the United States, Canada, Australia, New Zealand and white South Africa, soccer lingered as the poor second cousin to other forms of football. Worse, as soccer became essentially a working-class game in the late eighteenth century, it acquired a debilitating association with migrants seeking social advancement and national identity in another country.[30]

On the field in Europe, during the early years of the twentieth century, the city teams of Vienna, Budapest and Prague (where representatives of the British Empire also largely instigated the development of soccer) dominated the game. Ironically, the attempts to ban soccer by the Russian and Ottoman Empires – due to a fear that soccer might be used as a cover for revolutionary action – only led to the formation of more soccer teams. In Austria, Hungary, and neighbouring countries such as Russia, Romania, Bulgaria, Yugoslavia and Turkey (all of which had recently been, or were still, involved in wars or struggles for independence from imperial rule), soccer became an expression of freedom, particularly for the young.

The developing economies of some of the South American countries late in the nineteenth century encouraged the arrival of English sailors and railway workers to the shores of Argentina. The Argentine Association Football League was set up in 1891 and in the first decade of the twentieth century it had four divisions, making it the most prosperous league outside the United Kingdom.[31] A professor of English literature, William Leslie Poole, founded the first soccer club in Uruguay in 1891, and shortly afterwards the first Brazilian club was founded in São Paulo in 1898. Brazilian football started its development towards becoming the dominant force in world football in the second part of the twentieth century. Interestingly, the club which won the first World Championship for club teams, organised by FIFA in January 2000, was Corinthians from Brazil. The club was founded in 1910 and was named after the famous English amateur club that had recently toured the country.

On the occasion of a match between two of the most popular Brazilian clubs, Flamengo and Fluminense, a world record for attendance at an ordinary league game was set in 1963 when 177,656 people attended. The first confederational soccer controlling body to be founded (in 1916) was the South American confederation, the *Confederacion Sudamericana de Futbol* (CONMEBOL). In other words:

> soccer had arrived in Europe, with its warring nationalities and culture clashes. It was already well entrenched in South America, and as it embraced the world, it also embraced the world's problems, not only bringing the joy of sport but also encouraging the enmity of nationals and individuals who could not leave their cultural baggage behind.[32]

Soccer was played throughout the First World War with match attendances continuing to increase. In 1923, a crowd of 85,000 turned up in Vienna to see Austria play Italy and up to 65,000 attended multiple matches of Austria against Hungary. Continued increases in spectator numbers coincided with growing numbers of participants. In 1919, Germany had 150,000 registered players and by 1932 this number had grown to over a million. In 1920 there were 650 clubs affiliated to the French Football Association, but only four years later this number had grown to 3,983. In Poland, registered player numbers increased from 485 in 1920 to 17,558 in 1925.[33]

South American soccer made a real impact in Europe when Uruguay won gold medals at the Olympic Games in Paris (1924) and Amsterdam

(1928), where they defeated Argentina in the final. According to Murray, 'throughout the 1920's soccer prospered along with the cinema and dancing as the most popular leisure pursuits. It reigned supreme across Europe and in the Americas from the tip of Tierra Del Fuego to the border between Mexico and the United States',[34] and this led to the creation of international competitions for club teams and national teams. It was in games between countries that the intensity of identifying with geographic location and related culture – similar to the rivalries between local communities in folk football – surfaced again at the level of national identity. Put another way:

> the potential for violence in games between teams representing nations whose political relations were tense was easily realized, and one contemporary observer commented dryly that no *Mitropa Cup* game [contested by teams from Austria, Czechoslovakia, Hungary and Yugoslavia] was really decided until the final appeal had been heard from the appropriate foreign embassy'.[35]

The first World Cup tournament was organised (and won) by Uruguay in 1930 and, henceforth, the sport was blatantly used by both democratic leaders and dictators in their political public relations and propaganda campaigns:

> Mussolini's Fascist regime was the first to use sports as an integral part of government, and Hitler copied much of Mussolini's work in his Nazi regime. Stalin, on the other hand, reserved sports for national unification and defence preparation, unwilling to put the Soviet athletes to the test of international competition until he was sure that they would win.[36]

However, throughout the Second World War international soccer (and many of Europe's domestic competitions) came to a standstill. The first World Cup after the war, in 1950 in Brazil, kick-started the post-war growth of the sport. From the mid-1950s, 'with the spread of floodlights, improvements in air travel, and advances in television, new European club competitions were inaugurated...'.[37] The *Union Européenne de Football Associations* (UEFA) was founded in 1954 and it organised competitions for winners of the domestic leagues (1955) and for the domestic Cup winners (1958); it also installed the UEFA cup (1960) as a competition for teams that had just missed out qualification for the other two competitions. In South America a similar continental competition, the *Copa*

Libertadores, was started in 1960, and in the same year the winner of the 'Copa' played the winner of the European Cup for the title of Club World Champion.

The surprisingly strong performance of the North Korean team at the 1966 World Cup drew attention to the development of the game in Asia again. Although the soccer powers in Europe and South America continued largely to ignore what happened in Asia and Africa, the election of João Havelange to the presidency of FIFA in 1974 changed the tide for the less developed (Third World) soccer nations. He was elected with the support of many of the 39 countries from Africa and 33 countries from Asia, which represented just over half of FIFA's member countries in 1974. In the late 1960s, the combined votes of African and Asian nations made up less than 25 per cent of all votes, but in 1974 they collectively amounted to more than 50 per cent. By that time successful international competitions were organised in Asia as well. The Asian Champions Cup started in 1966, the Asian Youth Cup was organised annually between 1959 and 1980; and some regional competitions in Seoul, Bangkok and Kuala Lumpur in particular were very successful. Soccer took off in the Middle East (which for FIFA purposes is part of the Asian confederation) in the 1970s during the sharp rise of world oil prices. To this day countries such as Saudi Arabia, Iraq and Iran are home to well organised and high-level competitions. 'Havelange has been criticized for overcommercializing soccer, but under his presidency many of the weaker soccer countries have benefited from the provision of coaches and equipment and, perhaps above all, by the institution of youth competitions weighted in favour of the weaker confederations'.[38] However, with successful leagues in Japan, Korea, China and Malaysia, to name just a few, the enthusiasm of the millions of Asian soccer followers has yet to be converted to international commercial success, though performances in the 2002 World Cup are promising platforms. Asia and Africa are the sleeping giants of world soccer.

Entering the Era of Contemporary Football

The first World Cup tournament to be widely televised was hosted and won by England in 1966. It also drew attention to the emerging problem of hooliganism in British soccer (a phenomenon that prior to the 1960s was dismissed by the British as a 'continental problem'). Throughout the next three decades European soccer in general, and English soccer in particular, became better known (and feared) for the behaviour of its fans off the field than team performance on the field. To combat this problem most English grounds were fenced, which in turn partly contributed to some of the major disasters in modern football. For example, at Bradford, in 1985, some 56 people were killed in a fire in the stadium, and in 1989 at Hillsborough stadium in Sheffield, 96 people were crushed to death against a security fence. By no means, however, can hooliganism be described as an 'English problem'. Statistics show that the number of deaths and injuries as a result of crowd violence outside England are equally substantial.[39] Since the 1960s the statistical evidence[40] clearly shows that 'while hooligans come from all levels in the class hierarchy, the majority, some 80–90 percent, come from the working class; manual workers with low levels of formal education'.[41]

Dunning, Murphy and Williams explain how five popular causes of soccer hooliganism at best can only be assumed to be *contributing* to the phenomenon. These causes include excessive alcohol consumption, violent incidents on the field and/or incompetent refereeing, unemployment, affluence and permissiveness. Although the authors do not simply discard the (sometimes limited) contribution of four academic explanations for hooliganism – the anthropological explanation (a proxy for tribalism), the Marxist explanation (working-class resistance movement), the ethological explanation (sport as ritual violence) and the psychological reversal theory (the assumption that 'the quest for excitement', through hooliganism, can be explained as a reversal from one metamotivational state, such as boredom, to another, such as excitement) – they put forward the 'figurational' explanation of soccer hooliganism. Based on extensive research they proposed the following working hypothesis:

A quest for pleasurable excitement is a common feature of leisure activities in all societies. Particularly in industrial societies, what is involved is a search for a counter to the emotional staleness which tends to be engendered by the routines of non-leisure life. Furthermore, present-day England is a patriarchal society in which males generally are expected under certain circumstances to fight, and high status is legitimately conferred on good fighters in particular occupational contexts, for example the military and the police. However, the dominant norms in English society demand that males should not be the initiators of fights and require them to confine their fighting to self-defense, defense of their families and loved ones, defense of the 'realm', and sports such as boxing. The 'core' soccer hooligans, those who engage in soccer hooliganism most regularly, seeking out confrontations with opposing fans rather than being drawn into fighting by the exigencies of particular situations, contravene these socially dominant norms. They are liable to initiate and plan attacks and to fight publicly in situations where, according to the dominant norms, fighting is taboo. For them, a quest for status as 'hard men' and the 'pleasurable battle-excitement' engendered in hooligan confrontations forms a central life interest.[42]

Beyond the origins of (and explanations for) hooliganism, the Bradford and Hillsborough disasters in England led to the installation of the Hillsborough Stadium Disaster inquiry chaired by Lord Justice Taylor. The results of this inquiry, outlined in the Taylor report, changed the face of English football:

> One of the most influential recommendations of the Taylor Report was the replacement of the terraces with seating, although the push for all-seater stadia was already in motion. Through the introduction of seating it was reasoned that crowd numbers could be controlled and effectively monitored. Taylor advised the improvement of the design and quality of football stadia commenting that the state of the grounds and the facilities available were lamentable. This reinforced ... concerns following Bradford and Brussels [where 39 Juventus supporters were crushed to death trying to escape an attack of Liverpool supporters during a European Cup match] four years earlier.[43]

As will be shown later, the renovation of old stadia and the construction of new stadia in England sparked (or coincided with) a stadium redevelopment and regeneration boom that extended throughout Europe, Australia and the United States. However, prior to the development of stadia which dramatically improved the levels of service quality provided to soccer spectators when attending matches live, the game further developed and prospered as a result of the integration of the mass medium of television. As Murray observed:

> In the late 1960s television coverage of soccer changed its focus to specially packaged highlights with more emphasis on off-the-field activities ... players were being courted as never before, and as 'personalities' in the new 'package' they expected to be paid an appropriate fee. The spectators, who provided the atmosphere without which televised sport can barely survive, developed their own interpretation of the new ethos in outbursts of triumphalism that owed less to greed than to a twisted sense of loyalty to the local team.[44]

Television has also been blamed for decreasing attendance at matches. Nevertheless, for better or worse, television has become an integral part of distributing the world game to people and locations never exposed to seeing the stars of world soccer. Not only does television allow for alternative distribution of soccer to the converted, it is also an excellent marketing tool to further 'preach' the soccer 'gospel'. However, as will be shown later, soccer clubs increasingly rely on income sources other than gate receipts to balance their budgets and to compete in the world market for soccer talent, where single players can cost as much as the total annual turnover of football leagues in smaller countries. As was shown earlier, television rights revenue is rapidly becoming the most important of all sources of income. The efforts of media conglomerates to gain control over the major sporting clubs in the world suggests a move towards corporate ownership of sporting clubs that were previously membership driven.

The Commercialism of Soccer in the 1990s

FIFA has 204 members and is by far the biggest single sport association in the world. Member nations are distributed over six confederations including the Confédération Africaine de Football (52 members), the Asian Football Confederation (45 members), the Union of European Football Associations (51 members), the Confederacion Norte-Centroamericana y del Caribe de Futbol, or CONCACAF (35 members), the Confederacion Sudamericana de Futbol (10 members), and the Oceania Football Confederation (11 members). Maarten van Bottenburg,[45] in one of the most comprehensive studies on the variation in popularity of different sports in Europe, identified that in 19 of the 22 European countries examined, soccer was the most popular participation sport. When soccer was not ranked first, it was the second most popular sport twice and the third most popular sport once. Registered soccer participants in those countries amounted to almost 16 million (15,879,800). The top five countries were Germany, France, Italy, England and the Netherlands, in that order,[46] all with more than 1 million registered participants. Data collected in FIFA's Football 2000 worldwide official survey (released in April 2001) indicated that globally 242,378,000 people are regular soccer players. This equates to 4.1 per cent of the world population. In relative terms soccer is most popular in the CONCACAF region where 8.4 per cent of the population plays the game.

They are followed by Europe (6.7 per cent), South America (6.5 per cent), Oceania (4.4 per cent), Asia (3 per cent) and Africa (2.9 per cent). Of all players, almost 22 million are female and 127,000 play the game professionally. Of all professional players, 75 per cent play in Europe or South America. These high participation numbers are also reflected in television spectatorship, another indicator of the global popularity of the game. Accumulated World Cup television audiences for the past four tournaments are presented in Figure 4.3.

It should be noted that the numbers in Figure 4.3 are slightly misleading as the 1998 World Cup in France hosted 64 matches whereas the previous three World Cups only consisted of 52. The average accumulated audiences per 10 games presented in Figure 4.3 accounts for this difference in games played. Since the early 1990s, television audiences for the World Cup have plateaued. However, this does not detract from the fact that the average television audience for any World Cup match throughout the 1990s was nearly one-tenth of the world's population (assuming a global population of approximately 6 billion).

Some of the France 1998 matches were ratings winners in selected countries. For example, 24.1 million Germans watched the final, a share of 33.7 per cent of all households. Italy versus Cameroon rated 42.8 per cent in Italy but the Dutch Broadcasting Association (NOS) presented the highest ratings when 63.7 per cent of the nation tuned in to watch the Netherlands versus Brazil semi-final. Even after being knocked out of the final, 50 per cent of Dutch households watched the final.[47]

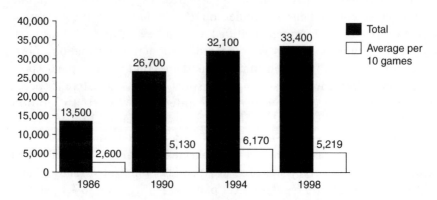

Figure 4.3 Accumulated World Cup TV audiences (millions)

Source: Adapted from factsheet at http://www.fifa.com (2002).

It may come as no surprise that of the top 100 European sports programmes broadcast in 1998 (in the major TV markets of the UK, France, Germany, the Netherlands, Spain and Italy), 72.3 per cent were soccer programmes.[48] Research by Sponsorship Research International (1999) shows that the top sponsored sports in 1998 in Europe were soccer (US$917 million), the Olympics (US$910 million), tennis (US$197 million), Formula 1 racing (US$158 million) and basketball (US$145 million). Of the top 20 European television sport deals, 16 involve soccer competitions.

Audiences for the World Cup, combined with the value of soccer competitions to television broadcasters, provide compelling evidence of the popularity and dominance of soccer as a mass television spectator sport. Soccer is also the most popular spectator sport on almost all continents as measured by 'live' attendance. The only exceptions are North America and Australia. This is also reflected in the main user purposes of the largest sporting venues built around the world. Only in North America, where stadia are built to host American football and baseball matches, and in Australia, where the largest stadia host a mix of Australian Rules football (the biggest spectator sport in the country), rugby league and cricket, is soccer not the primary occupant of the stadium. An inventory of the world's largest stadia specifically built for soccer is presented in Table 4.1.

The world record for the biggest crowd ever to watch a 'live' sporting event is still held by Estadio Marqacana in Rio de Janeiro, where on the

Table 4.1 The world's largest soccer stadia (seated capacity only)

Name of Stadium	Location	Capacity
Azadi Football Stadium	Tehran, Iran	128,000
Marqacana	Rio de Janeiro, Brazil	125,000
Krirangan Stadium	Salt Lake, Calcutta, India	120,000
Estadio Azteca	Mexico City, Mexico	114,000
Senayan Main Stadium	Jakarta, Indonesia	110,000
Nou Camp	Barcelona, Spain	109,815
Rose Bowl*	Los Angeles, USA	100,092
Central Stadium	Kiev, Ukraine	100,062
Estadio Maghalhaes Pinto	Belo Horizonte, Brazil	100,000
National Stadium of Malaysia	Kuala Lumpur, Malaysia	100,000

* The Rose Bowl was purpose-built to host American Football but is currently used by the Los Angeles Galaxy, playing in the Major League Soccer, as their home stadium.

Source: Adapted from www.geocities.com (2002).

Table 4.2 Most popular sports (% of viewers) on television during the 1998 Asian Games (Thailand)

Rank	China	Hong Kong	India	Korea	Thailand
1	Soccer (73)	Soccer (39)	Athletics (39)	Soccer (80)	Soccer (89)
2	Swimming (65)	Swimming (34)	Soccer (35)	Baseball (72)	Swimming (73)
3	Gymnastics (55)	Gymnastics (22)	Swimming (31)	Basketball (32)	Boxing (70)
4	Volleyball (55)	Volleyball (21)	Tennis (29)	Archery (28)	Sepak takrow (60)
5	Table tennis (54)	Athletics (20)	Hockey (28)	Judo (24)	Gymnastics (55)

Source: Adapted from Sponsorship Research International (1999).

16 July 1950, some 199,854 spectators witnessed Brazil play Uruguay in the final of the World Cup. This figure is as high as 205,000[49] when non-paying customers are included. On the 10 July 1999, the biggest crowd to ever watch a 'live' women's sporting event was recorded at the Women's World Cup soccer final at the Rose Bowl in Los Angeles. A crowd in excess of 90,000 saw the United States defeat China.[50] Although the popularity of soccer in Asia has only recently been reflected in international success where South Korea reached the semi-finals of the 2002 World Cup, soccer featured highly amongst the most popular sports watched on television during the 1998 Asian games, as summarised in Table 4.2.

It can be reasonably concluded that soccer is a popular sport from both a participation and spectator (event attendance and television) point of view. The next section will introduce a number of issues affecting attendance at football matches (soccer, American football, Australian Rules football) around the world, with the intention of highlighting the role of spectators and their attendance in the commercial development of sport in general, and football in particular.

Issues of Attendance

Australian-based research[51] has tested the impact of different variables on the attendance at minor round Australian Football League/Victorian Football League football games played in Victoria (Melbourne and Geelong) and South Australia (Adelaide), during 1948 to 1992. They found the following variables to be statistically significant:

- the minimum real price of admission for minor round games
- the number of different days on which games are played during the season

- the construction of the Great Southern Stand at the Melbourne Cricket Ground (the Australian Football League's premier venue in Melbourne, seating close to 100,000 spectators and home ground of four Melbourne clubs) which suggests that ground capacity is important
- the competitiveness index (by calculating the standard deviation of wins of teams in the competition at the completion of each season, a perfectly competitive season would imply each team winning and losing precisely the same number of matches, a competitiveness index of 0).

In an examination of total attendance figures for domestic football competitions around the world (including American football and Australian Rules football) it may be observed that average 'football' crowds in the major leagues do not differ greatly. However, it is interesting to observe that in equally populated countries such as the Netherlands (16 million) and Australia (19 million), the average attendances per 'football' match do differ significantly, as is shown in Table 4.3.

This may partly be the result of rationalisation efforts by the Australian Football League (AFL) throughout the late 1980s and 1990s. These actions led to relatively few teams (16) in the competition (compared to 36 professional soccer teams in two Dutch professional leagues), and hence fewer matches in larger shared stadia (capacity and function of stadia), as opposed to the Netherlands where all teams have an independent 'home' stadium. Rationalisation efforts have an important impact on attendance figures and will be discussed later.

Table 4.3 Total crowds and average crowds per match in selected domestic 'football' competitions around the world (2000/2001 figures)

Country	Competition and Sport	Total Crowds	Average Crowd/Match	Number of Games Played
England	*Premier League* soccer	12,505,200	32,904	380
Germany	*Bundesliga* soccer	8,696,712	28,421	306
Australia	*National Soccer League*	1,180,445	5,621	210
Netherlands	*Eredivisie* soccer	4,715,154	15,409	306
USA	*Major League Soccer*	2,641,085	13,756	192
Australia	*Australian Football League*	5,740,811	32,618	176
USA	*National Football League*	16,387,289	66,078	248

Sources: Adapted from www.afl.com.au (2002), www.nfl.com (2002), www.dfb.de (2002), www.4thegame.com (2002), www.soccerstats.com (2002), www.mls.com (2002), www.knvb.nl (2002).

It should also be noted that in Australia, competition within football codes for 'live' spectators is restricted to metropolitan (city) markets because of the large distances between Australian cities. For example, in Melbourne with a market size of approximately 3.5 million people, nine professional AFL teams reside next to one rugby league team and two professional soccer teams. The Australian domestic soccer competition finishes midway through the AFL season. In most European countries, domestic soccer leagues not only face stiff competition within their own codes but also from many other professional sports. The domestic leagues compete for spectators with 'feeder' professional leagues, the knock-out domestic cup competitions, international club competitions such as the UEFA cup and the Champions League organised by the European soccer federation (UEFA), the European Championship qualifying competition for national representative sides organised by UEFA and the World Championship qualifying competition for national representative sides organised by FIFA. Most European countries also have top-level amateur leagues attracting considerable spectator numbers.

In North America, the domestic soccer leagues do not face major competition from other soccer competitions, but rather from the 'big four' professional sports of NFL (American Football), Major League Baseball (MLB), NBA basketball (and the Women's NBA) and NHL ice hockey. It is worth noting that the Women's United Soccer Association, in their first year (2001) of operating a professional women's soccer league, attracted average crowds of 8,295 spectators. Some annual attendance figures for the 'big four' leagues and Major League Soccer (MLS) are presented in Table 4.4, showing the intensity of competition between the different sporting codes for the disposable spectator dollar.

Table 4.4 Total crowds and average crowds per match in major professional sporting competitions in North America (2000/2001 figures)

Competition and Sport	Total Crowds	Average Crowd/Match	Number of Games Played
MLB, baseball	72,566,416	30,073	2,413
NBA, basketball	19,955,981	16,784	1,189
NHL, hockey	20,373,379	16,564	1,230
NFL, football	16,387,289	66,078	248
MLS, soccer	2,641,085	13,756	192
Totals	**131,924,150**	**28,651**	**5,272**

Sources: Adapted from www.nfl.com (2002), www.mls.com (2002), www.nhl.com (2002), www.infoplease.com (2002).

Similar sporting competitions at the college level in the United States draw equally large crowds as those in European soccer. Second or third tier professional 'feeder' leagues (such as triple A or double A baseball teams) also attract significant spectator numbers. Dennis Howard[52] observed that:

> minor leagues across a number of sports are thriving. Minor league baseball has enjoyed sustained growth in the 1990s. In 1992, 168 minor league ball clubs drew 27 million fans. By 1997, attendance had reached 34.7 million ... perhaps the most surprising development of the decade has been the explosive growth of minor league [ice] hockey ... The East Coast Hockey League (ECHL), for example, has grown from 5 to 29 teams in just 9 years. Over the past four seasons, ECHL attendance has more than doubled, topping 4.7 million in 1997–1998.

Attending an ECHL Icebreakers game cost $156.34 less than taking the family to an NHL CAPs game at the MCI Center, an experience that was not $156.34 less pleasurable.[53]

Finally, there is the issue of the availability of 'prime-time' sporting events that can be watched (in real time) on television and the related process of the 'commedialisation' of sport.[54] Commedialisation refers to the usage of television packaged sport events as a means to sell a variety of other entertainments products. Vertical integration, a frequently adopted strategy by the main players in the global media industry, will be reviewed in that respect later. Broadcasting sport events live on television has an immediate impact on attendance figures as evidenced recently in the Australian Football League, when one club threatened to sue the league for allowing a non-sanctioned live pay-television broadcast. The club argued that the broadcast would negatively affect their gate takings.[55]

We have identified some issues affecting match attendance. They can be summarised under three main headings: economic rationalisation of competitions; capacity and function of football stadia; and live coverage of matches on television. The following section expands on these issues in more detail, and helps to place the sport fan of the future in greater focus.

Economic Rationalisation of Competitions

In North America it has long been common practice for professional sporting teams to move from one city to another. Recent examples in the NFL include the Cleveland Browns who moved to Baltimore to become the Ravens, and the Houston Oilers who relocated to Nashville in 2000.[56] In Australia the South Melbourne Football Club moved to Sydney in 1979, and in 1996 the Fitzroy Football Club was forced to merge with the Brisbane Bears, and was subsequently exiled to Brisbane. The motivation for these relocations is simple; the anticipated returns in the 'new' city or geographic region are higher than in the former. In other words, the logic underpinning the relocation or merger of teams is economic rationalism.

When fewer teams compete in a league or, alternatively, in a particular geographic catchment, the attention of the fans can be artificially concentrated. Rather than a highly cluttered market with an overload of 'team brands', fewer, clearly identifiable brands can be presented to sizeable target markets more capable of sustaining these brands. At the same time the league forces spectators to contribute to economies of scale (more fans for fewer teams leads to lower variable costs per attendee) when organising and operating the stadium for the match. This relates to most operational services such as ticket ushers, security, food and beverage outlets, merchandise outlets, cleaning and maintenance, and operational expenses such as lighting, sound and heating. Economies of scale and strong brand identification are especially important when considering the issue of market power, researched in the context of Australian Rules football by Hans Westerbeek and Paul Turner.[57]

Market power in sport can be defined as the power of a sport organisation to control the price they charge for their product(s). The highest prices an organisation can receive for its products will be charged when an organisation operates in the market conditions we commonly know as a monopoly. An organisation operates as a monopolist when that organisation is the sole supplier of a good, service or resource that has no close substitutes and in which there is a barrier to the entry of new firms. It may be observed[58] that some sport organisations have monopolistic characteristics,[59] and hence are in a position to exercise market power. In the case of the AFL, it is the most advanced supplier of the spectator product, Australian Rules football. There is a high brand affiliation, strong cultural and social identification and, through this, low cross-elasticity of demand (no close substitutes). Barriers to entry are high in that setting up a rival professional Australian Rules football competition requires significant investment and will also lead to considerable social opposition (of fans). The latter is exemplified by the failed efforts of Rupert Murdoch's News Limited to set up a rival Super League, in direct competition with the Australian Rugby League's professional competition. These characteristics suggest that the AFL, in a way, acts as a monopolist. Although there are substitute products (including basketball and soccer), sound strategies can reduce the likelihood of customers changing allegiance (switching brands).

From a marketing point of view, this exemplifies the fact that when an organisation is able to create a product, highly differentiated from possible substitutes and difficult to imitate by other producers, it can increase its market power. The AFL's decision to decrease the number of clubs in the Melbourne market and expand the competition to other cities in Australia was clearly aimed at increasing the market power of the individual club brands and of the league brand 'AFL'. It may be speculated that league management in North America makes relocation decisions based on similar economic rationales. From that point of view it is interesting to note that the power of most European domestic soccer governing bodies is not far-reaching enough to decide which teams can and cannot play at the highest level of competition. This is likely to be the result of a combination of factors such as the historic rights of individual clubs to play in the competition, traditional competition structures such as the promotion and relegation systems operating in most countries, and outdated structures of league governance such as the delegate system, where 'managers' of the league are more likely to be appointed on the basis of representation than professional expertise.

Capacity and Function of Football Stadia

All matches at the World Cup in France were sold out because of 'limited' stadium capacity. In the most lucrative domestic soccer competition in the world, the English Premier League, total attendance is (sometimes) restricted by stadium capacity. The Premier League provides another example of the importance of this variable when interpreting overall attendance figures per club and per league. When comparing average league attendance with ground capacity,[60] it is worth noting that although all clubs in the Premier League averaged an occupancy rate of 90 per cent, the top five clubs had occupancy rates exceeding 100 per cent, as illustrated in Table 4.5. These figures show the overselling of the official capacity of many of the smaller stadia in the English Premier League.

The importance for clubs to own and operate a modern stadium was further highlighted when US Major League Soccer boss, Don Garber, made the development of soccer-dedicated stadia for MLS clubs a strategic priority. In MLS-owned stadia, he argued, all revenue streams

Table 4.5 Top five stadium occupancy rates (%) of Premier League teams (UK)

Team	Stadium capacity	Occupancy rate
Charlton Athletic	20,043	116
West Ham United	26.054	116
Chelsea	35,421	108
Ipswich	22,559	104
Fulham	19,000	102

Source: Adapted from www.soccerstats.com (2002).

Table 4.6 Top five stadium occupancy rates (%) of National Football League teams (USA)

Team	Stadium capacity	Occupancy rate
Philadelphia Eagles	65,352	100
Kansas City Chiefs	78,451	100
St Louis Rams	66,000	100
Washington Redskins	80,166	100
Cleveland Browns	73,200	100

Source: Adapted from www.nfl.com (1999), www.infoplease.com (2002).

can be controlled, the scheduling of games in relation to television broadcast can be optimised and customers can be serviced according to the standards set by the league, not by the stadium operators.

A similar situation can be seen in American football (see Table 4.6) where the average occupancy rate for all 30 NFL teams was 91 per cent, with only a few teams performing at less than 80 per cent occupancy rates.

The reverse is the case for less successful teams in English football (often first, second, and third division teams). Increasing stadium capacity in order to increase gate receipts may well have a negative effect on attendance. Gary Boon noted that:

One serious conclusion to be drawn from this is the clear need for some lower division clubs to temper their dream stadium plans with a degree of realism. It may be great to have a 20,000 capacity stadium, but an average attendance of only 4,000 creates a negative atmosphere. A 10,000 or 12,000 capacity stadium can provide a better atmosphere and – paradoxically – increased support.[61]

The average occupancy rate of 90 per cent for Premier League teams drops to 69 per cent for Division One, 47 per cent for Division Two and

33 per cent for Division Three. Two recent examples of Dutch soccer clubs moving to new facilities with increased capacity show the potential these facilities hold when these clubs operate in unsaturated spectator markets. Ajax Amsterdam's move from the 29,500 capacity 'de Meer' stadium to the Amsterdam Arena with a capacity of 48,000 increased Ajax's average attendances from 29,000 to 41,275. When Vitesse Arnhem moved from 'Monnikehuize' (capacity 11,000) to the 'Gelredome' (capacity 26,500), average attendance increased from approximately 8,000 to 23,080. The particular significance of Boon's observation is that having 'excess capacity' in stadia is not necessarily a desirable situation for football clubs. Match day attendance can be positively stimulated by a limited supply of available seats in the stadium. It might therefore be better to talk about optimum capacity rather than maximum capacity. Optimum capacity assumes a marketing approach to revenue maximisation beyond maximising match day income. The Australian Football League, for whom (as highlighted before) stadium capacity in most cases is not a limiting factor when it comes to maximising the number of spectators at the game, characterises this approach.

One hundred of the 176 matches in the 1998 season of the AFL were played in stadia in the league's principal market, Melbourne. Eighty-one of those matches were played in the city's two major stadia: the Melbourne Cricket Ground (MCG), with a capacity just short of a 100,000, and Waverley Park, with a capacity of 75,000. The 26 games at Waverley Park averaged 34,549 spectators, whereas the 55 matches played at the MCG averaged 47,585 spectators. Only for the 1998 Grand Final (the final match for the 'Premiership' by the top two finishing teams) did demand for tickets exceed supply.[62] In this context some other issues demand attention from league administrators. The AFL indicated in their 1994 strategic plan that mass attendance at events is important because:

- crowd atmosphere is part of the entertainment experience; empty stadia create bad impressions
- large crowds indicate the health of the game and encourage others to become involved
- large crowds maintain the 'people's game' ethos, a significant advantage over other sports
- of necessity AFL stadia are large and need crowds to create interest and excitement
- large support bases underpin League and club finances through all forms of revenue generation.

In other words, rather than maximising gate receipts as an isolated source of club and league income, the AFL recognised that, given their market conditions (city markets for clubs rather than a domestic market, large stadia and limited domestic competition from other football codes), some income from gate receipts had to be sacrificed in order to maximise profit in other business areas. In describing the development from VFL (Victorian Football League, the previous State competition) to the national Australian Football League, and important strategic decisions in this process, Westerbeek and Turner[63] highlighted the deliberate decisions made by the AFL to increase the market power of both clubs and the league.

> Through equalisation efforts (salary cap and draft) and ground rationalisation, the AFL competition became more attractive for spectators which brought about an increase in match attendances. Together with an increase in televisual appeal and hence income, the AFL was able to devise strategies in which demand characteristics of their markets (like the inelastic demand for tickets) could be used to optimise net income. Mass attendance at games was deemed more important than maximum profit from gate receipts. By undercharging at the gate, income from TV and sponsorship could be raised, leading to greater total income rather than maximising gate receipts. It therefore can be concluded that the AFL have used their market power to optimise their total income.

The issue of stadium capacity is a double-edged sword. On the one hand stadia with limited capacity will lead to occupants not profiting from maximising their gate receipts. On the other hand, stadia that are too large contribute to increased operational costs, lack of atmosphere and, consequently, lack of support from the fans, impacting on other business areas of the club such as sponsorship, corporate hospitality and television revenue. For the time being, it still is important to have a stadium filled close to capacity. This is reinforced in Figure 4.4, which illustrates the importance of gate receipts in the overall revenue structure for soccer clubs in the major competitions in Europe. An interesting outlier is Holland, where corporate hospitality and sponsorship are by far the most important sources of revenue. Boon observed:

> Whether they are far-sighted visionaries or not, the school of thought that downplays the importance of income from the live event (and tends to disregard the fan – 'customer' – loyalty it creates) in favour of a

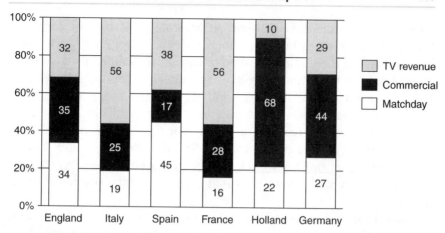

Figure 4.4 Income split by category in six major soccer leagues in Europe

Source: G. Boon (1999). *Deloitte & Touche Annual Review of Football Finance* (1997–1998 season), Deloitte & Touche, Manchester; G. Boon (2001). *Deloitte & Touche Annual Review of Football Finance* (1999–2000 season), Deloitte & Touche, Manchester.

greater impact from the (indirect) income for TV rights, is – in our view – putting the wrong emphasis on football's financial structure. It is the balance of the revenues from these different markets that is important.[64]

Individual clubs and leagues will continue their efforts to achieve full capacity for revenue maximisation purposes. As a matter of fact, in the 2001–2002 Premier League, the emphasis is back on expanding (or retaining) the fan base. In order to increase regular attendance and to turn young spectators into football devotees, half of all clubs have reduced prices. Sunderland, for example, discounted season tickets by 10 per cent and designed a special discount scheme for children younger than 12 and those aged under 22. The latter youngsters are in their first jobs and, having moved out of their parental homes, money is likely to be tight. To that end clubs still aim to maximise gate takings, while leagues aim to maximise total revenue from the product mix consisting of gate, sponsorship, merchandise and television revenues. Licensing revenues, which are another major source of income, can be considered as a separate issue when viewed in the context of stadium capacity.

Related to capacity are the required features of modern day stadia. As a result of the changing functionality of sporting arenas, the current (fourth) generation of stadia incorporate multi-purpose facilities with an increased focus on catering for corporate hospitality, which in turn impacts upon attendance patterns at matches. Not only is corporate funding an increasingly important source of revenue for facility operators, but the space in the stadium devoted to corporate facilities also requires a reassessment of the facility's positioning strategies. This logically leads to a reassessment of the facility's (and its tenants) target markets. As reported by *Sport Business International*,[65] 'England's bid for the 2006 World Cup [soccer] received a boost when plans for the new-look Wembley stadium were revealed. The US$700 million stadium will boast a retractable roof, athletics track, 200-bedroom hotel complex, state-of-the-art media centre and an increased capacity of 90,000 when it opens in 2003'.

Sport Business Group's editorial director, Kevin Roberts,[66] highlighted the change in the approach to funding fourth generation (contemporary) sport facilities. Because of the reluctance of sport fans and the local community to fund developments with tax dollars (as opposed to third-generation stadia developed two or three decades ago where funding often consisted of nearly 100 per cent public money), sport organisations have turned their attention to identifying alternative funding strategies. This has resulted in the 'unbundling' of commercial activities (concessions, alcohol-licensing rights, merchandising rights, media rights) that (can) operate through the facility. Corporations are prepared to pay 'top dollar' for luxury boxes and club seating. The values of stadium naming rights have dramatically increased and stadium precincts are 'increasingly becoming the beating heart of a total entertainment destination where in-stadium rights have been extended by the development of the surrounding zones with cinemas, other sports facilities, and restaurants. The common denominator is that each is forward contracted to deliver revenue at set times.'[67] As outlined by Chris Britcher,[68] the Staples Center in Los Angeles is a

> one million-square foot building [and] contains 20,000 seats, 160 luxury suites on three levels at the mid-level, 3000 premier club seats, premier club, grand reserve club, Fox Network Television studio, Fox Network Sports Bar and a large team store selling team apparel for all four professional sports franchises. The naming rights to the venue sold for more than US$120million.

Dan Meis and Ron Turner, of architects NBBJ Sports and Entertainment, were selected to build the stadium because they are always looking for ways to connect with sponsors over and above just selling a sign. It helps that the architects are sports fans as well. When they designed the first

Major League Soccer stadium in the USA (Columbus Crew, Ohio), the frustrating experience of missing out on a goal that was scored when getting some fast food made them build the concession stands to face the field.[69] The fan and sponsor are king in the new stadium.

Another example of a fourth-generation multi-purpose facility, the Telstra Dome in Melbourne, Australia, was selected 'as the site for Channel Seven's new digital broadcast centre'. The stadium was expected to become the vanguard of the television revolution.[70] This possibility was left unfulfilled as a result of Channel Seven's failure to win the bid for the AFL broadcast rights. Nevertheless, the commercial broadcaster had expected to fit the stadium with the most modern television facilities, so that it became the home of an AUD$100 million digital television broadcast and production centre which was to be the first of its type in Australia. Allied to the growing importance of television revenue for football clubs and the investment of media organisations in stadia comes the increase in power and influence media organisations will have on the operations of the clubs and sporting leagues.

Live Television Coverage of Matches

In the early days of US television, sporting franchises were primarily occupied with protecting their main source of revenue, gate receipts. Healthy attendances at games were secured as long as broadcasters were prevented from broadcasting home games. This initial battle of home game broadcasts versus the 'gate' occurred as a result of historical precedence. Minor league baseball attendance declined from 42 million before television broadcasts (1949) to a meagre 10 million 20 years later.[71] Attendance figures for British soccer, as presented in Figure 4.5, show a steady decline in Premier League attendance over a 50-year period, despite the fact that the 2002 Premier League is one of the most successful sporting leagues in the world and is slowly on the way up again. The decline coincides with increasing entertainment options over the past 50 years. It is therefore unlikely that the drop in attendance is solely the result of television broadcasts of soccer matches. However, most marketers will argue that a soccer match on television is a very close substitute for attending the soccer match 'live'.

Long before the advent of television there had always been an active and influential sports print media industry. Sport has always proved to be cheap and attractive content for newspapers. Apart from using publications to legislate and organise sport, early sport publications were used as

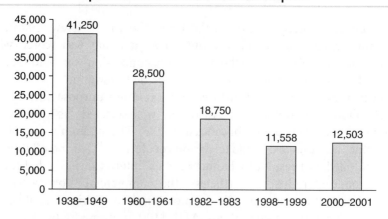

Figure 4.5 Seasonal premier league attendances (millions)

Sources: Adapted from www.sportStats.com (1999); A. Guttmann (1986), *Sports Spectators*, Columbia University Press, New York; www.4thegame.com (2002).

a forum for gambling. As early as 1868 a sporting paper (*The Field*) moved into sport sponsorship when they offered the All England Croquet Club a silver trophy to inaugurate the Wimbledon Championships.[72] Continental Europe, in particular, developed a strong presence in the daily sport newspaper market with the *Gazzetta dello Sport* launched in 1896 in Italy, followed by *L'Equipe* in France in 1900 and *El Mundo Deportivo* in Spain in 1906.

Not much different from contemporary sport, coverage of twentieth-century sport was dominated by men's sporting prowess. During the early 1900s sports coverage was advanced to moving images for the first time. During the 1920s the first 'major' sporting events such as Henley Regatta or yachting from Cowes were shown to mass audiences on newsreel in cinemas.[73] Sport was at the centre of competition between American newsreel companies who were so keen to secure exclusive film material of high-profile events that up to £2,000 was paid for the rights to the Grand National alone.[74]

In contemporary society, broadcasting companies around the world have rediscovered the attractiveness of major sporting contests as a means of attracting viewers. Major revenue streams for broadcasters are generated through the sales of advertising inventory around television shows or, in the case of many cable television operators, through the sale of subscriptions to their pay-television services. 'Prime time' is the viewing window where the largest proportion of watchers can conveniently enjoy television entertainment. It is also the most profitable time slot for advertising sales, and subsequently commands high-profile programming. According to Rupert Murdoch, 'sport is the universal language of entertainment'.[75] The money invested in sport by the major networks increases their control over the sport event. As we shall demonstrate later, corporate ownership of teams dramatically improves the bargaining position of the corporate owners with the league, for instance in regard to the scheduling of games. In the United States, athletes and event organisers must accept the fact that the 'live' broadcast will take place during the 'prime time' of the most lucrative domestic television market, the East Coast.[76] The same principles apply on the international scene.

In the world's most lucrative television markets of North America (including the sleeping giant of South America, which is in the North American time zone) and Europe, major sporting events and competitions are available in abundance. An implication of this availability is that when sporting contests are transformed into prime time television programming (broadcast in real time), these events become the direct competitors of other sporting events in need of 'live' spectators. The addition of 'real time' is critical in that an important part of the attractiveness of sporting contests resides in the uncertainty of outcome. Being part of the drama of watching a sporting contest as a spectator (even when it is 'only' through television), is an emotionally involved activity. Many hallmark sporting events are organised in North America (such as major professional sport leagues, US Open tennis and golf, and the US PGA golf tour) and Europe (such as Wimbledon, French Open tennis, the European PGA tour, the majority of Formula One Grand Prix races, and major professional sport leagues). Much more than in Australia and to a lesser extent, Asia, the availability of 'prime time' sporting events in real time is a significant competitive force that North American and European sporting leagues have to deal with. The television sport events compete directly with 'on-site' live events for the favour of spectators. Because Australia is in a different time zone, these events do not compete directly against the gate of domestic competitions for the simple reason that, most of the time, these events can only be watched in 'real time' at night. Because of its size, Asia has a number of continental sporting competitions and events (such as J-league soccer, Asian Games) and a number of lesser high-profile international tour events (tennis, golf) that compete through television for spectators in much of the same way as in Europe and North America.

In Australia, the main struggle between televised and live spectator sports takes place within football codes (for instance, soccer, rugby league, Australian Rules football). Television networks want to broadcast live into the main markets when the game is also being played in the stadium, resulting in people opting to watch the game on television at home rather than going to the game.

Murdoch famously argued that sport 'absolutely overpowers all other programming as an incentive for viewers to subscribe to cable and satellite TV'.[77] His Fox sports network has expanded to include 61 million subscribers. News Corporation's annual report[78] further reported that 'Fox broadcasting concluded a new multi-year agreement to broadcast National Football League games, including the rights to two Super Bowls over the next five years. In Australia, News Corporation helped form the National Rugby League, unifying the company's Super League with the Australian Rugby League'. The NFL deal, worth US$17.6 billion over eight years and split between a number of networks, can be described as one of News Corporation's most important victories. Their aggressive entry into football in 1994, when they outbid the opposition by half a billion dollars gave them access to the glamorous National Football Conference including the prized Green Bay Packers, San Francisco 49ers, Chicago Bears, Dallas Cowboys and New York Giants. The renewal of the contract cost News Corporation an increase of 39 per cent on the 1994 deal, a bargain considering the 'leftovers' that other media players had to buy 'because the strategic cost of not paying exorbitant broadcast fees for football was even higher than the actual cost of paying them'.[79] Disney committed almost US$10 billion to hang on to the ABC's most prized possession, 'Monday Night Football' and the football cable rights for their sport channel ESPN. Since the start of Monday Night Football in 1969 it has been one of the highest rating programs of the ABC, but at a cost of almost US$40 million per game it is unlikely to make any money. The reality of the professional sport broadcasting playing field is that:

> the strategic defense of the ESPN sports channel has come at an enormous cost. For many years, ESPN has been the dominant sport channel on cable TV, and a huge profit centre. But those days are over. Last year, Murdoch stitched together a complex alliance of 17 regional sports channels, now known as Fox sports, which should collectively out-rate ESPN'.[80]

We commented earlier that media experts suspect near-total corporate ownership of professional sport is inevitable; this proposition is illustrated by Murdoch's BSkyB bid to take over Manchester United. The Monopolies and Merger Commission (MMC) in the UK, however, described the attempt as anti-competitive. The MMC recommendation was based on the principle that a merger would enhance BSkyB's ability to secure Premier League rights in the future. This would in turn lead to further restrictions on entry into the sport pay-television market by new companies. The prices of BSkyB's sport channels would be higher, with overall choice and innovation in the market lower than it would be otherwise. Reduced entry by pay-television providers in the sports sector would also lead to reduced competition in the wider pay-television market. It is also important to assess the likely effects of the merger separately in relation to existing (that is, collective) or future (potentially individual) selling arrangements for Premier League rights:

> In the event of the continuation of collective selling arrangements on the existing basis, and no other mergers being precipitated by the BSkyB/Manchester United merger, the MMC concluded that BSkyB would gain influence over and information about the Premier League's selling of rights that together would be liable to significantly improve its chances of securing those rights in the future, whatever the response of its competitors might be ... On the alternative outcome to the case, that TV rights may in future be sold on an individual basis, the MMC concluded that the merger might be expected to give BSkyB an advantage over other broadcasters which would not otherwise have been enjoyed.[81]

In other words, ownership of Manchester United would have a significant impact when entering into negotiations for the acquisition of individual club rights (much more so than when only owning a smaller Premier League club). With the rights of the strongest club already in its possession, BSkyB would be more readily able to secure the rights of other leading clubs, because other clubs would naturally be inclined to link themselves with the strongest club in the league.

David Stotlar[82] discussed the developments in the global media industry from a vertical integration perspective. Vertical integration is a corporate growth strategy where acquisitions in the channel of distribution are the drivers of growth. According to Stotlar, the three main players in the global media industry are the Walt Disney Company, Time Warner (now AOL Time Warner) and News Corporation. All three organisations are moving towards producing, distributing and selling their own entertainment products (including sport), and subsequently obtaining full control over all elements/phases in the distribution channel. Ten years ago, none of these organisations even existed. ABC, CBS and NBC were the three major networks in the USA, but these have now been swallowed by global giants, all of which are vertically integrated conglomerates. A closer look at the strategies of these conglomerates reveals a delayed gratification philosophy. Although News Corporation failed to buy Manchester United outright, they (through subsidiaries) did succeed in securing a number of other high-profile sport properties:

> Australia's Seven network was able to secure the right to the 2000 Sydney Games and last year added the 2002, 2004, 2006 and 2008 Olympic Games at a price reported to be AUD$187 million ... 35% of Telecom Italia's Stream (digital TV operator) [was secured] which included partial ownership of four major soccer clubs. In Germany, Murdoch just purchased 66% of a small TV station, TM3, and then purchased the German rights of the UEFA's Champions [soccer] league for US$109 million as programming for TM3.[83]

In that regard it does 'seem certain that European soccer is headed the way of US professional sports, where some franchises are now in the hands of corporations, most of them in the entertainment business'.[84] Along the same lines as News Corporation, similar strategic moves have been undertaken by Disney and Time Warner (prior to the merger). In 1998 Disney purchased 43 per cent of Infoseek (an Internet search engine), ultimately creating their own Internet portal to provide them with the capacity to sell and 'promote their properties across the spectrum of telecommunication'.[85] Disney created their own sport-related content by developing sport properties the 'Disney way'. The Mighty Ducks of Anaheim (National Hockey League) and the Anaheim Angels (Major League Baseball) are as much cartoon characters as they are professional sporting franchises. As for Time Warner, their sports properties include the Atlanta Braves (Major League Baseball), Atlanta Hawks (National Basketball League), the Atlanta Thrashers (a 1999 addition to the National Hockey League) and *Sports Illustrated*, one of the widest distributed sport magazines in the world. Disney distribute their sport properties through channels such as ESPN, ESPN2 and ABC Sports, whereas Time Warner own the Warner Brothers studios, the Warner Brothers network, HBO, CNN, WTBS and TNT.[86] Of course, Time Warner's merger with Internet giant America Online is another example of communications conglomerates aiming to achieve the greatest global reach possible, and may shift the balance of power towards the new media giant.

In 1999 News Corporation aimed to attain a truly global reach, approaching 75 per cent of the world's population when launching their satellite platforms in Latin America and Japan.[87] However, as observed by James Santomier,[88] it is important to note that competition is lurking around the corner. In the Asia-Pacific region, media companies such as NHK, Fuji Television, Nippon Television Network, PBL Australia and China Entertainment Television, together with Bertelsmann in Germany, Havas and Canal Plus in France, Globo in Brazil and Televisa in Mexico, are all challengers in the global media arena. FIFA has announced that DirecTV Latin America have obtained the exclusive broadcast rights for the 2002 and 2006 World Cups and a number of other FIFA competitions, enabling them to air more than 1,000 hours of digital programming. Coverage will extend to include Argentina, Colombia, Chile, Uruguay, Venezuela and Mexico, and the agreement includes all television and radio broadcast rights. A subsidiary of the General Motors Corporation, the US-based Hughes Electronics Corporation, owns DirecTV. As we have already briefly mentioned, building mega-media companies may just be one step towards the fragmentation of vertically integrated conglomerates into highly specialised, separate companies that benefit from the creative economies of scale of their mother companies.

Given the enormous financial gains to be generated through broadcasting sport to mass markets, it is likely that the media conglomerates will find ways to encourage sport marketers to broadcast live into major spectator markets sooner rather than later, especially when considering the exorbitant salaries which the star players of popular television sports are currently demanding. As noted in an earlier chapter, in 2001 the average NFL player made close to US$1.2 million, hockey players made US$1.5, the MLB athletes pocketed US$2.3 million and the stars of the NBA US$4.2 million. In the English Premier League an average of 63 per cent of club turnover is paid out in salaries or wages. Average income on match days generates 34 per cent of total income of the clubs, indicating the inability of gate receipts to cover players' salary costs.[89] The fact that many sporting franchises and clubs have become involved in debt-funded facility construction and upgrade projects only increases the pressure placed upon the fund-seeking activities of sport marketers. HSBC analyst, Virginie Lannevere,[90] reportedly argued that:

if wages for soccer players continue to rise in Europe, some clubs might find themselves in financial ruin. Unless there is a cap on wages, a string of bankruptcies will be declared from clubs, which would trigger shock waves throughout the whole soccer industry. For institutional investors there is too much risk attached to piling money into soccer because clubs offer no liquidity. Nobody is interested in buying or selling soccer stocks at the moment.

Developments such as virtual advertising (the 'on screen' insertion of electronically generated advertisements over parts of the crowd and stadium) show the potential of simply superimposing 'virtual crowds' over empty seats in stadia. With the addition of some 'canned' crowd noises inserted at the appropriate times during the telecast, viewers in the comfort of their homes will not realise that the new corporate owners of sport do not need spectators in the stadium. In other words, 'at best, ballpark spectators have become the equivalent of studio guests; at worst, they are background, mere television props'.[91]

In the first part of this chapter it was shown that soccer is a globally popular participation and spectator sport. In the context of different football codes played around the world, three main issues affecting attendance at matches were identified: the professionalisation of league management and the consequent economic rationalisation of competitions; capacity and functionality of football stadia; and live coverage of matches on television. This last point was further discussed in the context of developments in the global media industry. In order to appreciate some of the broader drivers of the sport entertainment industry, it is necessary to consider some of the reasons explaining the rapid growth of the services sector.

Notes and references

1 Collins (1996), *Collins Cobuild Essential Dictionary*, HarperCollins, London, p. 147.
2 *The Economist* (1998), 'The world of sport: Not just a game', *The Economist*, June 6, pp. 3–19.
3 *The Economist* (1998), 'The world of sport: Not just a game'.
4 R. S. Johnson (1997), 'Take me out to the boardroom', *Time*, 4 August, pp. 44–7.
5 M. Glendinning (1998) *Sport Business Magazine*, October, pp. 22–6.
6 R. S. Johnson, 'Take me out to the boardroom'.
7 R. Boyle and R. Haynes (2000), *Power Play. Sport, the Media and Popular Culture*, Pearson Education, Harlow.
8 H. Gabler, H. J. Schulz and R. Weber (1982), 'Zuschaueraggressionen, eine feldstudie ueber fussballfans', in G. Pilz (ed.), *Sport und gewalt*, Hofmann, Schondorf, p. 23.
9 A. Guttmann (1986), *Sports Spectators*, Columbia University Press, New York.
10 R. Holt (1981), *Sport and Society in Modern France*, Macmillan, London, p. 138.
11 J. MacClancy (1996), *Sport, Identity and Ethnicity*. Berg, Oxford, p. 17.
12 H. Bredekamp (1993), *Florentiner fussball: die renaissance der spiele*, Campus, Frankfurt; A. Guttmann, *Sports Spectators*; B. Murray (1996), *The World's Game, A History of Soccer*, University of Illinois Press, Chicago.
13 E. Dunning (1999), *Sport Matters: Sociological Studies of Sport, Violence and Civilisation*, Routledge, London.

14 J. Huizinga (1971), 'The play element in contemporary sport', in E. Dunning (ed.), *The Sociology of Sport: A Selection of Readings*. Cass, London, p. 13.
15 E. Dunning, *Sport Matters*, p. 53.
16 Called sportification by M. Bottenburg (1994), *Verborgen competitie, over de uiteenlopende populariteit van sporten*, Uitgeverij Bert Bakker, Amsterdam.
17 N. Elias (1994), *The Civilizing Process: The History of Manner and State-Formation and Civilisation*, Blackwell, Oxford; N. Elias and E. Dunning (1986), *Quest for Excitement: Sport and Leisure in the Civilizing Process*, Blackwell, Oxford.
18 E. Dunning, *Sport Matters*, p. 89.
19 N. Elias (1986), 'The genesis of sport as a sociological problem', in N. Elias and E. Dunning, *Quest for Excitement*, p. 34.
20 E. Dunning, *Sport Matters*, p. 63.
21 E. Dunning, *Sport Matters*, p. 64.
22 E. Dunning, *Sport Matters*, p. 82.
23 B. Murray, *The World's Game*.
24 B. Murray, *The World's Game*.
25 N. Elias, 'The genesis of sport as a sociological problem'.
26 E. Dunning, *Sport Matters*.
27 B. Murray, *The World's Game*.
28 B. Murray, *The World's Game*.
29 B. Murray, *The World's Game*, p. 18.
30 B. Murray, *The World's Game*, p. 20.
31 B. Murray, *The World's Game*.
32 B. Murray, *The World's Game*, p. 43.
33 B. Murray, *The World's Game*.
34 B. Murray, *The World's Game*, p. 55.
35 B. Murray, *The World's Game*, p. 60.
36 B. Murray, *The World's Game*, p. 65.
37 B. Murray, *The World's Game*, p. 101.
38 B. Murray, *The World's Game*, p. 131.
39 E. Dunning, *Sport Matters*.
40 E. Dunning, P. Murphy and J. Williams (1988), *The Roots of Football Hooliganism*. Routledge, London.
41 E. Dunning, *Sport Matters*, p. 140.
42 E. Dunning, *Sport Matters*, pp. 147–8.
43 A. L. Spurling (1999), 'Hooligans or fans? Violence and culture in association football since the second world war', Bachelor of Arts (Honours) Thesis, Deakin University, Waurn Ponds, p. 49.
44 B. Murray, *The World's Game*, p. 127.
45 M. Bottenburg, *Verborgen competitie*.
46 M. Bottenburg, *Verborgen competitie*.
47 A. Fry (1998), 'France 98 sets new standard', *Sport Business*, August, 15–16.
48 Sponsorship Information Services (1998), 'Top 100 European sports programmes broadcast March to May 1998', *Sport Business*, September, 29.
49 B. Murray, *The World's Game*.
50 *Sport Business*, August 1992, p. 2.
51 P. Fuller and M. Stewart (1993) 'Attendance Patterns at Victorian and South Australian Football Games', *Working Papers Series in Economics and Finance*, RMIT, Melbourne, April, p. 9.

52   D. R. Howard (1999), 'The changing fanscape for big-league sports: Implications for sport managers', *Journal of Sport Management*, 13, 78–91, 89.

53   T. Knott (1998), 'Capping out?', *Washington Times*, 3 March, p. 3.

54   H. M. Westerbeek (2000), 'Sport in the global village: A product-based typology of the international sport industry', *International Journal of Sport Management*, 1(2), 103–20.

55   P. Smith and M. Ryan (2000), 'Blues may lose points',. The Age, 11 March, p. 20.

56   G. R. Milne and M. A. McDonald (1999), *Sport Marketing, Managing the Exchange Process*, Jones & Bartlett, Sudbury, Massachusetts.

57   H. M. Westerbeek and P. Turner (1996), 'Market power of an Australian sport organisation', in *Proceedings of the Fourth European Congress on Sport Management*, Montpellier, France, pp. 386–94.

58   R. B. Stewart, A. C. T. Smith and S. Quick (1995), 'The economic parameters of professional sport in Australia: lessons for sport administrators', paper presented at the first conference of the Sport Management Association of Australia and New Zealand, November, Melbourne.

59   P. Fuller and M. Stewart (1993), 'Attendance Patterns at Victorian and South Australian Football Games', *Working Papers Series in Economics and Finance*, RMIT, Melbourne, April.

60   G. Boon (1999), *Deloitte & Touche Annual Review of Football Finance* (1997–1998 season), Deloitte & Touche, Manchester.

61   G. Boon (1998), *Deloitte & Touche Annual Review of Football Finance* (1996–1997 season), Deloitte & Touche, Manchester, p. 15.

62   AFL (1999), *102nd Annual Report 1998*, Australian Football League, Melbourne, p. 133.

63   H. M. Westerbeek and P. Turner (1996), 'Market power of an Australian sport organisation', pp. 393–4.

64   G. Boon, *Deloitte & Touche Annual Review of Football Finance* (1997–1998 season), p. 62.

65   *Sport Business* (1999), 'A new Wembley', *Sport Business International*, September, p. 1.

66   K. Roberts (1999), 'Building finance options, how project financing is helping fund the US stadium boom', *Sport Business*, September.

67   K. Roberts, 'Building finance options', p. 18.

68   C. Britcher (2000), 'The new breed of indoor arenas', *Sport Business*, January, pp. 26–7.

69   J. Rawe, J. (2001), 'If these guys build it, fans will come', *Time*, 3 September, p. 67.

70   A. Rados (2000), 'Seven's big move', *Telstra Dome Guide, Herald Sun*, March, pp. 30–1.

71   A. Guttmann, *Sports Spectators*.

72   R. Boyle and R. Haynes, *Power Play*.

73   R. Boyle and R. Haynes, *Power Play*.

74   A. Aldgate (1979), *Cinema and History: British Newsreels and the Spanish Civil War*, London, Scolar Press.

75   News Corporation (1998), *News Corporation Ltd. Annual Report 1998*, News Corporation Ltd, New York, p. 5.

76   A. Guttmann, *Sports Spectators*.

77   *The Economist* (1998), 'The world of sport: Not just a game', *The Economist*, 6 June, p. 14.

78   News Corporation (1998), *News Corporation Ltd. Annual Report 1998*, p. 5.

79   P. Sheehan (1998), 'Game plan; how Murdoch became the champion of world sports', *The Age Green Guide*, 5 March, pp. 1–10

80   P. Sheehan, 'Game plan', pp. 1–10

81   R. Finbow (1999), 'United decision is not the end of the road', *Sport Business*, May, p. 11.

82   D. Stotlar (2000), 'Vertical integration in sport', *Journal of Sport Management*, 14(1), pp. 1–7.

83   D. Stotlar, 'Vertical integration in sport', pp. 7–8

84   S. Reed (1998), 'The new lords of soccer', *Business Week*, 5 October, p. 176.

85 D. Stotlar, 'Vertical integration in sport', p. 8.

86 D. Stotlar, 'Vertical integration in sport', pp. 1–7.

87 News Corporation, News Corporation Ltd. Annual Report 1998.

88 J. Santomier (2001), 'Sport mega-brands: global marketing strategies', Paper presented at the 7th annual conference of the Sport Management Association of Australia and New Zealand, November, Melbourne.

89 G. Boon, Deloitte & Touche Annual Review (1999–2000 season)

90 N. Wolstenhome (2001), 'Money to burn', Football Business International, 1, September, p. 14.

91 A. Guttmann, Sports Spectators, p. 141.

CHAPTER 5

Self Service: Sport and the Services Economy

First, I was suspicious of an advertising industry that manufactures needs, then sells products to foster those needs. Second, some offers were coming to me as a 'white hope', and that offended me. Third, basketball was an important part of my life. I wanted to keep it pure. Hair sprays and deodorants and popcorn poppers were not basketball.
Bill Bradley, basketball star (on why he refused to make television commercials)

We have already given an overview of the forces of globalisation that are likely to affect sport, retraced the relatively recent commercial development of the industry, examined its structure, revealed the origin of sport and considered the variables affecting the all important consumers of sport. In this chapter we introduce the first nexus dimension, the economy, or more specifically, the global sport services economy, which, when considered as a driving force of globalisation and change, has the capacity to affect sport business radically.

In what follows, we highlight the extraordinary growth of the services sector, particularly across developed nations. This is a fundamental trend that has bolstered the expansion of once parochial sport into international markets. In an effort to understand why this growth is occurring, we pay particular attention to the driving forces that have leveraged this escalation. One of the complications of selling sport products is that they are not products, at least in the traditional definition. This chapter also examines the evaluation process of consumers with the aim of coming to terms with the implications of marketing what are often intangible services, such as spectator sport. These implications demand recognition of the role that the media and broadcast mechanisms play in manipulating sport services.

It is common to classify spectator sport products as services and therefore as part of the ever-growing global services industry.[1] The metaphor of a theatre can be useful in describing service management, where service personnel are the actors in a play who deliver services to their audience, the customers, irrespective of whether those customers perceive they are buying an experience or a performance.[2] It was not until the early 1980s that marketers began to recognise that services were just as important as goods. Before that time, marketing theory was chiefly focused on selling physical goods such as food, clothing or cars. Only when the growth of services production and the expansion of services in terms of economic importance overtook the growth of physical goods production, was attention given to developing more sophisticated services marketing techniques. With the output of services now accounting for around 70 per cent of the gross domestic product (GDP) of most highly developed economies, it is estimated that over the next decade 90 per cent of all new jobs created in these countries will be in the service sector.[3]

There are several prevailing explanations for growth of the services industry, including increasing income levels, urbanisation, deregulation, women in the workforce, demographic shifts, growth of government, environmentalism, general growth in GDP and changes in demand composition.[4] The importance of the services industry in the United States and other developed nations is significant. Nine out of ten new jobs are in services,[5] and in highly developed Westernised countries service exports exceed imports markedly.[6] In contrast to the conservative explanations for services growth, another line of thought has concentrated on national and international specialisation as critical factors promoting the growth of the services sector.[7] These are, of course, critical factors that we have speculated will continue to proliferate in the more 'globalised' economy of the future.

The point was made in Chapter 1 that the apparent globalisation of sport seems to mirror the political economy of the world. In other words, it is not a radical notion that globalisation, and the future of sport, has something to do with the Americanisation or, at the very least, Westernisation of sport. While we have gone to some trouble in Chapter 7 to make it clear that it is vital to understand local cultural forces in order to really appreciate how the development of a sport occurs in a particular location, it is clear that the economic benchmark for the growth of the sport industry has come from developed nations, and in particular the United States. Even a cursory look at the international role of corporate sport in the USA reveals its ability to sell quite intangible services to a broad range of markets. A quick but not exhaustive inventory might note the National Football League (NFL) expansion in Europe, National Basketball Association (NBA) games in Japan and plenty of European players in the domestic US league, two summer Olympics within 12 years, the 1994 World Cup, a tennis Grand Slam and a host of ATP events, the most lucrative of professional golf tours, two massive motor racing competitions only rivalled by Formula One, the National Hockey League (NHL) stocked with the finest European players, and a university sport system which contains teams and individual athletes that in many cases perform at higher levels and have more resources at their disposal than most professional sport clubs in the rest of the world. Corporate sport in the USA has mastered the ability to sell sport services and to create niches and specialisations in an area that has historically been nebulous and difficult for consumers to 'uncluster'.

Increasing complexity in societies forces the workforce to specialise further. Task specialisation, in particular, allows organisations to cope with enhanced knowledge and innovations. Service tasks previously performed in the manufacturing industry are often detached from the core of these organisations. These special services, such as the maintenance of manufacturing equipment, for example, or the use of physiotherapists, masseurs and exercise scientists in sport clubs, exist in their own right and are 'bought' by producers. Such 'unbundling' of functions leads to increased specialisation for both the producers and those enterprises to which the work has been outsourced. In theory, this should lead to increased efficiencies and output.

Growth of service industries is not limited to domestic markets. Services industries in the global marketplace offer enormous potential for growth, especially for many of the developed, industrialised nations. Services account for more than 30 per cent of total world trade, growing at twice the pace of the international trade in goods.[8] The international services sector is an increasingly vital element in nations' strategies for economic development. This fact, married to the political leverage that sport can provide, makes investment in the development of domestic sport infrastructure an appealing use of finance for governments.

In understanding the impact of the global economy on the progress of sport, it is critical to chart the trends that have facilitated its development. If the services sector is as important as the figures we have quoted imply, then the factors (listed below) leading to the internationalisation and globalisation of service trade are drivers of the sport industry's evolution as well:[9]

1   The 'hollowing out effect' is the shift in economic activity to service industries, caused in part by the large-scale transfer of labour-intensive manufacturing activity from developed to low-wage countries. The hollowing out effect can be identified in sport equipment

and apparel manufacturing, particularly with sporting footwear. The celebrated example of Nike is perhaps a little unfair to the company trying to compete in a marketplace full of manufacturers using a similar strategy to minimise production costs. Without venturing into the ethical minefield of this strategy, it should perhaps be observed that the removal of these manufacturing 'sweatshops', en masse, could have a crushing effect on the host economies.

2 As manufacturers go global, their service suppliers (financiers, project engineers, legal advisers) are often forced to follow if they wish to continue their relationship with important global clients. More than one entrepreneurial sport enterprise has been carried into international prominence as an outcome of their affiliation with global sport event products. It is interesting that the sport industry has similar 'hangers-on' who prosper as their clients develop internationally. Mark McCormack, founder of the International Management Group, together with a handful of other pioneering athlete managers, consultants and financiers, has benefited enormously from the activities of their clients.

3 The deregulation of many key industries, such as telecommunications, media, banking and finance, and the airline industry, has acted as a catalyst for global competition. The decrease in regulatory barriers has encouraged sport enterprises to seek more competitive suppliers and to offer their wares in previously inaccessible markets. This process has been facilitated by the growth in large international sporting events. For example, significant contracts for support services to the Beijing Olympics have gone to Australian tenderers in the aftermath of their successful involvement in Sydney. The ability for sport events to lubricate the opportunities provided by deregulation should not be overlooked.

4 Growing leisure time and increased affluence has led to a demand for more services. This pressure for greater consumer choice has filtered down to the sport and entertainment world to the point where the range of sport which can be viewed either live, on free-to-air television, or on pay channels is surprisingly diverse, from lawn bowls in Hong Kong to camel racing in Australia.

5 Technology – in medicine, media, transportation, telecommunications or the Internet – is having a unifying effect and making national boundaries effectively disappear. Technology, as we argue later in more detail, is a second nexus factor, such is its influence over sport. Clearly, the impact of technology on the expansion and popularity of sport through television and the Internet is unquestioned.

'The hollowing out effect' implies that the specialisation principle for one nation also applies to multiple countries, culminating in an increase in international trade. Some countries (with lower knowledge bases) specialise in manufacturing, while others (with higher knowledge bases) specialise in services production. In addition, the so-called 'low-wage' countries have a comparative advantage in labour-intensive manufacturing where 'advanced countries' use the benefits of good infrastructure, higher education, communication and transportation to specialise in the production of services. The specialisation argument can be applied to countries with limited space for primary (agriculture) and secondary (manufacturing) industries. Indeed, countries such as Austria and the Netherlands produce around 17.01 per cent and 22.76 per cent respectively of the countries' GDP as services exports signalling the scope and importance of service industries for economic development.[10]

As we have already discussed, the technology trend will play a major role in transforming the world and, in this case, the provision of services and the penetration of sport. In an extensive review of the services sector, the Allen Consulting Group concluded that the Internet specifically, and e-commerce in general, are the most powerful vehicles of transformation and globalisation of services.[11] Organisations around the world are forced to re-engineer the services they provide to allow for electronic delivery, either as a result of price competition (deliver at lowest cost, for example, in banking), the need to personalise service provision (and hence the need to actively archive and 'mine' consumer records), or to achieve economies of scale and expand markets. The Organisation for Economic Co-operation and Development (OECD) forecast the turnover for e-commerce to grow from approximately €15 billion in 1997 to €300 billion in 2002 and €900 billion in 2005.[12] According to Michael Rubin, the Chief Executive Officer (CEO) of Global Sports Interactive (the multi-company e-commerce partner of US sports retailers like The Sports Authority) online sales of sporting goods will be worth an estimated US$4 billion in 2004 in the USA alone.[13] The implications for sport and the mechanisms for accumulating competitive advantage in sport through the strategic use of the Internet is so important that we have reserved Chapter 6 to discuss it fully.

Sport is a vast service industry that has been affected significantly by three pivotal trends; globalisation, specialisation and growing economic importance. To explore the place of sport as an entertainment product further, we will turn our attention to the most significant differences between goods and services in the industry.

Sporting Goods and Sport Services

One well-established method for conceptualising the differences between goods and services is to look at them from the perspective of the consumer's evaluation processes.[14] For example, a number of hypotheses can be formed based on an evaluation continuum for different types of products ranging from those easy to evaluate (pure goods) to those more difficult to evaluate (pure services). In this continuum, easy to evaluate products are high in search qualities: that is the attributes of the product (such as price, colour, fit of running shoes) which consumers can determine and evaluate prior to purchase. Difficult to evaluate products are high in credence qualities, which are the characteristics of products consumers might find hard to evaluate, even after purchase or consumption. Credence qualities imply a substantial knowledge base about the product and its delivery, such as the reconstruction of an athlete's knee or the repair of a sports car engine. Most consumers lack this knowledge base. Stuck in the middle of the continuum are those products that combine goods and services characteristics as a package. Evaluation of those products is inescapably based on 'experience qualities', or those attributes that can only be discerned after purchase or during the process of consuming the product (including taste of food, courtesy of personnel, result of a soccer match). Based on this continuum of evaluation, a number of statements can be made about how consumers go about this evaluation process:[15]

1   When evaluating services prior to purchase, consumers will rely more on personal sources (word-of-mouth) because objective evaluation standards are less available for products high on experience qualities. This means that, despite all the cunning marketing angles that can be conceived about a sports product, the most convincing evidence remains word of mouth endorsement.

2   Most evaluation of services and information-seeking about services will take place post-purchase because only then can the consumer develop an attitude towards the service. This evaluation will most often focus on an information search, supporting the choice of the consumer (cognitive dissonance) in order to decrease the number of uncertain alternatives to the purchased service. In practice, this means that post-sale marketing and consumer education about a service is critical to repeat purchasing decision and word of mouth approval.

3   Since price and physical facilities are often the only tangible clues available to consumers, these clues will feature in the process of assessing the quality of service. This characteristic is at play when the sport facility is positioned as the key element of the spectator sport product.

4   The number of service products consumers consider to be acceptable options are likely to be smaller because of the physical distance between competing retailers (such as banks) offering the service, and due to the labour-intensive process of collecting and comparing pre-purchase information.

5   Because of the evaluation difficulties, intangibility and user-specific preferences, consumers are less likely to adopt service innovations than innovations in goods. The risk of switching to another 'unknown' provider is high, which is why adopting an innovative service is less likely. Brand loyalty therefore is higher for service products. This is also applicable to sport fans who follow a club or a team.

6   Consumers are more likely to blame themselves for dissatisfaction with the service after consumption given their participation in the production process and the perceived lack of ability to sufficiently specify the required quality level. This is why consumers do not necessarily blame the instructor for a poor aerobics class or a coaching lesson for why they do not improve their skills.

A distinction can be made between sporting goods and sport services as described earlier in the product-based typology of the international sport industry. We identified three categories of facility dependent sport services. The typology makes a clear distinction between products that directly *involve the sporting contest* (facility dependent sport services) and products that merely *contribute to the sporting contest* (sporting goods and sport consultation services). This distinction allows for the further separation between three categories of facility dependent sport services (corporate sport, hybrid sport and participant sport) at level 2 of the model. Level 3 then distinguishes between corporate-related products (spectator services, sponsorship services, broad/narrow/Internetcasting rights and licence rights) and participant services. The next section further examines how these levels of sport presently interact and how they may subsequently be conceptualised.

Media Power and Perceptions of Sport

Raymond Boyle and Richard Haynes, in their epic work on sport, media and popular culture, discuss the relative centrality of media in the production, reproduction and amplification of information associated with sport in the modern world.[16] On the one hand, they argue that there has been some independent development of sporting structures and identities of people and nations in social spaces outside the media, where sport has developed from the roots of gender, race, ethnicity and nationality. On the other hand, they observe that the media has played an important, if not a central, role in communicating and disseminating sport's gospels from its modern beginnings. The study of media sport (or sport reported through mass media) is therefore likely to provide an in-depth insight into how popular culture (say, sport or pop music) is commodified by capital. Boyle and Haynes perhaps put it best when they noted that 'televised sport not only provides our main connection to sport itself, but also our ideas about nationality, class, race, gender, age and disability. It therefore presents a rich seam of material from which to investigate and understand our social, cultural, economic and political lives.' [17]

Some might argue that the media have artificially transformed some sport services into product units for better sale, and in the process have ruined the sport consumption experience. As major networks are forced to pay extraordinary sums for the rights to broadcast sport, they naturally feel inclined to maximise their investments. The result has been a trend towards pay-per-view as the solitary outlet for fans to access events remotely. For most large sports, the trend has not yet reached its natural conclusion, although there are already first movers, such as professional boxing, which have effectively become exclusive to pay television. For some the only remedy is through federal regulatory mechanisms such as those in Australia, where at least a portion of the television sport diet needs to be free-to-air, in the process 'protecting' the 'cultural rights' of sports fans. In the USA, Division I college sport is being held up more and more as the amateur ideal gone wrong, particularly as gambling on college sport is rampant, while 'sport entertainment' products such as professional wrestling continually find new ways of packaging the consumption experience together with other lucrative products such as merchandise and computer games. The failure of the XFL in the USA, however, demonstrates that the media is not all-powerful and that, as we discuss in Chapter 7, cultural identity remains a significant pivot point for sport. In addition, as we argue in the following chapter, while the media will always prove influential, the other nexus that will determine the future of sport is technology, which incorporates much of the muscle of the media.

We can see the relative impact and power of media representations of sport in the relationship between football (soccer) and collective identities in a city such as Glasgow. Irrespective of the ability of the media to reproduce and amplify the existence of collective identities – where supporting Rangers or Celtic serves as a badge of identity – club support in Glasgow is based on religious demarcation which is historically determined and unaffected by the media. In that regard, the real challenge when attempting to determine the impact of the media on sport is to consider the tug-of-war between 'traditional sport' and the 'change' brought about by the demands of the (new) media and its increasing power to rearrange (on and off) the playing field.[18] Within the context of a growing sport services economy, we must acknowledge the power of the media to influence consumers' perceptions of traditional sport and their subsequent ability to manipulate the playing field in favour of the strongest or smartest sport service suppliers. In other words, through strong media relations, or ownership, sport organisations can dramatically increase the value of their products and brands, in turn affecting the value of their corporate products such as sponsorship, licensing and broadcasting rights. Through global reach, deregulation of the media sector and the unifying effect of new technology, the value that is accumulated in the sponsorship and licensing markets can be significantly increased.

Globalisation, Sponsorship, Licensing and the Media

Organising an international sporting event has become such a prodigious undertaking that major sport enterprises are forced to look for substantial multinational sponsorship to secure the success of the event financially. We are essentially talking about global sporting events delivered to a global audience and supported by global corporations. The triangle between the sport, the sponsor and the media is underpinned by geographic scope in that only an event that can attract a global viewing audience will be picked up by a media outlet, in turn securing the interest of sponsors to invest in the event as a means of communication. It therefore comes as no surprise that the growth of sport sponsorship follows the development of the media industry as a global business.

Figure 5.1 shows the growth of sport sponsorship expenditure in the UK. These figures need to be considered in light of the global growth of sport sponsorship, increasing in value from US$1.5 billion in 1989, to US$5.5 billion in 1996 and US$10 billion in 1999.[19] The logic of a sponsorship link between multinational companies and sport is quite straightforward. The coverage attracted by domestic or international

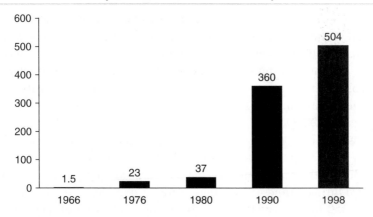

Figure 5.1 Sport sponsorship expenditure in the UK from 1966 to 1998 (US$ million)
Source: Adapted from R. Boyle and R. Haynes (2000). *Power Play. Sport, the Media and Popular Culture.* Pearson Education, Harlow, p. 49.

sporting events allows the sponsor to be associated with the event, in the process communicating to a variety of (potential) target markets. The main attractions of sport sponsorship are simply to increase or change the public profile of the company, to raise awareness of products or services of the company, or to (re)position a company's image in line with the action, excitement and sophistication of the sporting contest. Association at the domestic or global level can subsequently be translated and integrated at the level of local and national communities. Formula One motor racing is a good example of a sport that is highly attractive, glamorous, expensive, dangerous and exciting at the global level, and which also appeals to the competitive instinct. What better sport than Formula One to choose if a company wants to raise its profile and be associated with all the exciting characteristics of a sport being exposed to millions of spectators via television? With the Formula One 'circus' travelling from one continental region to the next every two weeks, there are plenty of opportunities to apply global sponsorship regionally or locally.

The globalisation of sport sponsorship is a logical development given the unique quality of popular commercial sport to cross borders without facing the difficulty of having to adjust to local language or culture. In the new millennium, businesses should 'use sport in marketing communications ... Sports symbolise an alternative to the gnawing complexity of postmodern life: the playing field is always level, and the rules stay the same.'[20] Furthermore, televised sporting events not only appeal to the committed sports fan but also, when put together well (camera angles, sound, close-ups, replays and so on), the peripheral sports viewer becomes interested in the narratives constructed around the event by broadcast and writing media. People follow televised sport because of its easy connection to issues dealing with national pride and hence, the identification with a wider collective experience. To that end, geographic popularity of the sport determines which organisations are most likely to sponsor the event (for instance, McDonald's and the 1984 Los Angeles Olympics) and indeed, when the event is broadcast into the main media market (high-profile World Cup matches during Mexico 1986 and USA 1994 were played during the hottest time of the day to accommodate the European market). During France 1998, there were 45 companies who collectively paid US$450 million for the right to call themselves an official sponsor, equipment or service supplier. Needless to say, most of these companies spend at least $1 for every $1 paid in sponsorship fees in order to leverage the effect of the sponsorship. Sponsors will simply not spend such amounts of money without the committed support of major broadcasters to the event. It is unsurprising therefore that sponsorship of youth sporting events accounts for as little as 0.5 per cent of all sport sponsorship.[21] Where sport at the local level is not necessarily changing dramatically, globally popular sports such as soccer, 'at the top level ... represent more and more graphically the triumph of the universal market, and whenever it is watched – live or in its transmitted forms – it is an increasingly commodified cultural product in a structured environment of an intensifying exclusive type'.[22] Football club sponsorship in Europe's biggest soccer markets shows the value corporations place on this exclusive product (see Figure 5.2).

The sporting goods industry and the sale of licensed sporting goods further exemplifies the triumph of the universal market. Sales of licensed sporting goods reached their peak during the mid-1990s in the United States. Partly due to the baseball strike and the NBA lockout in 1997/1998, sales dropped dramatically towards the end of the 1990s. However, the NFL and NBA are revitalising and reinvigorating the industry by entering previously untapped markets. For example, the NBA launched the Global Retail Environment Program through which they aimed to create 'unified NBA-branded visual impact zones at retail outlets all over the world ... looking at direct TV selling models, selling products in ad-spots during matches, and alternative retailing and merchandising, with the aim of getting the brand message at the point of sale'.[23] More recently, Manchester United have shown that their merchandising arm is almost as lucrative outside the UK as it is inside.

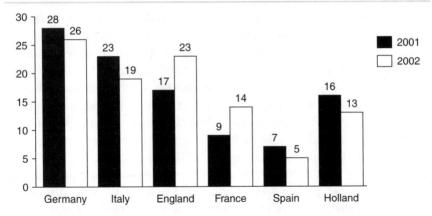

Figure 5.2 Value of club sponsorship as percentage of total market value (total market value: €248 million in 2001, €301 million in 2002)

Source: Football Business International, 2 (December 2001), p. 42.

The Copyright Promotions Group (CPG), in their association with the 1999 World Cup cricket event in England, represent a good example of licensing in the context of a one-off event. Of the five product categories that included apparel, toys and gifts, publishing, fast moving consumer goods and promotions, 60 per cent of revenue came from the apparel product category. The success of their licensing programmes was based on their integral involvement in discussions that ranged from television rights to on-site sales of products. This allowed them to come up with the best licensing strategies which not only protected and leveraged the rights of (often exclusive) licensees, but provided the best possible value and return for the licensor as well. Opportunities for cross-promotions were also maximised as a result of their integral involvement in the event organisation. Sales of event merchandise increasingly takes place through the Internet as well. Even when fans are not able to attend the event or purchase memorabilia from event-specific merchandise stores, online shopping allows them to 'be part of the event' by ordering merchandise unique to the event. It needs to be noted here that when event property owners become actively involved in the retail end of licensing agreements, they effectively become horizontally integrated sport businesses. They supply sporting goods and sport services.

The online shopping environment is increasingly explored and exploited by new sporting goods retailers, although it has not proved universally lucrative. FogDog Inc, located in San José, California, raised $30 million from investors such as Intel Corporation and Vertex to launch their e-commerce sporting retail services and are still going strong. London-based Boo.com enticed corporations such as Benetton and investment bank J.P. Morgan to invest $40 million in the launch of their company, but subsequently folded after losing $200 million. FogDog spent $10 million in 1999 on marketing in the USA alone. They sell their merchandise by arguing that choice, expert advice and speed of delivery will set them apart from traditional 'physical' retailers. For example, they offer a range of 110 tennis rackets, a broad selection of strings and stringing tensions, and delivery within 48 hours in the US. In the near future, Europe should boast several of their warehouses with multilingual sites catering for people from cabled countries with high disposable incomes.[24] In the context of this chapter, online retail can also increasingly be seen as a hybrid good/service product. An important part of the benefits sold to the consumers is the ease of online access, purchase and convenient delivery. The wireless Internet may play a crucial role in that regard.

New Technology: Sport and the Mobile (Wireless) Internet[25]

Mobile phones have become an integral part of life in most developed economies. In Europe the mobile telephony market is approaching the point of saturation with approximately 230 million people owning a mobile phone', in 2000, 89 per cent of mobile revenue was generated through voice traffic, only 8 per cent by SMS messaging and 3 per cent as a result of mobile Internet services. In Europe mobile phone companies have paid an estimated US$190 billion for so-called 3G licences, or the right to use the new Universal Mobile Telecommunication System (UMTS), the third-generation mobile phone standard able to deliver data downloads some 200 times faster than the current GSM standard (global standard for mobile communications). In order to recoup this massive investment, which does not include the cost of the necessary infrastructure, mobile Internet revenues need to grow by 25 per cent in 2003. Voice calls are likely to become a standardised service, billed at a flat, all-you-can-use rate. If the IBM forecast that two billion people will be using mobile devices to access the Internet by 2005 is to prove accurate, quality content and access anytime and anywhere are the key success factors. Especially when 'only' 700 million people will be online through a personal computer.

If the near future of wireless Internet services is to be extrapolated from the recent European and American experience, the prospect is bleak.

Short-term failure of WAP technology (Wireless Application Protocol) to capture the imagination (and application) of mobile customers has led to a 'wait and see' attitude in most markets before adopting the expensive new technology. Although the WAP technology is very good, and certainly capable of delivering mobile Internet services through 'older' technology, less than 20 per cent of phones are WAP enabled in Europe and, even when they are, only 20 per cent of those phones are used to access the Internet. In the USA only 6 per cent of phones are Internet-able and 1 per cent of Americans actually use their phone to access Internet information. The unique selling proposition, of course, of wireless data networking is to roam anywhere, accessing anytime wherever the network has local coverage; the challenge being the trade-off between bandwidth (amount of data) and distance (data travel). Although technologies such as Bluetooth, supporting wireless voice and data applications at speeds of 2Mbps with a range of 100 meters (through local servers) are a threat to the new 3G technology, the real benefit of wireless technology is for network operators and content providers to communicate with customers one-on-one at the customer's convenience.

The introduction of WAP as a replacement of fixed device access to the Internet was unfortunate because mobile phones and networks were simply not fully equipped to handle the transition of HTML (the *de facto* Internet protocol) to the phone display. WAP uses Wireless Markup Language (WML) to specify the core WAP coding. In that regard, WAP should have been marketed as delivering unique content (mostly text information) that is optimised for wireless devices, not as a direct replacement for the PC-accessed Internet. With the arrival of high speed 3G standards and handsets, WAP might still re-launch its applications successfully. However, the Japanese company NTT DoCoMo is much more likely to dominate the wireless market in years to come. Already hugely successful in Japan (where, since the introduction of their wireless technology I-mode, 80 per cent of NTT's 20-odd million subscribers access the Internet from their mobile telephones), I-mode is a one button access point on users' mobile phones. It is always online, users are charged for information downloads only, and, in contrast to WAP, they have made it genuinely easy for outside web developers to make their sites I-mode friendly. NTT are actively developing strategic alliances (for example, in Holland and Italy) to enter the European market. They need to be in the European market to remain competitive, especially given the fact that wholesale 3G technology will be launched in Europe around 2004, and the American mobile market is lagging behind because of its fragmentation. Ironically, the enormous success of the Internet largely resulted from its openness (that is, the opportunity for any individual or business to create its own content and distribute this to the rest of the world). In the wireless world hardware manufacturers are still controlling which data may or may not reach the customer. It seems that those providers using the traditional Internet business model are more likely to succeed in the wireless future.

S-commerce as the Key to Wireless Success

As noted earlier, because of the gigantic investment costs in 3G licences, there is simply no way back for those organisations that have focused their businesses upon mobile data services. To prosper in a saturated and highly competitive marketplace, the answer lies in successfully conducting mobile commerce (m-commerce). It is widely acknowledged by industry observers that entertainment will make up an important part of m-commerce, and in particular a specific form of entertainment: s-commerce. For sport organisations in particular, the opportunities that sport-commerce will present need to be considered carefully, at both the global and the local level. The mobile Internet allows for sport organisations to have contact with their fans anywhere at any time of the day. They will access databanks with information about their team and the players, chat with other supporters and players, order merchandise, bet on the outcome of sporting contests, buy tickets, be updated on matches in progress and be invited to view the latest goal scored just seconds after the event has occurred in real time.

One of the great features of wireless technology is that fans can be offered information that is highly personalised, such as BSkyB's service which requires the simple entering of a postcode in order to get directions to the nearest pub equipped with BSkyB's sports television services. Vodafone's four-year, US$48 million deal with Manchester United is only partly to do with putting their logo on the United shirt. With a global supporter base of about 300 million, Manchester United fans will watch highlights of games and be presented with exclusive up-to-date information about the team and its stars through Vodafone products.

In-stadium wireless Internet access also offers some great opportunities as evidenced by 3Com's efforts at 3Com Park, home of NFL franchise the San Francisco 49ers. They have installed a LAN (Local Area Network) in the stadium that operates a wireless commerce information and communication system. It adds significant value to the sports watching experience in the stadium by offering instant replays of match highlights, updates on progress of play at other venues, in-seat purchasing of merchandise and food, the sending and receiving of instant messages and e-mail, the opportunity to respond to polls and trivia questions or to play games with other fans. One of the main features of 49ersConnect is that it provides highly specific profile information of its users, allowing potential advertisers to refine their messages to the point where they can almost be sure they provide information that is relevant to the receiver.

Even for smaller niche sports, the one-on-one connective capabilities of wireless technology offers opportunities to deliver highly 'targetable' groups of consumers to specific sponsor partners. In particular the wireless companies themselves will seek sport to showcase their product capabilities. Sport content offers a highly involved, brand-loyal opportunity to maintain intensive contact with consumers through required technology. Each wireless brand needs to find (or is finding) its brand-specific sports positioning. For example, Motorola through American football (and Siemens through soccer) sell team-logo phones and accessories. The future of wireless technology will offer near universal mobility of access to information, whenever and wherever it is needed. Not only is sport one source of information that is in high demand, irrespective of its marketing 'pull' capability, but in the next ten years or so sport will also be a vital tool for technology advocates and entrepreneurs to convince laggard consumers to adopt the technology and accelerate the necessary revenue to keep wireless providers afloat. S-commerce remains king of content! However, where wireless success is dependent on sport, sport's success in turn will be largely dependent on the development of broadband Internet and interactive television.

New Technology: Sport, Broadband and Interactive Television[26]

Good partnerships and strategic alliances will be the key success factors broadband's success. Within the next five years broadband technology will largely replace current 'dial-up' narrowband access to the Internet, effectively enabling the convergence of a range of media such as television, radio, video and the Internet to be delivered through an 'always on', highly interactive multimedia platform. It is predicted that close to 200 million subscribers will be broadband connected worldwide by 2005. No better example in relation to a broadband-driven strategic alliance exists than the AOL and Time Warner merger. Time Warner, with huge content resources (film, television – CNN – music, books, magazines) will turn this asset into cash through the 34 million[27] subscribers to the AOL ISP (Internet Service Provider), the holders of the number one narrowband market position in the world. AOL will gain access to broadband through the Time Warner cable, which already has 13 million subscribers. However, as already noted in Chapter 1, the broadband advantage can easily turn against AOL Time Warner when other cable companies deny the giant access to their distribution networks or when consumers increasingly download films and music, a probable occurrence given the 24-hour online connection in combination with the increased speed of the download. AOL Time Warner's stock value has shown a steady decline that may indicate that investors' patience is diminishing.

Broadband, through its high-speed data download capability, will offer sport fans all around the world almost absolute control over what they want to watch as well as when and how they watch it. On top of that, they may choose to become actively involved in the event in a way that could ultimately lead to an influence on the outcome of the event. Visual and data properties of sport will be leveraged to the maximum because quality is similar to current television and compact disc standards, unlike the low bandwidth, primarily text-driven narrowband environment. With newly developed software applications, broadband operators will be able to narrow consumer patterns down to an individual profile, offering enormous opportunities for highly customised marketing, sponsoring and e-commerce activities. Growth of the broadband business is crucial from other perspectives as well. Research has shown that not only are broadband adopters young, well-paid professionals, but they also spend about three times as much time on the Internet compared to their narrowband counterparts, increasing the opportunities for generating online revenues.

For sport organisations, the arrival of broadband adopted by a mass market may truly change the face of their businesses forever. Before we go any further in discussing how this may occur it is important to qualify the difference between broadband Internet and interactive television applications. Although some industry observers may see the broadband Internet as the more advanced version of interactive television technology, the reality is that interactive television is principally built upon the benefits of digital technology, whereas broadcast data is compressed to the extent that more data can be transmitted and that more channels and functionality become available. Where 'self production at convenience' may be the key to success in relation to broadband, interactive betting during live events is considered to be the key revenue stream in regard to interactive television.

Historically, broadcast corporations have had an insatiable appetite for sports programming. Sport is cheap (or at least some sport properties still are) with a high level of inherent drama. With the advent of digital platforms, television programmers will not only be struggling to find sufficient content for what are potentially hundreds of channels, but they will also feel the heat of competition from sport organisations themselves. Along with the widespread introduction of broadband will come the falling costs of broadcast technology, where production companies (such as international sport federations) can record, produce and broadcast directly from the location where the sport event is being hosted. These developments are combined with the rapid growth of multimedia platforms, the simultaneous production of different broadcast products (for multiple markets) of the same event, the use of fibre-optic cable, and the art of digital compression, which allows for greater satellite capacity, lower production costs, a reduction in the size of transmission equipment and the constant quality of the digital picture (which can be relayed without loss of quality).[28] As can be observed from this section, although the near future may suggest the separate development of interactive television and broadband Internet, the move towards convergence of technologies will see these two elements meet at the time that is most convenient for both.

In regard to broadband in particular, sport organisations in the very near future may not need the 'middleman' broadcasting companies in order to deliver sport to the end consumer, the fan. In fact, media companies have recognised this issue and some have already acquired significant equity in strategic sport properties. For example, Granada Media has set up 50/50 joint venture businesses with both Liverpool and Arsenal football clubs. Liverpool FC Broadband will exploit the club's media and commercial rights and the portal will be turned into a one-stop-shop delivering delayed broadcasts of Premier League matches of the club, provide video archival services, online games and betting, an online merchandise shop, educational products and software, live memorabilia auctions, personal e-mail addresses for fans, interfan audio and conferencing and other special events. Arsenal FC Broadband is based upon the same principles. The reach of the businesses will be truly global, allowing fans all over the world access to television quality matches of the teams through the Internet.

This also signifies one of the major complexities of providing optimal value to the traditional owners of exclusive television rights. If sports fans in the USA can access event coverage through broadband in real time rather than await the broadcast of, for example, the Olympic 100 metre final to take place during US prime-time, the choice is easy. It will prove difficult to protect the exclusive rights owners (the traditional broadcasters) from broadband pirating, as examples in the music industry (such as napster.com) have already shown.

However, it can be argued that the level of interactivity offered by sport content providers will distinguish success from failure.[29] It is simply not enough for spectators to passively sit and watch a sporting contest on their television screens. People want to be drawn into the action and have a sense of active involvement and participation in the event, even if it is from the comfort of their own homes. Former Internet entrepreneurs Quokka Sports have already offered such an experience, which can be compared to being the producer of a sport programme. Their website offered the 'spectator' several images and provided different camera angles of the event at the same time, which could be manipulated by the viewer. These views were combined with interesting background information on the event and its participants. Not only could the viewer decide when he or she wanted to see the event, but the images could also be accessed from anywhere in the world, unlike television pictures that are still typically regionally based. Quokka Sports added value for the viewer by presenting lead-up information to the event: for example, counting down the minutes to the start of the 100 metres at the Sydney Olympics, or showing Michael Johnson's heart rate before, during and after his 400 metres race. As noted earlier in regard to AOL Time Warner, great enthusiasm for the introduction of broadband technology needs to be mediated by a great deal of patience, and significant financial resources in order for the technology to be adopted and accepted by the wider marketplace. Unfortunately for Quokka, enthusiasm could not be combined with cashflow, but Quokka's legacy lives on in MSNBC (a joint venture between Microsoft and NBC), the company that very successfully operates the website NBCOlympics.com. Similar initiatives by FIFA during the World Cup in South Korea and Japan gave football fanatics all over the world the opportunity to subscribe to a service that included short replays (4 minutes), only hours after the finish of the match and access to an image database that allowed views to 'query' for an overview of, for example, all goals by the Japanese team. The cost of this service was US$20.

Opportunities do exist for smaller, less popular sports to communicate their products to a bigger marketplace. Niche sports that have not received the airtime of the bigger, global sports, but which do have communities of fanatic followers, will be given the opportunity to reach out to those who have not been able to tune in on network television. Content may be provided for free, but sponsorship and advertising revenue is likely to increase significantly if larger, highly segmented groups of sport fans can access the broadband service. For example, the International Badminton Federation has 55 million players in 145 associations, but players have no access to competition broadcasts. How broadband will change their fortunes! Broadband applications are unlikely to be limited to sports watching. Imagine the opportunities offered to the top European soccer clubs when their talent scouts obtain access to webcasts of amateur games in Latin American soccer leagues, and can 'check out' the next Ronaldo online.

Optimism should not be exaggerated, however, in the end it is still the inherent attractiveness of the core sport product that determines whether people are entertained. If smaller sports do not add value to their existing product in an effort to draw traffic to their site or interactive/pay-television programme, then sport consumers will remain loyal to the 'big' sports which have already proved they provide the best content and value to their viewers.[30] The challenge for enterprises that offer innovative technology for sports viewing remains the same as for any business: they must understand the trends in the market and the best ways to meet the needs of their customers and other potential consumers. Broadband will take the television medium from local to global, and interactive features will allow sport fans to be drawn into the sport experience and consequently become more involved with the sport organisation. With interactivity as the key success factor for both interactive television and broadband, the match can become a marriage made in heaven. New broadcasting technology signifies the emergence of what will become a vital component of the sport entertainment industry: the market for novel experiences.

Customers and Marketing Trends Driving Sport Services

In the so called 'experience' economy, a number of trends will dominate the ways in which marketers will have to deal with customers in the next decade. The first trend, *paradox and oscillation*,[31] relates to the old and the new century, old and new technologies, the passivity of television and the interactivity of the Internet. Tips for marketers may include keeping the future friendly or, in other words, user-friendliness and customer service are more important than the uncertainty of the overly 'futuristic' unknown, in that regard it also seems important to respect (an organisation's proud) history and communicate this as part of sport marketing programmes.

In relation to a second trend, *overload and stress*, it can be argued that in the Information Age new technology enables us to 'keep in touch' all the time. However, information presented to us through new technology increases exponentially in quantity but not in quality. It is becoming harder to determine what is and is not useful to our personal lives. Many people find it hard to deal with information overload. Marketers can take advantage of these trends by keeping things simple. With the rapid pace of change in society it needs to be realised that in principle, very few human beings enjoy (big) changes. Keeping things simple, clear and with few surprises is the key to success, especially when 'minor' change leads to greater simplicity, greater service, convenience and flexibility. A late twentieth-century lesson still holds true: the customer is always right, and should therefore be given a sense of control in the purchase and consumption process. This can only be facilitated by offering service representatives of the organisation the power to act on the spot, with problems best solved if service representatives have learned how to deal with the 'psychology of the difficult customer' or the irrational fan.

A third trend refers to *giantism and grandiosity*. As outlined earlier in this book, multinational organisations continue to increase their size at the sort of frightening pace exemplified by the mega-merger between America Online and Time Warner. Cities try to outperform each other by building the tallest skyscraper in the world and television brings us the best, biggest, worst, tallest, most successful, most bizarre, stupidest, funniest and most radical, interactive programmes, many of which are founded on an artificially contrived 'reality". In this world of giantism, marketers should keep things small, even when they are big. Personalisation and customisation is the key to success, and it is more effective to communicate this through animals, cartoon characters, or sport which all offer simple symbols understood by people all over the world. In that sense people should be told what they can expect to be delivered and the actual delivery should surpass the consumer's expectations. One of the difficulties associated with new technologies is that it is sometimes unclear what can be offered to consumers, because companies are unsure how to best utilise the technology to meet customer expectations and achieve competitive advantage.

More than any other futurist, we believe that Rolf Jensen has eloquently expressed a realistic and comprehensive scenario of the future that in many ways will determine how marketers will go about producing products and selling them into different markets. He argues that wealthy, developed nations are on the verge of entering the 'Dream Society'. Humankind took about 100,000 years to move from being hunters and gatherers to farmers in an agricultural society that subsequently existed for another 10,000 years. Less than 200 years ago, as a result of the industrial revolution, the USA and Western European nations progressed to what has been named the industrial society. This was a period in which wealth increased exponentially as a result of dramatic technological advances and led to the movement of people from the country to urban centres resulted in the construction of cities which in turn facilitated improved transport infrastructure. Another result of the industrial society is the idea of progress or planning. People and organisations increasingly expanded their time horizons, allowing them to forgo short-term results for longer-term prosperity. Only some 30 years ago did the nations that entered the industrial age as leaders move into becoming information societies. Production jobs were automated and knowledge became more important than capital. Indeed, power was transferred back to the workers because the capital that is valued by the information society is intellectual, not physical. It resides in people's heads, not in the physical assets of companies. However, success in the information society is still measured in tangible, materialistic wealth. Jensen believes that the Dream Society will drive people towards achieving the emotional wealth that typified the very early human societies. According to Jensen, the Dream Society is the ultimate societal type because it combines material wealth (we no longer struggle to survive) with emotional wealth and fulfilment. In the Dream Society, marketers are required to satisfy people's emotional needs in six marketplaces:

- the market for adventures
- the market for togetherness, friendship and love
- the market for care
- the who-am-I market
- the market for peace of mind
- the market for convictions.[32]

The market for adventures is dominated by sport organisations. We let athletes, clubs and events tell us the stories about success, failure, and overcoming difficulty. Successful Olympic athletes and professional sporting teams are becoming wealthy because of the value of the stories they are able to tell.

Togetherness and friendship is sold by companies that sell tangible products such as coffee, beer or mobile phones. The products can bring people together. Sporting theme parks or museums may serve as an example of sport organisations tapping into the market for togetherness.

Organisations such as the Red Cross and the Salvation Army operate in the care market; they 'sell' opportunities for people to show they care and, in that regard, non-profit and profit sport organisations alike can offer 'volunteer' opportunities to people who 'care' about the club, in the process building a more committed and extensive network of supporters and clients.

Once again, sport organisations are important suppliers to the who-am-I marketplace. The teams people associate themselves with (whether blue-collar or white-collar teams), the club merchandise they choose to wear, the brand of trainers they showcase to their peers and the athletes they openly admire and support, tell more about the consumer than the 'products'.

People buy 'peace of mind' when they are brought back to times and places they recognise as the 'good old times'. Values that instil confidence and trust in buyers are communicated through the physical setting in which products are sold, for example, by decorating sporting stadia with memorabilia commemorating great sporting moments. Financial institutions will go back to servicing clients personally in a non-technical setting where people feel they are valued as an individual customer.

Finally, the market for convictions relates to a growing global, yet emanating from the individual moral conscience. Politicians who have fought moral and welfare battles on behalf of voters will increasingly compete with for-profit and not-for-profit (non-political) organisations that are forced to think and act beyond achieving organisational objectives. How companies can become good 'corporate (global) citizens' will become equally important compared to how individuals can become or remain good citizens in their respective societies. The challenge for General Motors to sell environmentally friendly cars will be as big as Nike's challenge to sell shoes that consumers perceive were produced in an appropriate work environment.

However, Jensen argues that most nations that are currently information societies will need some time before truly becoming Dream Societies. Nevertheless, the transition will be facilitated by the fervour with which consumers have embraced sport as a mechanism to achieve the emotional needs highlighted by Jensen. In Chapter 7 we go further with these needs, the cultural links and how they are manifested and discharged through sport.

This chapter has explored the importance of the economic factors by focusing on the development of the service sector as a 'switching point'

which will determine the future of sport. Current trends unambiguously support a future system that will be driven by sport services, lubricated by the media and culminating in the realisation of consumers' emotional needs. Some of these needs will be facilitated through technological means. Throughout the next 10 years the importance and ubiquity of information technology in sport business will be so significant that we feel it is justified to spend the next chapter examining the strategic importance of technologies such as the Internet.

Notes and references

1 P. Chelladurai (1994), 'Sport management: defining the field', *European Journal for Sport Management*, 1(1), pp. 7–21; G. R. Milne and M. A. McDonald (1999), *Sport Marketing, Managing the Exchange Process*, Jones & Bartlett, Sudbury, Massachusetts; B. J. Mullin, S. Hardy and W. A. Sutton (1993), *Sport Marketing*, Human Kinetics, Champaign; D. Shilbury, S. Quick and H. M. Westerbeek (1998), *Strategic Sport Marketing*, Allen & Unwin, Sydney.
2 T. A. Schwartz, D. E. Bowen and S. W. Brown (1992), *Advances in Services Marketing and Management*, JAI Press, Greenwich, CT.
3 C. H. Lovelock, P. G. Patterson and R. H. Walker (1998), *Services Marketing Australia and New Zealand*, Prentice Hall, Sydney, p. 6.
4 S. M. Shugan (1994), 'Explanations for the growth of services', in R. T. Rust and R. L. Oliver (eds), *Service Quality: New Directions in Theory and Practice*, Sage, Thousand Oaks, pp. 223–40.
5 S. M. Shugan,' Explanations for the growth of services'.
6 S. Samiee (1999), 'The internationalization of services: trends, obstacles and issues', *Journal of Services Marketing*, 13(4/5), pp. 319–28.
7 S. M. Shugan, Explanations for the growth of services'.
8 C. H. Lovelock, P. G. Patterson and R. H. Walker, *Services marketing Australia and New Zealand*.
9 C. H. Lovelock, P. G. Patterson and R. H. Walker, *Services marketing Australia and New Zealand*, p. 470.
10 S. Samiee, 'The internationalization of services: trends, obstacles and issues'.
11 Allen Consulting Group (1999), *Policies for Growth, the Australian Service Sector Review 2000* (Volume 2), The Australian Services Network, Melbourne, p. 15.
12 Allen Consulting Group, *Policies for Growth*.
13 M. Glendinning (1999), 'New Media', *Sport Business*, December, pp. 17–21.
14 V. Zeithaml (1981), 'How consumer evaluation processes differ between goods and services', in J. H. Donnely and W. R. George (eds), *Marketing of Services*, American Marketing Association, Chicago.
15 V. Zeithaml, 'How consumer evaluation processes differ between goods and services'.
16 R. Boyle and R. Haynes (2000), *Power Play. Sport, the Media and Popular Culture*, Pearson Education, Harlow.
17 R. Boyle and R. Haynes, *Power Play. Sport, the Media and Popular Culture*, p. 11.
18 R. Boyle (1995), 'Football and Cultural Identity in Glasgow and Liverpool', PhD Thesis, University of Stirling, Scotland.

19   R. Boyle and R. Haynes, *Power Play. Sport, the Media and Popular Culture*; A. Kolah (1999), 'Maximising the value of sports sponsorship', *Financial Times Media*, London.

20   J. Rosenfield (2000) *Marketing and ebusiness*, June, p. 21.

21   R. Boyle and R. Haynes, *Power Play. Sport, the Media and Popular Culture*.

22   J. Sugden and A. Tomlinson (1998), *FIFA and the Contest for World Football*, Polity Press, Cambridge, p. 98.

23   M. Glendinning (1999), 'Mapping out the future of sports licensing', *Sport Business*, September, p. 10

24   *Sport Business* (1999), 'On-line sporting goods retail', *Sport Business*, August, p. 10.

25   The contents of this section are largely derived from A. Gellatly and D. Lambton (2001), 'Sport and Wireless: how the mobile Internet is changing sport', one of the many excellent special research reports produced by SportsBusiness Information Resources, a division of the SportBusiness Group.

26   The contents of this section are largely derived from A. Gellatly and D. Lambton (2001), 'Sport and Broadband', and 'Interactive TV and sport: an introduction to a revolutionary technology', two of the many excellent special research reports produced by SportsBusiness Information Resources, a division of the SportBusiness Group.

27   BBC News. 'The AOL-Time Warner merger, 26 January 2000.

28   *Sport Business*, Special Report on Broadcast Technology, August, 1999

29   M. Glendinning, 'New Media', pp. 17–21.

30   M. Glendinning, 'New Media', pp. 17–21.

31   J. Rosenfield, *Marketing and ebusiness*, June 2000, 17–23.

32   R. Jensen (1999) *The Dream Society*, McGraw-Hill, New York.

CHAPTER 6

In the Spider's Web: The Internet and Competitive Advantage in Global Sport

Daniel Evans

Gentleman, you are looking at more than a million dollars worth of obsolete racing equipment.
Art Lathrop, US racing car team owner, 1961
(referring to his front-engined cars following Jack Brabham's successful debut in a rear-engined car)

We have identified technology as a shaping factor at the nexus of alternative global sport futures, and as such it is a pivotal driver of sport's global evolution. Although the impacts of a range of technologies are reviewed and integrated into other chapters, it is the Internet which is the focus of this chapter. As the World Wide Web spreads, the sport product is proving the stickiest of gossamer. However, the search for competitive advantage via the Internet has changed radically, even in the last 12 months. A dose of reality has brought many well-resourced Internet-based initiatives to their knees. Does this mean that the Internet is not capable of delivering on our expectations of a business revolution? We will argue that despite the Internet disasters of the last two years it remains, at the very least, an essential sport business tool, and at the most, a radically innovative platform for interactive sport experiences. Perhaps most importantly, we will insist that the sport business is amongst the best placed of industries to capitalise upon the opportunities for competitive advantage that the Internet offers.

The Internet is an extraordinarily powerful network that can be compared to the superorganism that is the human social network. It is an evolutionary learning machine.[1] The Internet, like the human brain, is a neural net that connects its electronic cells in a vast web of knowledge that accumulates, and perpetuates. That web of knowledge, the World Wide Web, is wired together in a series of connections that form a mass brain capable of infinitely more than the individual. Like its arachnid analogy, it links its electronic components into a vast array of communal power. To continue this analogy, consider this captivating medieval poem:

> Much like a subtle spider which doth sit
> In middle of her web, which spreadeth wide;
> If aught do touch the utmost thread of it,
> She feels it instantly on every side.

> Sir John Davies, *The Immortality of the Soul*

This absorbing web parallel elucidates the intrinsic character of the World Wide Web.[2] You can picture the individual in front of a computer screen; recognising fellow supporters that come online, checking scores and viewing highlights, communicating; each person an individual spider in the World Wide Web. Through this web we are indeed all connected, with the Internet also interacting with the other two shaping factors affecting our future: the global economy and culture.

We have explained that for both economic and cultural-political reasons, the distribution of infrastructure and access to the Internet, is not equitable. Criminal laws in Libya, Iraq, North Korea, Burma and Syria, for example, prohibit the use of the Internet entirely. Saudi Arabia forbids access to sites offering 'information contrary to Islamic values', and China, recognised as a major potential market, has erected a similar 'fire wall' in what Geoffrey Robertson, QC, observes is a 'fascinating surf war'.[3] He observed that the Chinese Falun Gong cult was banned more for its ability to organise demonstrations by e-mail than for its meditation techniques!

The Internet is the most complete and efficient method of seeking, receiving and imparting information ever developed. It is in fact difficult to imagine a more complete method of information transfer, with the exception of the ongoing evolution of the human brain's neural network to a stage where it could realise conscious telepathy and communal thought. Like bee colonies that pool their activities in an interconnected mass, or Star Trek's Borg (the half-biological and half-technological race united by a singular consciousness and motivated by the assimilation of other species and technologies), the possibility of a human hive working within a connectionist web might not be so far fetched.[4] Researchers are already developing computers integrated within clothing, and are making significant progress in constructing devices which interact with, or are controlled directly by, the brain. Undoubtedly, we will use technology to complement our biology at the neural level. Technology and thinking will be interconnected in the same way that artificial hearts can become the core of a body's circulatory system. The purpose of this chapter is not to consider the more distant future, however, we are more interested in the Internet as a 'pivot-point' for the future of sport business. Specifically, we will focus on the opportunities the Internet facilitates, and how these might be capitalised upon.

The Internet Opportunity

Tectonic shifts, revolutionary changes, a new paradigm, a tsunami of transformation:[5] these are all examples of the rhetoric that has been used to characterise the 'new world' we have entered. The description of a new world (dis)order created by the Internet revolution is itself part of the inexhaustible superlatives attached to the Internet opportunity. While superlatives are to be expected for any trend where calculable benefits are sometimes difficult to judge, the growing statistics available to explain the Internet phenomenon are irrefutable.

The First Quarter 2001 Global Internet Trends report from Nielsen/ NetRatings measured Internet use in 27 countries around the world and determined that 420 million people have Internet access. CyberAtlas estimates that this represents commerce of US$220 billion. At present North America still accounts for the largest proportion of the world's Internet users, with 53 per cent of the global audience located in these countries. Europe is next with 20 per cent, followed by Asia (15 per cent), Oceania (6 per cent), South America (4 per cent), Africa (1 per cent) and Central America (1 per cent). If we use the projected uptake of broadband technology (as a percentage of all households in 2005) as an indicator of Internet access leadership, then Sweden (40 per cent), Denmark (37 per cent), Norway (36 per cent) and the Netherlands (28 per cent) are well ahead of the pack in Europe. In Asia, Korea is the leader (currently 38 per cent of households are already broadband connected), followed by Hong Kong with 8 per cent and Singapore with 4 per cent.[6] It is expected that the number of broadband connected households in the USA will also approach 40 per cent in 2005.

In early 2002, the partly public, partly government-owned Australian telecommunications giant Telstra aggressively started marketing their broadband access packages. Ironically, this campaign coincided with the re-launch of the Australian Football League's website, in which the AFL promises users a range of interactive features (interactive gambling, match replays) that fundamentally assume broadband Internet access capabilities. It may not come as a big surprise that Telstra and the AFL have entered into a strategic partnership which enables both organisations to achieve financial gain by contributing their specific resources to an Internet venture.

In the previous chapter we outlined a number of organisations that successfully operate their business through, or at least with the help of the broadband enabled Internet. Joint ventures such as Liverpool FC Broadband are examples of Internet dependent businesses that are on the verge of becoming very successful and sustainable ventures. Traditional narrowband sites have, for a number of years, also achieved significant traffic. Sportsline USA was reporting seven million page views per day in 1998, and had 55,000 subscribers paying US$45 per year for sport content. Similarly, US Major League Baseball has been able to attract over 110,000 online subscribers to MLB.com and ESPN.com was registering in excess of seven million users a month in 2001. The effects of the merger between AOL and Time Warner, as we have already highlighted, will become increasingly transparent and, to a great extent, showcase the role sport can play on the Internet.

There is ample evidence that sport boasts some of the most popular and well-trafficked websites. This relationship leads us to an interesting observation. The basic demographic profile of sport fans and web users is remarkably similar. The sporting industry appears to have an excellent platform from which to launch an aggressive assault on Internet activities. Table 6.1 summarises these statistics.

Table 6.1 Demographics of Internet users and sports fans

	Internet User	Sports Fan
Sex – Male	70 per cent	64 per cent
Sex – Female	30 per cent	36 per cent
Average Age	32.7	34
Median Income	US$50,000–60,000	US$50,000+

Source: Adapted from L. Delpy (1998), 'Sport Management and Marketing via the World Wide Web', *Sport Marketing Quarterly*, Vol. 7, No. 1, pp. 21–7.

The typical online sports visitor also has a higher net-worth and propensity to buy online compared to visitors of other sites.[7] In addition, the 'stickiness' of sports sites (their ability to hold a visitor for longer, making them more attractive to advertisers and sponsors), the growing popularity of online gambling, and the power of major sports to attract global audiences are contributing to their success. Sporting enthusiasts also present many of the key attributes associated with the development of online communities, which is a key strategy for online success and will be discussed later in this chapter.

As noted earlier, the impact of the Internet on sports broadcasting may prove to be monumental, affecting both the traditional broadcasting industry and the online sports industry, making the impact of the Internet on sports communication 'absolute'.[8] Briefly stated, as high quality Internet broadcasts with interactive capacity increasingly challenge television's monopoly of event vision, the flow of consumers through sporting dotcoms will continue to multiply. There is already evidence of a growing convergence between the multi-billion dollar television industry and the Internet, in the form of Netcasting.[9] According to the US National Football League (NFL) commissioner, Paul Tagliabue, the Internet will be as important in the first half of this century as television was in the second half of the 1900s. The uptake of broadband technology will largely determine the speed with which technology convergence and a re-arrangement of the broadcasting playing field will take place.

Given that Internet broadcasting rights represent a massive revenue source, the online success of sporting organisations largely depends on their ability to tap into the growing flow of Internet traffic through offering a range of (interactive) e-products. That said, while much of the discussion regarding Internet opportunities inevitably is drawn to traditional financial rewards, this could only occur if organisations have identified how to achieve competitive advantage through the Internet. And this, in turn, requires acknowledgment of the many roads that may lead to this goal. Added to this there is the complication that being the 'first mover' has not, in the Internet and technology context, always proved an advantage: consider the situation with pay-television.

The vision of unlimited growth for television sport needs to be curtailed with the obligatory touch of reality. Pay sport television is already on shaky ground in Britain, Germany, France and Japan. Profits are difficult to obtain. This is the very opposite of pay sport television in America. Why, then, is there a difference? It is always difficult to suggest reasons why a concept that is so popular in one country may fail in others. For our money there are three major reasons for the difficulty of establishing profitable pay sport television outside America. First, people are not willing to pay to see relatively second-class games. Many of the football games being screened in Europe feature lesser known teams with correspondingly lesser known players. In some countries pay sport televises games from an overall group of up to 60 or 70 teams. Compare this to the United States where there are only 34 NFL teams, all of whom are well known and well supported.

The second reason we believe that the concept may not be so successful in Europe and elsewhere, when compared to the United States, is due to differences in culture. In the United States, people are conditioned to watching sport on days other than Saturday. Sunday sport is highly accepted, while Monday night football consistently achieves extremely high television ratings. In Europe, only in recent years has football (or, indeed, any sport) been consistently featured live on television other than on a Saturday. It will take some time to change this culture and may require an acceptance by pay sport television companies of greater investment and of lower profits for some time while the culture is developed.

The third reason is simple. In the USA, even pay-television contains advertising. Consequently, costs are shared between advertiser and customer. This means a lower cost for customers and the opportunity for higher profits for the television company. In April 2002 the football fraternity in Britain was shocked to discover that ITV Digital had been placed in the hands of administrators. The digital joint venture between television networks Carlton and Granada had turned out to be a financial disaster, having lost £900 million. Unfortunately, the service could not compete with the comprehensive satellite platform offered by BSkyB, majority owned by News Corporation, and clearly the market leader with 5.7 million subscribers compared to ITV Digital's 1.3 million. The death blow for ITV was the cost of television rights. ITV Digital owes £178 million to the Football League for the broadcast rights to First Division through to Fourth Division matches. The payments were critical for clubs in the lower divisions and, in some cases, represented as much as 30 per cent of their total expected revenues.

Pay-television is not likely to be the only casualty of any potential failure of pay sport. We might well expect that a number of teams will collapse, many having spent money not yet earned on higher wages and payments for players.

Our point in the first part of this chapter is that the Internet has connected billions of people in most of the developed nations around the globe. People are now free to obtain any information that is provided through the World Wide Web at their convenience. The key to success for sport businesses in providing this information lies in getting to consumers first with a superior offering, or, in other words, achieving competitive advantage. This is so important because the other reality of the Internet is that any organisation can distribute information to whomever they choose to target. The worst aspect of the Internet is also its best: anyone can 'go online'.

The Road to Online Success

Leadership is critical during the introduction of an organisation's Internet-driven business activities. Interestingly, sport regularly provides examples of the immeasurable value of quality leadership, with sporting team captains lauded for their contribution above and beyond their personal performances. These athletes often possess several of the six traits associated with leadership in any organisation; drive, the desire to lead, honesty and integrity, self-confidence, intelligence and job-relevant knowledge.[10]

Online strategy authors are increasingly considering leadership in the digital estate,[11] with sport businesses searching for a white-collar Michael Jordan or Joe Montana to steer them to online success and deliver the financial riches that often are associated with Internet ventures. Within the framework of a new medium and unpredictable customer responses, three elements are central to online success:[12] first, a willingness to commit the resources (including money, talent, and executive-level interest) necessary to make the Internet a valuable part of the revenue mix; second, an overriding interest in experimentation, leading to the following practical necessities – success measuring techniques (such as hits/sales), goal setting (to be discussed later) and varying alternatives (constant experimentation), and, third, the ability to respond quickly to anything learnt.

Strategy Implementation

Although information technology (IT) leaders might recognise and value the competitive potential of their technology, such a sentiment is not necessarily widely shared by sport business leaders.[13] Certainly, there is a common perception that many organisations initially adopted a Web presence out of fear that they might be left behind, or simply as a fashion statement.[14] Naturally, there are a number of risks associated with implementing a strategy based on joining a bandwagon, however, the reality is that the initial uptake of every major contemporary technological development (such as telecommunication, radio, television) resembled a bandwagon approach to strategy. Conversely, there has been growing concern amongst a number of south-east Asian countries, based on fears that companies are *not* jumping on the Internet bandwagon. Government incentives in Malaysia, for example, are failing to entice significant investment in Internet-based strategies as firms are leery of the Net because they have heard about disappointing results from exising Web sites.[15]

The atmosphere of early electronic commerce has been compared to a gold rush.[16] Some organisations though, including existing site proprietors who are hesitant to commit additional resources without evidence of profitable websites, have become disillusioned with this industry analysis going into 2002, a sentiment echoed by Wall Street investor chagrin that has turned expectations of dotcoms to 'dot bombs'. For example, Robert Shiller, in his US stock-market review, *Irrational Exuberance*, takes a swipe at the Internet.[17] He speculates that the economic impact of the medium may be far less dramatic than expected, and that 'as time goes on the Internet may seem less and less a symbol of the promise of new technology, and more and more like a phone book'. Some, who insisted that television would never be a viable alternative to radio, advocated similar caution.

The upshot of this deliberation therefore, is that the key players within sporting organisations need to determine with clarity the path their organisations will take with regard to online commerce. Although understandable at its inception, sport organisations avoiding any formal Internet policy, or remaining conspicuous by their absence, for example, are no longer viable, and risk competitive disadvantage.

Information Technology Assimilation

One critical component of IT strategy gaining credence is the concept of merging online strategies with the primary strategic thrust of the sport business,[18] and incorporating IT into the entire spectrum of organisational activities. Where the Internet was still separated from traditional business activities, the emergence of the electronic economy has provided an environment where IT permeates every aspect of an organisation. The World Wide Web can literally link every component of an organisation, as well as its existing and potential customers. At the start of this chapter Sir

John Davies provided a medieval poem that exemplified this concept, and we have also argued that integration is a theme that runs through globalisation and the future of sport. In the future, successful Internet strategies will be based on this understanding of the integrative capacity of the World Wide Web, and will assimilate IT applications such as websites into the fabric of company operations. For example, IT applications such as organisational websites have the ability to create value for sports businesses in ways that will create a shift in business planning from conventional strategy to value innovation. These opportunities for innovation are likely to become clearer as sport businesses integrate their activities. To paraphrase a Zen proverb, the beginner sees many choices while the expert sees few.

Part of the problem for sport businesses has been the lack of accountability assigned to Internet strategies. Websites, for example, should have measurable financial objectives that are clearly defined and tied to the organisation's wider business objectives. These measures should include recognition of cost savings generated through the application. The notion of measuring return on investment (ROI) is certainly not new in business. Sporting organisations should not be afraid to apply traditional balance sheet measures of success to their online commitment. Indeed specific, measurable goals will help to stop companies 'flopping around in cyberspace because their goals aren't focused enough'.[19] This type of analysis could include income statistics such as merchandise revenues, ticket sales or advertising, and can be weighed equally with cost savings. These savings may include reduced communication expenses, and the savings associated with disintermediation, where 'middlemen' wholesale companies (such as media organisations) are 'bypassed by the Internet revolution as more companies that create the goods and services interact directly with the consumer without the aid of intermediaries'.[20] Sports organisations conducting their own ticketing, merchandising and/or broadcasting via the Internet can significantly affect the financial structure of the organisation, in the process leading to improved vertical integration.

Internet Project Teams

The team-based philosophy is perhaps even more relevant in the digital age, and also in the sport business, with the inherent capabilities of the Internet, its suitability to team-based strategies, and sport's cultural association with teams. The Internet has the power and capacity to utilise its networks and open new channels for human communication and collaboration, and is not constrained by geography or time. Teams then provide an excellent parallel with the human social network, and the concepts of superorganisms and knowledge management.

Who should be in an Internet project team? Just as a balanced on-field team is critical to football clubs, research has shown the importance of incorporating both IT and managerial skills into a project team.[21] There is sufficient evidence that the critical dimensions of human IT resources are both technical skills (such as programming and design), and managerial IT skills (which include coordination and interaction with the user community, and project and leadership skills). There is a need to provide both elements in a project team in order to align IT resources with organisational strategy.

In other words, for a project team to be successful it must have a synthesis of human capital with both IT and management expertise. With the growing financial importance placed on the Internet by sporting organisations, it appears likely that dedicated IT executives, as part of Internet project teams that have Board level representation, may soon be considered crucial for professional sporting organisations. As a matter of fact, some professional sport organisations in both Europe and the USA have set up executive positions and departments that are exclusively devoted to dealing with Internet and IT-related business activity.

Partnerships and Alliances

The bringing together of complimentary assets, defraying costs, and sharing risks are incentives to forming alliances, as exemplified by Manchester United and the New York Yankees.[22] While there is a perception that Internet technologies are easily replicable, it has been noted that IT systems which create linkages and interdependencies beyond a single organisation can often shift the balance of power in an industry in ways that can be difficult for competitors to duplicate or overcome.[23]

The peculiar economies of sport have been well established wherein the mutual interdependencies of competing teams requires organisations to have some level of cooperation to ensure a stable environment.[24] In other words, the competitive lines typically drawn for many organisations are blurred by the unique nature of sport. Indeed, management models assessing competitive strategy, including Porter's 'five forces' model, highlight the special circumstances of sport, particularly in the assessment of 'rivalry'.[25] Unlike in the automotive, banking or white-goods industries, sport businesses, particularly in a league environment, do not necessarily benefit from the demise of direct competitors. The Lakers need the Celtics, Manchester United needs Liverpool, and Collingwood needs Carlton. They may not like each other, but they depend on the relative strength of their counterpart. This is the kind of interdependency that enables sport organisations, more than any other businesses, to enter into partnerships and alliances in a competitive environment. A number of online commentators identify both the benefits of strategic online alliances, and the Internet's intrinsic suitability to such arrangements.[26]

Given that the peculiar economies of sport add complexity to partnership formations, much of the strategic alliance research suggests that organisations competing in both product and location are better suited to cooperative practices. Indeed, the best alliance opportunities often arise between businesses with a virtual overlap in product and geographic market.[27] Both sport and the Internet are intrinsically suited to alliances. The sporting industry demonstrates a reliance on direct competitors (teams or athletes in the same sport), and therefore an opportunity exists to pool resources for a greater good. In this industry, as opposed to most, healthy competition is crucial to the success of individual organisations. Similarly, strategic use of the Internet is conducive to partnering. If true, enlightened sport organisations would benefit from putting aside on-field rivalries in order to develop some business opportunities together, the greatest of which may be the Internet opportunity.

Having established that competing sport businesses might be well suited to strategic alliances, it is also important to note that these partnerships should not be limited to league-associated sports, professional sports, or high-profile sports. International, national and regional sporting bodies, amateur sports and participation-based activities, as well as organisations with commercial links to sport including information, apparel and gambling businesses, might also consider the benefits of partnering.

An excellent example of sporting organisations using a strategic alliance to help achieve competitive advantage in the Internet business environment can be found in the United States-based National Football League. In March 2000 the NFL's 31 owners agreed to pool their resources and split revenues from the NFL's website for the following two years. Given the famously disparate reputation of owners within the league, this partnership, allowing each team to run its own site and retain local advertising, with all national revenue shared, was a significant development. With 30-second television commercials during the Super Bowl set to break US$3 million, advertisers are clearly desperate to take advantage of the sport's exposure, auguring well for the Internet arm of NFL revenues.

To demonstrate further the opportunities that online partnership and alliances can present, we will discuss another two sporting examples: the Sydney Organising Committee for the Olympic Games (SOCOG), and the Australian Football League.

SOCOG's spectacular delivery of the world's highest-profile event showcased every element of Australia's array of assets, in particular its professional sport management capabilities and world class venues. Central to the completion of SOCOG's objectives, both internally and in the provision of information to consumers, was its use of electronic commerce. The digital preludes to Sydney, the 1998 Nagano Olympic Winter Games and the 1996 Atlanta Olympics, provided an indication of what SOCOG's cyber planners could expect. Atlanta's official website registered 187 million hits during the event. Two years later the Nagano site, with 650 million event hits (including a peak of 103,429 hits per minute) prompted some commentators to suggest that it was the first occasion where television and the Internet went head-to-head, with the Internet presenting a significant challenge. FIFA's official website registered 1 billion hits over the duration of the 2002 World Cup.

Pivotal to SOCOG's operations was an all-encompassing Internet strategy based on a number of critical partnerships and alliances designed to tackle the phenomenal logistics of an event catering for more than 5,000 officials, 15,000 accredited media staff and 10,200 athletes. Some specific examples of the Internet's application by SOCOG during the event, and the partnerships employed, are shown below:

- *Info2000* (developed by IBM): this intranet service was available only to the Olympic 'family' of athletes, media, sponsors and officials during the Games.
- *Athena* was a comprehensive information Intranet for SOCOG staff developed by Lotus Consulting.
- *Infopoint* (a program developed with IBM) consisted of a network of touch-screen multimedia kiosks located in public places all over Australia, such as libraries and shopping centres, providing free information to the public (also involved in this project were the Sydney firm, Brainwave Interactive, and Lotus Consulting).

By November 2000 it became clear that SOCOG and the International Olympic Committee (IOC) had met the challenges of the Internet and its borderless nature. Olympic sponsors, tourism bodies, government agencies and the media all played a part in both contributing to, and benefiting from, the most sophisticated and popular website ever established, sporting or otherwise. New online relationships among the Olympic 'family' have been created, and new business models and modes of operation have successfully been tested, demonstrating the power of the Internet. SOCOG and a host of Australian enterprises were at the forefront of this push deeper into cyberspace. There is, however, an engaging paradox that emerges in the business of sport. Irrespective of the theoretically intrinsic suitability of sport to Internet alliances, separating on-field rivalries from business practice does not always come naturally for sport managers. In fact, in many instances it runs decidedly against the grain.

In comparison with the US NFL example, the premier Australian Football League and its member clubs presented an example of a less cooperative approach to strategic use of the Internet. It was an extremely fragmented position that resulted in the AFL being roundly criticised for its failure to 'tie up' Internet rights, and provided private companies such as Sportsview (with stakeholders including Microsoft co-founder Paul Allen) with an enormous opportunity. Sportsview represented five of the league's 16 clubs, with each of the remaining 11 clubs dealing with a private Internet Service Provider (ISP). The deal delivered Sportsview 65 per cent of all club revenues, and meant that the AFL could not sell any exclusive Internet package without either granting Sportsview equity, or buying them out, which would cost tens of millions of dollars.

By 2002, the AFL had moved to better align its member clubs, albeit at a cost. A five-year Internet rights contract for a reported A$30 million was negotiated with the telecommunications company, Telstra, with all of the Sportsview-contracted clubs disengaging those contracts for undisclosed sums. One club still remains outside the AFL banner with a rival network, and the exact details of the agreement with the other 15 clubs are not public; however on the surface the AFL now appears to present a more united approach to Internet opportunities.

A Missing Link

Individual clubs that have global reach do hold reasonable arguments for maintaining control of certain revenue-generating elements of their websites. However, there is no doubt that a lack of collaboration between sport organisations operating in a single league is likely to lead to missed opportunities associated with the massive personnel, sponsorship, and marketing synergies that could be provided by a united approach to Internet exploitation. The NFL example has shown that the league and its constituting teams can reach a negotiated agreement.

This is not to suggest that the intricate issues facing clubs globally, such as broadcasting revenues, are easily digested, or that individual clubs are wrong to avoid arbitrarily signing away real or potential future opportunities. However, while an opportunity exists to take advantage of alliance synergies that will assist in developing a league brand, and still maintain a negotiated level of club control, it remains difficult to identify the balance between the two. Presumably clubs either fundamentally disagree with alliance theory or, more likely, are engaged in a struggle between a business theory that identifies inherent advantages in teamwork, and a team sport where the stakeholders maintain a passionate competitive rivalry with the proposed partners; a rivalry that is perhaps in this instance intensified by the perceived magnitude of potential opportunities for the single club entity.

In Australia, the AFL is not the sole example of a league struggling to come to terms with its member clubs in regard to Internet issues. A lack of cooperation to growing the Internet business is evident throughout Australia's major sporting leagues, including the National Rugby League (NRL), the National Soccer League (NSL) and the National Basketball League (NBL). Individual sporting clubs appear to be developing Internet strategies that do not include the traditional league-based partnership approaches to issues such as television rights. This departure from alliance strategy clearly indicates underlying problems in the relationships between the leagues and their clubs. Even a basic analysis of current Internet practice reveals numerous inefficiencies regarding economies of scale. In addition, the missed brand leveraging opportunity is perplexing, especially considering the strategic energies that leagues such as the AFL have focused on their brands.

It is worth noting that individual clubs plan their organisational approach to the Internet based on their perceptions of optimum competitive advantage. In this respect many major sporting clubs appear to be unwilling to relinquish their individual rights to the Internet, not realising that partnering may deliver greater benefits. Although this constitutes an admission about the tremendous future importance of the Internet, it is an issue that may impact upon the full realisation of that potential, should a partnership-based strategy fail to develop.

The peculiar interdependencies of sport have already been noted. Clubs participating in league-based competitions therefore need to consider strategy on two levels – club and league – and should focus on a combined approach to leveraging resources. Indeed, both management and the Internet team need to agree on the role of Internet strategy if the sport business is to develop strategies that effectively leverage the potential of the Internet.[28] With this in mind, league-based clubs are no different from international, national and regional sports governing bodies in terms of the benefits of a common approach to Internet applications.

Online Communities

The loyal affiliation of supporters to teams, and sport enthusiasts' natural tendency to form tight groups, puts sporting organisations in a unique position to develop online communities. Quite simply, the passion and commitment generated by the sporting product provides the industry with unmatchable brand loyalty in cyberspace. Digital communities are the Internet version of the loyal audiences eagerly sought after by newspapers, trade publications, interest-based magazines and television stations. The ability to hold an audience is crucial to success in these businesses, with product sales and advertising revenue inexplicably tied to consumer numbers. The development of loyal communities has been identified as just as critical in developing successful Internet operations.[29] In sport, physical communities already exist; making them virtual seems natural. Internet communities are like online 'Barmy Armies'. They are places where supporters, fans, or enthusiasts can gather and develop even stronger connections to their team; such connections will always remain difficult to manufacture for Sony, or McDonald's. English cricket supporters already band together, as do Swedish tennis fans and New Zealand rugby followers. The Internet facilitates these relationships in the online environment and presents sport businesses with an enormous opportunity. In the future, these communities will be the lifeblood of the net,[30] providing a place where people can satisfy their human need to be part of a group, regardless of their geographic location. It is also a place where sport managers can generate revenue in a multitude of ways. Traditional sources such as merchandising and ticketing can be replicated, and new revenue streams can be created, such as netcasting, online memberships, or selling space in the new community environment to zealous advertisers looking to reach a clearly defined market. The 'culture' of sport provides its businesses with a head start.

Accessing information concerning the demographics of the Internet communities will provide the key to a new advertising world with hitherto untapped one-on-one marketing communication opportunities. The creation of online communities takes a backdoor approach to this development by attracting fans based on their interests, such as online chat groups and net memberships. This has not always been achieved successfully to date. Perhaps the greatest player, and ultimately one of the greatest Internet 'bombs', was Sportal, the once ubiquitous but now disintegrated platform that delivered interactive football coverage, sport gambling and access to online sport communities. It was designed as the ultimate sports network which would embrace the latest technological possibilities. The brand never had time to mature, however, as the company lost money with alarming rapidity. This was largely because the uptake of Internet technology was too slow for the magnificent opportunities that were being offered, rather than consumers' lack of interest in interactivity and control of the broadcast or because of unwillingness to engage with other fans in online communication. As we have discussed in the previous chapter, the Internet mass market has not adopted wireless and broadband technology at the rate predicted by industry analysts.

Online relationships are a resource capable of leading to new sales, repeat sales and increased profits. In addition, some of the attractive benefits online community techniques can provide include giving fans an emotional stake in the business (arousing curiosity, empathy, or excitement), multiplying the number of times they make contact with the organisation, and increasing the quality of each contact made. Along with these come increases in revenue associated with the sale of primary and associated products, the creation of a new, accessible segment attractive to sponsors, and the cultivation of a group of human advertisements for the sport business. The promotion of an organisational strategy that both expands and enhances the richness of customer databases is prudent. In today's marketplace, there are few comprehensive databases that are not valuable assets, which (at worst) can be sold or rented to other organisations.

Generally, media companies and marketers view the aggregation of audiences as either geographic or 'special interest', and in both cases consumers have little influence (except in massive numbers) over the content that is offered to them.[31] The expansion of extreme sports' presence on the Internet reinforces the 'special interest' or cult/niche market possibilities for sport. The fragmented nature of the activities that comprise 'X' sports has not stopped a massive number of fans from communicating online in specialised chat rooms. These online community niches are impossible to replicate with traditional marketing, media and events. The interactive and 'access to all' nature of the Internet allows consumers to sift through the massive and diverse content available on the web, captive to neither geography nor editor bias, and even empowers them to create their own content. This paradigm shift from distributor to consumer has challenged sport enterprises to unlearn traditional models of community building using other media.[32] Another interesting feature is the deconstruction of marketing control so that traditionally conveyed, intrusive advertisements are reversed on the web, where consumers have complete control over the messages with which they choose to interact.

The potential for sporting organisations to generate significant revenue through e-commerce may well be defined by their ability to build communities that are hungry for their products, in turn attracting zealous sponsors. Sport business observers may be pondering why all sports with large memberships are not actively pursuing this strategy. Nevertheless, sport's natural 'membership' base seems to be the key to unlocking substantial competitive advantage in the online business environment through the Internet sport community.

Using the Internet in the Global Sport Marketplace

That the application of the Internet has the potential to lead to competitive advantage is beyond dispute. However, online commerce has gained a slippery reputation in terms of its potential for return on investment. In many instances, sport organisations feel compelled to have a web presence, but have remained uncertain about the volume of resources to throw at it.

The development of online sport communities may well prove to be the most profitable and sustainable way of achieving online success. These communities are the life-blood of organisational websites, and are well suited to the sporting industry and its high involvement products. To enhance and extend these internal, practical measures for building competitive advantage via the Internet, communication amongst potential online partners can facilitate an improved position by all. It should be emphasised to potential participants however, that any forum convened to discuss partnership and alliance opportunities is not analogous to reducing individual control of Internet rights or revenues. As has been demonstrated by some leagues in the USA, it is possible for clubs to retain independent control of their websites, and still generate significant alliance-based competitive advantages. Defraying costs and leveraging brands should be high on the agenda.

Final Comments

The Internet is potentially a formidable source of competitive advantage, and a shaping factor at the nexus of alternative global sport futures. As business leaders globally search for successful methods of tapping its riches, contemporary sport managers are in the enviable position of controlling a product that is inherently suited to the core strengths of the medium. People are passionate about the sporting product. They desire information about the sporting product. Sport is global, and sport is marketable. The Internet is a new form of community that has radically altered communication methods, overcome international borders, and developed mechanisms to distribute its products and generate revenue. In short, the Internet and sport are intrinsically linked. However, the willingness of sport businesses to commit resources to entrepreneurial Internet activities, in concert with the rapidity of technological uptake amongst sport consumers, will determine how much of a switching factor within technology the Internet proves to be.

One of the difficulties that bold, pioneering sport organisations have discovered in utilising the Internet as a marketing tool is that generic sites do not necessarily appeal to different national audiences. In other words, the potential for sports to 'go global' hinges upon their ability to transcend national barriers. Successful global sports of the future will be characterised not only by their capacity to balance upon the sticky threads of the spider's web, but also by their ability to manage disparate cultural sensitivities.

Notes and references

1   H. Bloom (1995), *The Lucifer Principle: A Scientific Expedition into the Forces of History*, Allen & Unwin, Australia.

2   O. A. El Sawy, A. Malhotra, S. Gosain and K. M. Young (1999), 'IT-intensive value innovation in the electronic economy: Insights from marshall industries', *MIS Quarterly*, 23(3), pp. 305–35.

3   G. Robertson (2000), *Crimes against Humanity: The Struggle for Global Justice*, Penguin Books, Australia.

4   H. Bloom, *The Lucifer principle*.

5   D. Tapscott (1996) *The Digital Economy: Promise and Peril in the Age of Networked Intelligence*, McGraw-Hill, USA.

6   A. Gellatly and D. Lambton (2001), 'Sport and Broadband: an introduction to a revolutionary technology', *SportsBusiness Information Resources*, SportBusiness Group, London.

7   R. Church (2000), *Sport on the Internet*, Screen Digest, USA.

8   C. A. Pratt (1998), 'Sport Communication', in J. Parkes, B. Zanger and J. Quarterman (eds), *Contemporary Sport Management*, Human Kinetics, Champaign, p. 167.

9   P. Turner (1999), 'Television and Internet convergence: Implications for sport broadcasting', *Sport Marketing Quarterly*, 8(2), pp. 43–9.

10 S. Kirkpatrick and E. Locke (1991), 'Leadership: Do traits really matter?', *Academy of Management Executive*, May, pp. 48–60.

11 B. Judson and K. Kelly (1999), *Hyperwars – Eleven Strategies for Survival and Profit in the Era of Online Business*, Scribner, New York.

12 B. Judson and K. Kelly, *Hyperwars*.

13 R. Roepke, R. Agarwal and T. W. Ferratt (2000), 'Aligning the IT human resource with business vision: The leadership initiative at 3M', *MIS Quarterly*, 24(2), pp. 327–53.

14 C. Martin (1997), *The Digital Estate – Strategies for Competing, Surviving, and Thriving in an Internetworked World*, McGraw-Hill, USA.

15 D. Bullis (1999), *Preparing for Electronic Commerce in Asia*, Quorum Books, USA.

16 M. J. Cronin (1996), *Global Advantage on the Internet – From Corporate Connectivity to International Competitiveness*, Van Nostrand Reinhold, USA, Chicago.

17 R. Shiller (2000), *Irrational Exuberance*, Scribe, Australia. p. 206.

18 B. Raghunathan and T. S. Raghunathan (1994), 'Adaptation of a planning system success model to information systems planning', *Information Systems Research*, 5(3), pp. 326–40.

19 J. Levinson and C. Rubin (1995), *Guerrilla marketing online: The entrepreneurs' guide to earning profits on the Internet*, Houghton Mifflin, Boston, MA, p. 214.

20 C. Standing (2000), *Internet Commerce Development*, Artech House, p. 4.

21 A. S. Bharadwaj (2000), 'A resource-based perspective on information technology capability and firm performance: An empirical investigation', *MIS Quarterly*, 24(1) pp. 169–96.

22 T. Stuart (2000), 'Interorganisational alliances and the performance of firms: A study of growth and innovation rates in a high-technology industry', *Strategic Management Journal*, 21(8), pp. 791–811.

23 J. C. Westland and T. H. K. Clark (2000), *Global Electronic Commerce: Theory and Case Studies*, MIT Press, London, p. 145.

24 B. Stewart (1984), 'The economic development of the Victorian Football League 1960–1984', *Sporting Traditions*, 1(2), pp. 2–26.

25 M. Porter (1985), *Competitive Advantage – Creating and Sustaining Superior Performance*, The Free Press, New York.

26 C. Martin, *The Digital Estate*.

27 A. Inkpen (2000), 'A note on the dynamics of learning alliances: Competition, co-operation, and relative scope', *Strategic Management Journal*, 21(7) pp. 775–9.

28 T. Teo and B. Too (2000), 'Information systems orientation and business use of the Internet: An empirical study', *International Journal of Electronic Commerce*, 4(4), pp. 105–30.

29 P. Bickerton, M. Bickerton and K. Simpson-Holley (1998), *Cyberstrategy – Business Strategy for Extranets, Intranets and the Internet*, Butterworth-Heinemann, Oxford.

30 C. Martin, *The Digital Estate*.

31 C. Martin, *The Digital Estate*.

32 F. Wang, M. Head and N. Archer (2000), 'A relationship-building model for the Web retail marketplace', *Internet Research: Electronic Networking Applications And Policy*, 10(5), pp. 374–84.

CHAPTER 7

Speaking in Tongues: Global Sport Marketing across Cultures

I think the Olympics should be a contest for all sportsmen, regardless of colour, race or wealth.
Carl Schranz, 1972, Austrian skier on his disqualification from the winter Games for commercialism (his income exceeded $50,000 pa)

In this chapter we argue that globalisation does not equate to homogenisation of markets. Put another way, we believe that markets are inherently different in different locations, and the ability to overcome these differences will prove a critical success factor for 'want to be' international sports. This cultural factor is the third and final nexus or window that will determine the fate of sport.

The misperceived assumption that markets are basically the same is commonly described as the 'global-local paradox'; 'one cannot think globally, every human being thinks according to their own culturally defined pattern'.[1] This is the first clue as to why culture may be considered a future sport nexus. Organisations can produce and distribute globally, but communication has to focus on the local habits and ways in which people relate to each other.

Knowledge of a local culture largely determines how well people and their subsequent behaviours can be understood. 'Local' culture is a relative measure. It can be based on criteria such as geography (for example, region, nation), ethnicity (for example, Jewish, Greek), religion (for example, Islam, Christianity) or organisational entity (for example, local branch, headquarters, organisation-wide). However, we are not talking about the work of cultural anthropologists and organisational psychologists as it applies to what has been named organisational or corporate culture; instead, we are interested in the dimensions of culture, irrespective of the local setting, be it a society, organisation or ethnic group. In this chapter, we shall provide an overview of how culture can be observed and measured in dissimilar settings.[2] In particular, we are interested in the ways in which culture impacts upon the perceptions and behaviours of sports consumers. It is important to understand this because culture can sometimes have an opposing, or at least mitigating, effect on globalisation, and can subsequently create some eclectic sport properties. The marketing of these sport properties has become the cutting edge of international sport business. To that end, before introducing the culture concept, we shall set the scene with a look at the broader context: marketing across cultures, or (the more common term) international marketing.

International Marketing and Culture

Culture and the comparison of cultures has been the almost exclusive domain of anthropologists for the last century. Only recently, since mass communication has extended beyond the borders of countries and continents, have marketers shown an interest in understanding cultures that are different from their own. With increasing globalisation of leading international companies in the late 1970s came the need to develop international marketing campaigns directed at consumers all over the world.[3] During that period it was believed that standardised products and marketing campaigns for a global mass market would deliver attractive economies of scale, assuming that in the process global communication would also lead to the standardisation of different (cultural or country) markets.

We outlined in Chapter 2 the multitude of reasons why people attend sporting contests. For example, spectators watching a tennis Grand Slam on television might be considered aficionados or theatregoers. However, is an English theatregoer the same as a Japanese theatregoer? They may share the same fundamental motivations for sports watching, but are they entertained by the same content? In other words, can a spectator segment in one country be replicated in another country? Can a sports marketer attract the Japanese theatregoer to tennis with the same communications messages that will work on an English tennis fan? If we were to base the answer to these questions on current practice, we might come to believe that there is one best set of marketing communications to attract tennis fans from anywhere in the world. After all, tennis is an international sport, and screaming fans come from all over the world to enjoy each of the Grand Slams. In making this assumption, we risk falling into the culture trap. A good spectator segmentation model can be applied to a range of cultural settings, with each category still reflecting the same motivations and behaviours. However, it is the way these motivations are manifested and the way that the behaviours are elicited that can be vastly different. For example, a theatregoer from any nation might watch the tennis on television, motivated fundamentally by the desire and expectation of entertainment. However, can we be sure that perceptions of entertainment are not affected by cultural influences? It is our contention that they are. This issue becomes more complex when we try to understand the impact of other variables that manipulate perception. The simple demographic variable of gender can serve as an example. For instance, spectator segments in the UK are made up of a mix of males and females, while in a number of Islamic countries it is forbidden for women to attend events such as soccer matches.

International marketing is usually introduced as marketing in more than one nation and is defined as 'the performance of business activities designed to plan, price, promote and direct the flow of a company's goods and services to consumers or users in more than one nation for a profit'.[4] A much more direct approach to identifying the aspects that set international marketing apart from marketing in general is put forward by Jean Claude Usunier:[5] 'International marketing automatically accords a prominent place to the cultural variable, despite the difficulties of isolating it for direct implementation. One of the principal aims is to identify, categorise, evaluate and finally select market segments.' The point here is that on an ethnic, linguistic and religious level, national states are different.

The uniqueness of international marketing comes from the range of unfamiliar problems and the variety of strategies necessary to cope with different levels of uncertainty encountered in foreign markets. International marketing from that perspective is about using the controllable elements of marketing (the marketing mix) within the framework of uncontrollable environmental elements such as competition, politics, legal issues, consumer behaviour, and the level of local technology (infrastructure). International marketing can therefore probably better be described as intercultural marketing, because marketing needs to be tailored to the local situation. This may seem obvious to the contemporary marketer, but it has been less than 20 years since Theodore Levitt published 'The globalisation of markets', advocating the standardisation of products and pricing, promotion and distribution strategies in order to reap the benefits of 'economies of scale'. In his own words:

gone are accustomed differences in national or regional preference ... the multinational world nears its end, and so does the multinational corporation ... the global corporation operates with resolute constancy —at low relative cost—as if the entire world (or major regions of it) were a single entity, it sells the same things in the same way everywhere.[6]

Levitt's contentions were based on the assumption that international travel and global communication would lead to the standardisation of needs and preferences of consumers all over the world. It is appealing to assume that markets are converging towards similar global structures (that is, market segments with similar needs for standardised products). Nike shoes, McDonald's hamburgers, Coca-Cola soft drinks, Levi Strauss jeans and Body Shop cosmetics are just a few examples of companies that sell the same core products all over the world. Their efforts are supported by mass communication media, introducing potential consumers from all corners of the globe to their products. They are truly global organisations. However, this does not mean that their marketing activities are always similarly standardised. Fast food giant McDonald's standardises processes, advertising, logos (symbols), store interior and layout; however, 'you will find wine on the menu in France and beer in Germany, a Filipino-style spicy burger in Manilla, pork burgers in Thailand, vegetable McNuggets and vegetable McBurgers in New Delhi [and a McOz burger in Australia with beetroot], all to accommodate local tastes and customs'.[7]

Along the same lines the influence of television acted as a global homogenising force from the perspective of advertising. However, there has been a limit to the penetration of these messages. While the same messages can travel successfully across the USA, language and cultural differences have prevented this from happening in Europe, Asia, South America and Africa.[8]

It might be concluded that globalisation as a process is actually happening, but much more at the level of competition (between producers) than at the level of consumer behaviour and needs and preferences patterns. For example, language differences will continue to exist. In culture-bound industries (such as food and sport), it is of the utmost importance to generate local knowledge and adjust marketing actions to local customs.

Globalisation can be viewed as a global–local paradox: global markets are products, but local markets are people. Because of the increasing technological opportunities to communicate to large groups of people in different ways, it is even more important to create distinctive advertising that stands out from the clutter. From that perspective it seems odd that advertisers try to develop strategies highlighting what people universally prefer, rather than what appeals to specific groups of people. For example:

the desire of women to be beautiful is universal, but the expression of beauty varies. Perspiration is a universal condition, but attitudes toward it differ throughout Europe. Continental Europe, particularly the hotter countries, tends to see perspiration as the body's natural cooling mechanism; the United Kingdom tends to see it as an embarrassment. The word average is probably the greatest enemy of quality. The customer wants it her or his way.[9]

Given that sports' consumers want it their way, it becomes a little clearer why culture can help us understand what their way is. Culture consists of the values, attitudes, beliefs, artefacts and other meaningful symbols represented in the pattern of life adopted by people that help them interpret, evaluate and communicate as members of a society. In this definition culture predominantly is positioned as the underpinning principle towards achieving successful communication.

However, the individual member of a cultural group also retains a considerable amount of independence. Because societies exist in an ever-changing world, their ability to adjust is dependent upon its constituent elements. In other words, if members of a society are completely conditioned through culture, the (cultural survival) system loses its flexibility, and its purpose for existing in the first place. This requires the introduction of the concept of 'operational culture'.[10] Operational culture refers to individuals sharing different cultures with different groups. They will switch to the most 'operational' culture when with a particular group of people (for example, from the family group to a group of soccer spectators), suggesting that people are part of different groups within a society. The term 'operational' refers to the sharing of beliefs, standards and practices that are necessary to complete a task within a particular context or situation.

It is the search for 'cultural universals' that has led to a sharper definition of the culture concept. Cultural universals are modes of behaviour that exist in all cultures because people may do the same things for different reasons, or indeed, do different things to achieve the same result. By focusing on behaviour, it is hard to detect universal patterns, but culture can represent the collective behaviour of groups of people to solve common (universal) problems. Although all people in general are confronted with similar problems, culture determines how these problems are solved.

The behaviour of sport fans can differ widely between cultures. For instance, is the fan expected to identify with a group or to operate as an individual? Should fans paint their faces and scream, or dress conservatively and politely applaud? Are males and females expected to behave alike? In other words, responses contain a 'cognitive dimension (people think it works that way), an affective dimension (people like it that way), and a directive dimension (people will do it that way)'.[11] We may assume that there is a single human nature (we all have the same nervous system or hardware), but we must be cautious in interpreting the differences in 'external circumstances' that have led to cultural diversity: that is, variations in physical appearance, customs, beliefs and temperament.[12]

Levels, Sources and/or Manifestations of Culture

Sports can be used to fulfil a plethora of functions that relate to expressing what an individual deems to be of great importance. Sports can be used 'to define more sharply the already established boundaries of moral and political communities ... sports are vehicles and embodiments of meaning, whose status and interpretation is continually open to negotiation and subject to conflict'.[13]

The 'operational culture' perspective helps us to understand the importance of cultural sources. These sources refer to groupings of people who share a common source of beliefs, standards or practices, strong enough to separate them clearly from other groups of people. With the possibility of individuals being members of more than one of these groups, as individuals they can be 'cultured' in a unique way. A number of sources of culture can be identified, including language, nationality, education (general), profession (specialised education), group (ethnicity), religion, family, sex, social class and corporate or organisational culture.[14]

Geert Hofstede defined culture as 'the collective programming of the mind which distinguishes the members of one human group from another'.[15] Culture, in Hofstede's research, refers to societies where nations represent 'societies'. He argued that societies are the highest level of cultural analysis because they are the largest known self-sufficient social systems in relation to their environment. Irrespective of the strength of subcultures (as groups within a society) in some societies that have their own cultural traits, subcultures still share common traits (at the level of society or nation) with other subcultures. These common traits make members of different subcultures identifiable to foreigners. However, more recent arguments challenge this view. For example, Samuel Huntington[16] argued that culture allows us to distinguish between seven different world civilisations (or mega-tribes) that he described as 'the highest levels of culture'. However, from the international marketing perspective of, for example the Federation of International Football Associations (FIFA), it is important to have knowledge of the ways in which soccer spectators differ between countries, given the fact that FIFA's direct 'customers' are 204 nation state members. This is why Hofstede's nation-by-nation comparison is one approach that may assist international sport marketers in coming to grips with the cultural variable.

Let us use the Sony Walkman as an example of a global (standardised) product for global customers who would use the product with similar motives.[17] In the Western world the primary reason for using a Walkman is to listen to music without being disturbed. The co-founder of the Japan-based Sony corporation, however, foresaw the Walkman as a means to listen to music without disturbing others. In other words, one cultural orientation places the onus on the individual and therefore is motivated (value-driven) by 'individualism', whereas the other culture places 'the group' at the centre of attention, thereby valuing the product (Walkman) from a 'collectivist' point of view. Obviously people not only use similar products in different ways, but they also choose different products to express differences in value orientation. Examples include British soccer fans naming their children after the leading players of their clubs, members of the middle class joining expensive golf or tennis clubs for social reasons and the 'black power' salute by two African-American athletes during the 1968 Olympic Games. In other words, when looking at sport as a way to express what one deems right and wrong, that behaviour contains rich information about what one does and does not value and, hence, a person's cultural orientation.

According to Hofstede[18] culture is visually expressed in behaviour much like the rings of an onion. The different layers of the onion illustrate the different ways in which culture becomes manifest from the more superficial indications of cultural belonging (the outside layer of the onion) through symbols such as words, pictures, language or objects to the deeper, intangible and invisible sense of a cultural group (the core of the onion) and what is valued as 'right' or 'wrong' behaviour. In between these two extremes, Hofstede distinguishes between heroes (the dead or still living, real or symbolic [non-existent] persons who are held in high regard in a culture and who more or less serve as role models), and rituals, which are those activities that are unnecessary to achieve a certain (organisational) goal but are vital to the collective perception of what is socially right. Rituals, for example, can be ways in which people pay respect to the deceased, how people greet each other or perform religious ceremonies such as baptism. Symbols, heroes and rituals together can be described as the actual activities or practices within a cultural setting, whereas the values are implicitly learned and exercised without physical manifestations. Outsiders can only derive values from the way people handle things in that culture. There are few better examples of manifestations of culture then the rituals of (folk) sport, especially when they can be dated back to pre-modern times. The chance of the rituals having evolved from day-to-day life (rather then having developed separated in time and space: that is, being time and place specific, as for example in the environment of the sport stadium) is much greater. The latter is important from the point of view that the values expressed in the activities of the ritual are likely to be, in Hofstede's words, more important software of the mind than in the case of more 'recent' rituals. In other words, the values underpinning the ritual are 'more important' for the survival of the individual in that particular social context. Consider a classic example from Afghanistan:

> where, in the traditional game of *Buzkashi*, tens of men on horseback compete for the possession of a calf carcass. *Buzkashi*, which commemorates the past equestrian culture of the area (on which the most glorious periods of Afghan history are based), provides the most dramatic sanctioned opportunity for the expression of the local version of masculine values: courage; strength; and dominance. It also serves as a metaphor for otherwise unacknowledged aspects of experience, for the chaotic, uninhibited and uncontrollable competition which 'lurks below the apparently co-operative surface'.[19]

Clearly, for people to express themselves, their cultural orientation to a large extent determines what are and what are not appropriate means of communication. Research into the differential popularity of sports led to the recognition that popularity of a sport is highly determined by the social circumstances and relationships between different societies, rather than being the result of the inherent characteristics of the sport.[20] In other words, if a sport is able to express a (sub)culture's dominant value orientation, it is more likely it will become popular in a society than others that do not have an equal expressive ability.

Cultural Dynamics

Culture is oriented towards finding solutions for common human problems. Attitudes towards action can best be seen in perceptions of time, space and the perception of the self and others. How people deal with the concept of time is probably one area where cultures differ most dramatically. There are, in principle, four common problems concerning time-related cultural assumptions. The economics of time relates to how time in different cultures is perceived as a commodity that is either scarce or plentiful. How people tend to schedule the different tasks they have in a day relates to the monochronic (one thing at a time) as opposed to the polychronic (dealing with multiple tasks simultaneously) view of time.[21] Time can be seen as either a single continuous line or as being cyclical, ensuring ever recurring patterns (daily, yearly, seasonal). In the context of sport in Western society, 'sports embody the sacred cycle of mythic time and provide a needed psychic relief from the tedium of Western linear time ... Their newness-sameness offers the spectator a strange sense of continuity within change',[22] which is why we cannot wait for the new football season to start every year.

How are people oriented towards time? Do they emphasise the past? Is the 'here and now' most important or are people striving towards long-term future goals? How people are oriented towards time relates to their supposed mastery of nature. The more the future can be controlled and (scientifically) predicted, the more likely it is that people will take a futuristic perspective. On the other hand, the more 'history' a people have, the more likely it is that the past will play an important role in explaining where they are now.

Space relates to the three-dimensional territories that people move through, intrude into and live and reside within. It deals with who owns and controls certain areas of space. Usunier identified four basic 'space-related' problems that help explain why it is important for sport. The first problem deals with being an insider or outsider. Do people belong 'in that space' or not, and are people assessed on what they do or what they are? This problem is of particular importance for members of (hooligan) supporter fringes of soccer clubs; not only do they claim certain parts of their club's home ground as their territory (Ajax Amsterdam's hard-liners are also known as F-siders, named after 'their' section in Ajax' old stadium 'de Meer'), but also initiation ceremonies and overt participation in 'stadium rituals' are required for acceptance into the group.[23] Second, if people are members of an 'in-group', what then does it take to become part of that group? Moreover, irrespective of behaviour in the group, what are the relevant in-groups (family, tribe, clan, club) in a certain culture that an individual has to be a member of in order to be seen as successful? The third problem then logically becomes how one gains membership of a particular group. The fourth problem deals with physical space in relation to group versus individualistic cultures. In group cultures it is more likely that close physical contact (proximity) is readily accepted as a prerequisite to healthy social relations whereas individualistic cultures will place a high value on sufficient private space around one's body.

The concept of self and others deals with 'how the organization of a society is internalised by people and reflected in the view that they hold of themselves in comparison with others'.[24] As with time, four basic problems regarding the concept of self and others can be stated. First, is human nature good or bad? This relates to how we generally treat people we do not know; do we show confidence or suspicion? Second, how do we appraise people, particularly in relation to their age, sex and social class? For example, is trustworthiness dependent on age, sex or social class and if so, in which direction? The second problem then leads to the third, which relates to appraising oneself in relation to self-esteem, perceived potency and level of activity (energy). Finally, how does the individual relate to the group and in that respect, what is being valued most as the principal resource of energy and activity? In other words, is the individual or the group most important in the ultimate efforts of people to survive in the context of a society?

In the context of the sport industry the problems associated with the self and others are aptly used to marketers' advantage. What people are (ought to be) and what is the ideal conduct in particular roles, is often expressed powerfully by successful, high-profile athletes. The athletes feature in highly-scripted commercials and public relations programmes that convey subliminal messages of what (success, achievement, the perfect role model for kids) is being valued in a society. Sport celebrities can be role models and, hence, if they 'fit' culturally they are used to endorse a wide variety of products. It was clear from the beginning that the highest-profile athlete endorser of the 1990s, Michael Jordan, 'was a made-for-the-media athlete. He had natural ability to communicate, to provide intelligent answers to questions, to delicately handle the tough questions. The 1984 Olympic gold medal enhanced Jordan's image as an all-American-kid.'[25]

Cultural Interaction

It is not by coincidence that the problem of what is the basic resource of energy and action, the individual or the group (introduced in the section on the self and others), returns as a principal problem in interaction models. Usunier observed:

> individualism is based on the principle of asserting one's independence and individuality. All societies have individuals and groups, but individualism stresses the smallest unit as being that where the solution lies ... collectivism is associated to 'traditional culture' whereas individualism is a strong component of 'modern culture', especially in the area of consumption, a splendid domain for enjoying individual freedom and expressing difference from others.[26]

A comparison of the prevalence of team sports and individual sports in both collectivistic and individualistic societies would be an interesting extension of this problem in the context of the sport industry. However, to date there is no empirical evidence in relation to this matter. Huntington noted that in respect to supposed cultural differences on matters such as individualism/collectivism, many researchers and politicians make the unfortunate mistake of distinguishing between countries as 'Western' or 'Eastern'. He argued that although certain cultural characteristics are shared among 'Western' and among 'Eastern' countries, they can also differ significantly in respect to dimensions such as individualism/collectivism. For example, the fact that the majority of Southern Europe is Catholic and the Northern countries Protestant probably accounts for bigger cultural differences (within Europe) than the difference between Southern European nations and South American nations (many of which are Catholic as well). Huntington argued that it is better to speak of the 'West' and the 'Rest', where the separation is based on economic activity and wealth (the West is rich and the rest are poor). However, with the rapid economic development of some of the non-West nations, any separation based on economic wealth will become increasingly irrelevant. Categorisation of nations is also dependent upon the 'power distance' of a particular culture.

The problem of power distance may be understood as necessity to rely on oneself and find power and motivation within, as opposed to the need for group support and dependence. Power distance separates interaction in societies where centralised power is more common. In these cases, there is a greater acceptance of power distance versus 'equality', which in turn leads to opposition when there is unequal distribution of power. There is ample evidence[27] that links societies where power distance is more readily accepted to the use of sport as a means of manipulation and propaganda. MacClancy saw this manifestation of power distance in the former Soviet Union:

> Sports may be used as a resource by which the powerful attempt to dominate others. The forgers of the Soviet State were well aware of its potential. To them, sport was a tool for socialising the population into the newly established system of values. It could encourage compliance and co-operation in both work and politics, and be used as a way to combat 'unhealthy, deviant, anti-social behaviour such as drunkenness, delinquency, prostitution, religiosity, and intellectual dissidence. Also, if deployed skilfully, it could unite wider sections of the population more than any other social activity, transcending differences of nationality, sex, age, social position, geographical location and political attitudes.[28]

However, apart from sport being used by the powerful in an effort to gain even greater control, it also needs to be acknowledged that the suppressed can use sport effectively as a means to resist control and achieve their own goals.

The issue of power distance closely relates to the problem of developing appropriate communication styles, the latter applying to the cultural persistence in Australian soccer, where the forced abandonment of communication through ethnic symbols was heavily opposed by the clubs involved. There are also problems that relate to interaction in societies stressing 'masculine' values (assertiveness, aggression, achievement) versus those that reinforce 'feminine' values (caring, nurturing, quality of life), and the difficulties of uncertainty avoidance where in some societies there is a tendency to avoid risks (high uncertainty avoidance) while others are willing to take risks in order to facilitate change (low uncertainty avoidance). For example, sports gambling highlights these alternative, culturally reinforced tendencies. After the identification of the basic cultural assumptions and their context (interaction models), the culturally-based attitudes people have towards taking 'corrective' action may be considered. After all, we must be clear about how people eventually 'solve' the problems that their unique cultural sensitivities create.

Cultural Diversity and the Future of Sport Businesses

So far we have illustrated the complex and surprisingly dynamic nature of culture as a powerful sport business variable. In the final section of this chapter we aim to summarise the issues and propose three main challenges when appreciating cultural diversity during trade in the sport-economy. It was proposed at the beginning of the chapter, that culture, as a system of learned, shared, compelling, interrelated set of symbols, heroes, rituals and values, provides meaningful orientations for members of a society. These orientations, considered together, provide solutions to problems that all societies must solve if they are to remain viable.[29] In other words, culture helps us to solve problems. Sport as a social and cultural activity is no different. It may be argued that sport, as a specific set of operational activities, also solves a specific set of (social) problems. From the perspective of the sport business entrepreneur it is of obvious importance to know which problems need to be (or can be) solved by the provision of sport products. At the level of the individual or smaller groups of people (whether participating or spectating), sport may assist in:

- the development of a sense of belonging
- the development of a positive self concept
- the appreciation of time and space (us versus them) concepts
- the development of social interaction skills.

At the level of the nation state, or indeed, larger ethnic groupings, sport assists in:

- the development of a sense of national identification
- the working towards national integration
- the development of a sense of social inclusion
- the enhancement of national cultures and values
- the development of sport as an international symbol of a country's identity and culture.[30]

Recent research into the influence of culture on service quality perceptions of soccer spectators in four different countries found that spectators in the Netherlands and Australia were significantly different in orientation compared to spectators from Malaysia and the USA, the former being more feminine in their orientation compared to the latter.[31] In that regard the impact of cultural orientation on sport consumption may be further exemplified in the activities of soccer 'hooligans'.

Most soccer hooligans are men and an important reason for becoming involved in fights is to express their 'maleness'.[32] Most hooligans openly express their perceived importance of the soccer club's home ground and, within the confines of the stadium, they violently defend their own strictly defined territory (the cultural problem of space).[33] It might seem a small leap to assume that violence in the stands is more likely to eventuate in culturally 'masculine' countries. On the other hand, it may also be argued that males in 'feminine' societies are not expected to express their maleness overtly in 'normal' life, and hence use the football stadium to do so. These extrapolations, of course, can only be made based on the assumption that sport spectators in general are reflected in the population of soccer spectators. However, this example naturally leads us to the identification of cultural challenges that sport entrepreneurs are facing. Although we are by no means claiming to be exhaustive in our discussion of these challenges, the following suggest themselves as priorities:

- within and across countries' cultural sensitivity
- scope of international sport branding
- the identification of sport consumption benefits within and across cultures.

In regard to these challenges, it should now be clear that sporting goods in general, and sport service products in particular, hold an advantage over many other products in that the consumers' emotional attachment to sport tends to drive them into non-rational purchasing behaviour. In other words, their decision to buy is strongly mediated by their love for the sport, their passion for a club or their admiration of an athlete. When emotional attachment is combined with the relative importance of sport in a particular society, the sport marketer can achieve a competitive advantage. The flipside of the coin, of course, is the risk of a significant loss, when the inherent marketing power of the sport product is manipulated and exploited with little understanding of emotional and cultural interplay. The latter is evidenced in the continuing struggle of soccer to become a nationally popular and accepted sport in the USA and Australia.

Cultural Sensitivity in Sport: A Case Study of Soccer in Australia and the USA[34]

Australian and American soccer has always suffered from an image problem. In Australia in particular, some of that stems from the persistent challenges the national squad has encountered in international competition, and some seems to be founded on an unrelenting crisis of identity.

Although the 'world game' enjoys excellent participation levels in both countries, particularly at the youth level, migrants who follow European and South American football leagues and maintain strong ethnic ties to their cultural heritage hold the chief interest in elite competition. It is these 'football migrants' who formed many of the clubs in Australia and local unaffiliated competitions in the USA; ironically, despite their passion, commitment and technical skill, they have instilled the Australian and North American versions of the game with an indissoluble ethnic flavour.

Sport clubs or sporting communities are, of course, powerful vehicles for social identity, refuelling historical images, shaping a sense of belonging and providing avenues for collective expression. As a traditional sport of the non-British Europeans in Australia, and of South Americans and non-British in the USA, soccer provided the microcosm that was required to preserve familiar traditions and provide belonging in a new land.

In Australia's sporting infrastructure clubs provided a range of socially-useful benefits: social interaction with those sharing a first language, physical challenge and emotional catharsis through team support, the opportunity for club patronage, support networks and business connections, personal prominence and prestige and the retention of youth support for cultural continuity and ethnic re-affirmation. The soccer club became a cultural safe haven for ethnic migrants. More recently, professional soccer teams in the USA have provided similar benefits for supporter groups. At the Los Angeles Galaxy, it is common for large supporter groups (for instance, those with Mexican or El Salvador heritage) to establish camp outside the Rosebowl hours before a match, set up the barbecue, and socialise with friends and family while having a beer and kicking around a ball with the kids.

Close to two-thirds of all Australians and Americans are of mixed ethnic origins. The nations' plural populations present sport managers with a unique juxtaposition of demographic factors: an Anglo-dominant culture, a diversity of minority cultures and quite similar national policy support for a multicultural society with a relatively high emphasis on continued immigration. Given the likelihood that sport managers will work in culturally resonant settings, it is imperative that their cultural sensitivities are adequately developed. Indeed their capacity for success in management and marketing may hinge upon such qualities.

Survival (or indeed the thriving success) of soccer in Australia and the USA is dependent upon a range of factors. Concern has been expressed about the low rates of transfer of participation from junior levels to senior ranks, the relatively small amount of interest paid to the sport by the commercial media, the lack of international success of the national mens' teams (in Australia in particular, while the US national team performed admirably in the 2002 World Cup) and the general public's perception of the sport. The fact that most clubs in Australia's National Soccer League (NSL) and in the USA's Major League Soccer (MLS) rely on support from specific ethnic groups, and that the sport is seen as a game for 'ethnics', may be viewed as a grave weakness.

In Australia, despite attempts to change the ethnic symbolism in many soccer clubs, recent research shows that the sport remains predominantly ethnic in its identity and support base. The disinterest from mainstream Australia has been attributed to various sources, including educational institutions grounded in British history, and media sensationalism of interethnic violence in soccer. Each contributed to the phobias of the dominant British culture and reinforced the 'ethnic' notions of an Australian Rules fixated sporting public. It is worth noting that Australia's lack of success in the international soccer arena is likely to be a significant contributing factor as well. When qualification for the 1998 World Cup was at stake, 90,000 fans showed up for the match against Iran in November 1997. Similar interest was generated four years later in the same situation against Uruguay. On neither occasion did the team succeed in qualifying.

Australia's top club teams do not play in an international club competition such as, for example, the European Champions League. Without pride and national identity being at stake, most Australian sport fans direct their passion to traditional club rivalries in Australian Rules football or the National Rugby League competition. The cultural orientations of soccer spectators differ significantly depending on ethnic backgrounds, and reflect the deeper values from their 'home' countries. This means that a 'general' approach to the formulation of management and marketing strategies for soccer organisations is likely to fail. From a strategic viewpoint, the individual clubs of the NSL and MLS can be seen as components (or business units) of the larger organisation, which collectively target and serve different market segments. From this perspective it may be prudent to allow clubs to focus on (ethnic) niche markets. Letting business units supply to a range of niche markets enables the parent organisation, at least to a certain extent, to pursue a strategy of full market coverage.

In the USA there is ample evidence from other professional sporting leagues, such as the National Football League (NFL) and the National Basketball Association (NBA), that it is not the clubs but the league as a whole that is the point of strategic departure. In other words, the teams that make up the league basically serve two main purposes: first, they have to be competitive enough to be in a position to provide sufficient opposition to rival teams to ensure a reasonably equal contest; and second, they have to satisfy the needs for sporting entertainment of a geographically dispersed market. Sporting franchises are strategically located in those areas with relatively little competition from franchises providing the same brand (for instance, NBA or NFL). As highlighted before for the LA Galaxy, who operate in a market with a disproportionately (compared to the rest of the USA) high number of Hispanics, it seems only logical that they provide their product to this (originally South American) audience deliberately, rather than aiming to 'Americanise' their product and approach to marketing. The Australian Football League and the big four in the USA (NFL, NBA, NHL and MLB) approach their licence-holding teams similarly. The number of teams in the league is based on their ability to serve significant geographic spectator markets, in turn ensuring their financial viability and creating intercity and interstate rivalry between clubs aimed at increasing the attractiveness of the competition as a whole. Teams with marginal supporter bases are forced to merge, move to another city, or remove themselves from the pre-eminent competition.

At the amateur soccer level the focus remains on 'broad' participation. Amateur competitions in Australia are mainly organised for the same reasons they were organised some 50 years ago. Large groups of non-British European immigrants came to Australia to play with and be among peers, and to create 'culturally safe' environments where a passion for sport could be shared. Even more than at the professional level (national) of the sport, multiculturalism is a fundamental characteristic of state-based amateur soccer infrastructure. In the USA this is rather different where amateur soccer is popular in universities, particularly among females. At the youth level a massive number of American children play in little-league style formats. However, this potential has yet to be transferred to senior level participation, even though the women's team are the world champions.

Based on market characteristics, soccer in both Australia and the USA must embrace multiculturalism (in both its competitions and its constituent clubs) as a vital characteristic. In the United States, the Chief Executive Officer (CEO) of Major League Soccer has argued that soccer may never appeal to American football fans,[35] and that indeed this may not be a bad thing. America's immigration rate is producing a melting pot of cultures, resulting in more than enough people wanting to attend soccer games, assuming that their cultural intelligence is not constantly insulted. It seems that when aiming to ensure the sport's healthy development,

careful management and recognition of the cultural values of the different nationalities and ethnic groupings (and, for that matter, clubs) needs to be considered.

As history has already shown, revolutionary change is likely to fail and evolutionary change is likely to take generations. Until soccer can formulate a strategy for managing its cultural affiliations without crushing them, and generate domestic, mainstream interest without alienating Anglo-Australians and Americans, it will remain a poor cousin of the countries' leading football codes. In other words, FIFA, as a global sport governing body has yet to achieve universal branding of their core product. Can this branding be achieved by sport governing bodies that have few national stories to tell, and few heroes to sell? Sports that want to become genuinely international successful cannot afford to be empty cultural 'shells'.

Scope of International Sport Branding

The impacts of national and/or ethnic culture can surface within a country, as outlined in the example above, or internationally, when sport organisations distribute products in more than one country. When the latter occurs, the way the organisation brands itself becomes an increasingly important matter. A brand is the extended story of a product, expressed in a logo and extended visual imagery. It is symbolism that is widely understood by the (to be) converted members of the product clan. Global organisations, through their branding, attempt to tell stories about their products that will capture the imagination of the global clan. Global clan members are all familiar with the 'meta' story. However, geographically dispersed tribes have their own rituals, their own heroes and, to a certain extent, their own symbols as well.

Brand equity, as the combined tangible and intangible value of the brand, can be broken down into four constituent components.[36] These components are perceived quality (of the brand), brand awareness (recall, recognition), brand associations (in sport often emotionally loaded), and brand loyalty (the ability of the brand to retain customers). In the sport industry, the antecedents to brand equity are team-related (success, star players), organisation-related (reputation and tradition, overall entertainment package, service reputation), and market-related (media coverage and reach, competitive forces).

The challenge of truly international brands therefore is to stand for something that appeals to 'all' people, while incorporating opportunities to extend the brand for cultural niche markets. McDonald's stands for

hamburgers (or fast food standardised in quality) all over the world, but the ingredients are adjusted to local customs. FIFA stands for soccer (standardised rules and regulations) all over the world, but the development, style and organisation of the game are adjusted to local needs. Of course, it needs to be noted that 'local adjustment' in soccer is conducted by 'national franchisees' who have branded themselves quite distinct from FIFA, a challenge that is specific to the 'delegate system' of sport governance which typifies many international sport governing bodies. Down at the club level the situation becomes even more complicated. Some of the soccer club brands are as strong as, if not stronger than, the FIFA brand. Clubs such as Manchester United, AC Milan, Barcelona and Ajax Amsterdam have fan clubs all over the world and their respective merchandise can be bought from specialty and department stores in many nations and on the internet. This is likely to be the greatest threat (or challenge) facing the wealthy sport governing bodies such as the IOC, FIFA, and the International Amateur Athletics Federation (IAAF): to remain the controlling body of the sport. Their brand equity is low compared to clubs and athletes, largely because they are support organisations, not the producers of the 'end' sport product. Commercial clout and independence of wealthy clubs and athletes, and their ability to form cartel-style alliances, are likely to erode the power of the umbrella brand and to form smaller, yet very powerful, subbrands in their own right. This is strongly exemplified by the G14 (or future G24) alliance of Europe's strongest soccer clubs. Until 2006 the G14 have agreed with the UEFA about keeping the European Champions League as a two-group stage, 32-team competition. But the G14 general manager, Thomas Kurth, is pushing for a Champions League with fewer weak teams. If they so choose, the G14 could form their own competition, without the involvement of governing bodies such as the Union Européenne de Football Associations (UEFA) or FIFA. As major stakeholders in Europe's (and for that matter global) football industry, they are taken very seriously by UEFA as partners in their European-based competitions. The G14 are still keeping the option of forming a European Super League alive and Kurth has proposed that the group stages of the Champions League be replaced by mini-leagues in which 12 teams play a full competition. The G14 also has its own media rights strategy where live and interactive live, highlights and news will be sold as a consortium with clubs individually negotiating delayed broadcast, mobile (wireless) and archive rights. In the near future, Europe's football landscape may change dramatically into a European Super league, a number of regional (multiple countries) leagues and downsized domestic (feeder) leagues.[37]

The expansion of the G14 to become the G24 has been anticipated for some time. This organisation, which overtly represents the interests of the backbone of successful football competition in Europe, shows the increasing power of 'market driven' sport organisations. The clubs speculated to be included in the prospective G24 are shown below:

The G14

Manchester United, Liverpool, Real Madrid, Barcelona, Juventus, AC Milan, Inter Milan, Bayern Munich, Borussia Dortmund, l'Olympique Marseille, Paris St-Germain, Ajax Amsterdam, PSV Eindhoven and FC Porto.

and the next 10 in line ...

Glasgow Rangers, Lazio, AS Roma, Parma, Hertha Berlin, Chelsea, Celtic, Sporting Lisbon, Arsenal and Anderlecht.

Figure 7.1 shows which countries are most powerful in European soccer when power is expressed as the top 24 clubs based on their annual turnover.

As hyperdeveloped corporate sport entities, US professional leagues may be the blueprint examples for future international governing bodies, or competitions such as the proposed European Super league. They control competition, stimulate development and legislate in relation to the rules, regulations and format of the game. It may prove too hard to control branding of nations and/or athletes and their subsequent

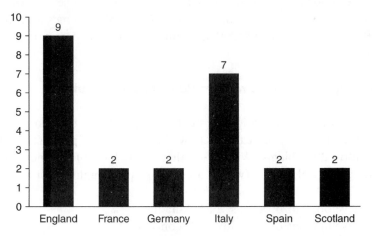

Figure 7.1 Football 'power' expressed as the top 24 clubs, by turnover, in Europe

Source: Based on data presented by the SportBusiness Group, December 2001.

commercialisation efforts, let alone to control the clubs that play professional sport at the national or regional level. Clubs are increasingly owned by investors, many of them with massive commercial clout, making it hard for governing bodies to tell them what they can and cannot do. As touched on earlier in this book, there are great benefits in using established brands as a means to sell new products (into new markets). Global entertainment conglomerates are successfully using the established brand power of sport organisations to increase (the profitability of) their sales, and increasingly they are building their own sport properties (teams and events) from scratch for the purpose of harnessing the inherent branding power of sport. It goes beyond the scope of this chapter to develop branding theory in sport further. However, it is worth reinforcing that it will be a great challenge for international sport governing bodies to remain in (or gain) control of their international branding. Governing bodies may turn out to be little more than culturally empty shells that will struggle to excite sport consumers with the stories they may have to tell.

We discussed Hofstede's view on culture, including how culture manifests itself in societies and for that matter, in organisations as well. Superficial manifestations in sport organisations include symbols (logos), heroes (champion players) and rituals (terrace songs in British soccer). In Chapter 5, we also outlined Jensen's view[38] that the stories behind the product, the history and culture of the product and the organisation that delivers the product will gain prominence in the minds of consumers. This leads us to the final section of this chapter in which we outline the challenge of identifying which benefits sport consumers seek in the sport products of the future. Again, the cultural variable assumes a prominent place as a result of the cultural segmentation of sport consumers.

Identifying Sport Consumption Benefits across Cultures

Earlier in this section we looked at the perspective of the sport business entrepreneur, and specifically at how they can create products that will solve cultural problems. We argued that at the level of the individual or smaller groups of people (within a culture), sport might assist in:

- the development of a sense of belonging
- the development of a positive self concept
- the appreciation of time and space (us versus them) concepts
- the development of social interaction skills.

At the level of nation states or, indeed, larger ethnic groupings (across cultures), sport assists in:

- the development of a sense of national identification
- the working towards national integration
- the development of a sense of social inclusion
- the enhancement of national cultures and values
- the development of sport as an international symbol of a country's identity and culture.

As a conceptual exercise at the end of this chapter we are proposing a framework in which we combine the need to solve cultural problems with the six marketplaces suggested by Jensen. These six markets were:

- the market for adventures
- the market for togetherness, friendship and love
- the market for care
- the who-am-I market
- the market for peace of mind
- the market for convictions.

The resultant matrix is presented in Table 7.1. It outlines (or hypothesises) which type of sport products are best suited to solving particular (within or across) cultural problems. Hence the matrix combines the identification of Dream Society marketplaces for sport products with cultural segmentation, the latter being proposed as an increasingly important segmentation variable in the sport business economy. In other words, some sport products are more suited to solving 'within' cultural problems and therefore need to be localised, whereas other products need to appeal to 'all' cultures and therefore are global products. The overview is not meant to be exhaustive; it only serves as an initial attempt to visualise the new economy marketplace for culturally sensitive sport products. It might also be noted that suggested products do not necessarily fit exclusively into one category.

The way we propose to look at segmented sport products, based on the cultural problems which they may help to solve, leads us into the final chapter of this book. In that chapter we will return to the discussion of the future of sport business in the global marketplace which we began in Chapter 1 and, amongst other things, we will develop four global scenarios for the future of sport that are partly based on how culture, as a nexus factor, will influence these scenarios.

Table 7.1 Examples of culturally segmented sport products

Dream Society marketplaces	Sport products solving 'within' cultural problems: localised products	Sport products solving 'across' cultural problems: global products
Adventure	• Sport participation products (local club membership, intramural sports) • Sport themed consumption (theme park, museum, facility tours)	• Sport tourism products (sport adventure packages to Queenstown, New Zealand including rafting, bungee jumping, etc.)
Togetherness	• Team-based spectatorship (Newcastle United, Los Angeles Lakers, Collingwood Football Club)	• International event-based spectatorship (at the Olympic Games or at the World University Games)
Care	• Team-based volunteerism (domestic teams, ethnically based teams, local clubs)	• International event-based volunteerism (the Sydney Olympic Games need to be mentioned as a spectacular success in that regard)
'Who am I' and 'Who are we'	• Sport participation products (Auskick, as a national participation programme marketed by the Australian Football League) • Sport spectator products (sepak takrow, immensely popular in Thailand and Malaysia) • Packaged athlete (and team) products (Dutch speed-skating teams and Gianni Romme, a Dutch speed-skating star)	• Sport spectatorship products (FIFA World Cup and fanatic country team support) • Packaged athlete (and team) products (Tiger Woods, Manchester United, the Brazilian soccer team)
Peace of mind	• Membership participation products (club) • Membership spectator products (club, corporate hospitality) • Sport themed consumption (theme park, museum, facility tours)	• Hallmark sporting events (Wimbledon) • Broadcast and film produced sporting entertainment (the FA Cup final) • Sport tourism (the British Lions Rugby Union tour)
Convictions	• Culturally specific convictions sport sponsorship (e.g. sun protection products and surf lifesaving in Australia)	• Culturally global convictions sport sponsorship (Coca-Cola and the Olympic Games)

Notes and references

1   M. de Mooy (1998), *Global Marketing and Advertising: Understanding Cultural Paradoxes*, Sage, Thousand Oaks, p. 12.

2   G. Hofstede (1980), *Culture's Consequences: International Differences in Work-related Values*, Sage, Beverly Hills, CA; G. Hofstede (1984), *Culture's Consequences, International Differences in Work-related Values*. (abridged edn), Sage, Newbury Park; G. Hofstede (1991), *Allemaal andersdenkenden. Omgaan met cultuurverschillen*, Uitgeverij Contact, Amsterdam; G. Hofstede (1991), *Cultures and Organisations, Software of the Mind*, McGraw-Hill, London; G. Hofstede (ed.) (1998), *Masculinity and Femininity: The Taboo Dimension of National Cultures*, Sage, Thousand Oaks.

3   M. de Mooy, *Global Marketing and Advertising*.

4   P. R. Cateora and J. L. Graham (1999), *International Marketing* (10th edn), Irwin McGraw-Hill, Boston, MA, p. 6.

5   J. C. Usunier (1996), *Marketing across Cultures* (2nd edn), Prentice Hall Europe, Hemel Hempstead, p. 3.

6   T. Levitt (1983), 'The globalization of markets', *Harvard Business Review*, 61(3), pp. 92–3.

7   P. R. Cateora and J. L. Graham, *International Marketing*, p. 22.

8   M. de Mooy, *Global Marketing and Advertising*, p. 17.

9   M. de Mooy, *Global Marketing and Advertising*, p. 26.

10 W. H. Goodenough (1971), *Culture, Language and Society*, Addison-Wesley, Reading, MA.

11 J. C. Usunier, *Marketing across Cultures*, p. 30.

12 B. Shore (1996), *Culture in Mind: Cognition, Culture and the Problem of Meaning*, Oxford University Press, New York.

13 J. MacClancy (1996), *Sport, Identity and Ethnicity*. Berg, Oxford, pp. 7–8.

14 J. C. Usunier, *Marketing across Cultures*.

15 G. Hofstede, *Culture's Consequences* (abridged edn), p. 21.

16 S. Huntington (1997), *The Clash of Civilisations and the Remaking of World Order*, Simon & Schuster, New York.

17 M. de Mooy, *Global Marketing and Advertising*.

18 G. Hofstede, *Cultures and Organisations, Software of the mind*.

19 J. MacClancy, *Sport, Identity and Ethnicity*, p. 3.

20 M. Bottenburg (1994), *Verborgen competitie, over de uiteenlopende populariteit van sporten*. Uitgeverij Bert Bakker, Amsterdam.

21 E. T. Hall (1983), *The Dance of Life*, Anchor Press, New York.

22 A. Guttmann (1986) *Sports Spectators*, Columbia University Press, New York, p. 178.

23 J. Bale, 1993, 'The spatial development of the modern stadium', *International Review for Sociology of Sport, 28(2), pp. 121–33*; Canter, Comber and Uzzell (1989), *Football in its Place, An Environmental Psychology of Football Grounds*, Routledge, London; E. Dunning, P. Murphy and J. Williams (1988), *The Roots of Football Hooliganism*. Routledge, London; Spurling, 1999.

24 J. C. Usunier, *Marketing across Cultures*, p. 66.

25 D. Shilbury, S. Quick and H. M. Westerbeek (1998), *Strategic Sport Marketing*, Allen & Unwin, Sydney, p. 205.

26 J. C. Usunier, *Marketing across Cultures*, p. 71.

27 W. J. Baker (1988), *Sports in the Western World* (revised edn), University of Illinois Press, Urbana; E. Dunning (1999), *Sport Matters: Sociological Studies of Sport, Violence and*

Civilisation. Routledge, London; Guttmann, *Sports Spectators*; MacClancy, *Sport, Identity and Ethnicity*.

28 J. MacClancy, *Sport, Identity and Ethnicity*, p. 10.
29 V. Terpstra and K. David (1991), *The Cultural Environment of International Business* (3rd edn), South Western, Cincinnati, p. 6.
30 A. C. T. Smith, H. M. Westerbeek and R. K. Stewart (in preparation), *Sport and International Investment*
31 H. M. Westerbeek (2001), 'Marketing across cultures: an investigation into place specific dimensions of service quality in sport', PhD Thesis, Deakin University, Melbourne, Australia.
32 E. Dunning, *Sport Matters*.
33 J. Bale, 1993; J. Bale (1994), *Landscapes of Modern Sport*, Leicester University Press, Leicester; Canter, Comber and Uzzell, 1989; E. Dunning, *Sport Matters*.
34 Large components of this section were published as an article by A. C. T. Smith, H. M. Westerbeek and J. Deane (2001), 'Soccer takes advantage of Australia's cultural mix', *Australia 2001: A Guide to Australian Sport Business*, SportBusiness Group, London, pp. 20–1.
35 T. Lusetich (2000), 'US glitz gives way to substance', *The Australian*, 20 March, p. 24.
36 J. Gladden, G. R. Milne and W. Sutton (1998), 'A conceptual framework for assessing brand equity in Division I college athletics', *Journal of Sport Management*, 12(1), pp. 1–19.
37 M. Glendinning (2002), 'The quiet radical', *Football Business International*, 3, March, pp. 18–20.
38 R. Jensen (1999) *The Dream Society*. McGraw-Hill, New York.

CHAPTER 8

Sport Trek: Future Sport Business in the Global Marketplace

Your hands get so filled with money, comes a time when there's nothing you can't imagine having. Everybody should be able to feel that way. I started to lose everything but money. And money wasn't that important. Because money doesn't help you sleep. Money doesn't help your mother be well, money don't make your brother still interested in his study, money don't help an argument when nobody knows what they're arguing about. Money don't help nothing. Money is only good when you got something else to do with it. A man can lose everything, family, all your dreams, and still have a pocketful of money. I don't want that.

George Foreman, world heavyweight champion, 1973

To conclude this book we have returned to where we began, which is ironically the future, or more specifically, the future of sport business. As before, we argue that examining the future of sport in isolation is both naive and misleading. The future of sport should be understood within a global context. In other words, we continue to argue that it is best to extrapolate the future for sport by applying trend analysis to the world as a whole first, before arguing sport's place in that future. Throughout this book, we have used the concept of globalisation as the key driver of change and have constructed our discussion around the impact of its continued and increasing importance in the world. The following section highlights the key uncertainties facing the world in general and sport in particular. We are able to identify the nexus points through which various scenarios may come into being. Specifically, we believe that the nexus points that will mediate change include the global economy, technology and culture (or the activities of a few pivotal regions and nations along with their communication and value systems).

The nexus factors work on two levels. Like the process of globalisation, they manifest on a macro level, but are also fed by micro events, trends and understandings. Just as the slogan, 'think global, act local' suggests, the influence of nexus variables can be seen in broad brush strokes on the world canvas, but are made up of the activities of billions of anonymous artists. As a result, in Chapter 1, we discussed the economy in broad terms and in Chapter 5, we discussed it in reference to the service sector, including the shift towards what Jensen described as the Dream Society.

Similarly, in Chapter 1, the development of technology was examined as a driver of the future. While this might be almost axiomatic, as we argued in Chapter 6, it is when the application and expansion of the Internet is considered as a key point of leverage to achieve competitive advantage that the impact it has upon sport is squarely observed.

Finally, in Chapter 7, the influence of culture in the advancement of sport was explored with particular interest paid to its aspects which make the generic distribution and promotion of certain sports troublesome or even impossible. The macro manifestation of this culture conundrum remains the impact of certain prominent societies, civilisations, corporations and spokespersons that represent these entities on the development and direction of the rest of the world's value systems.

The purpose of this chapter is to bring together these ideas to form a coherent snapshot of current sport as well as to provide a platform for peering into the future. We begin by discussing some macro issues that come into play as a result of the three nexus variables, keeping in mind the material covered in Chapter 1, and then look at the effect of the same variables upon the sport world.

The Economic Nexus

Globalisation promises much in terms of economic growth and development. Unfortunately, as we have counselled, economic growth is clearly not the panacea for quality of life improvement for some regions of the world that are unlikely to capitalise on the opportunities that globalisation affords. Nevertheless, given that the inevitable winners of globalisation will be the developed nations and a handful of economically developing nations, one of the most powerful impetuses for rapid change will be economic growth. To that end, we must recognise that the progress of the global economy is a key uncertainty. In particular, we can identify several potential constraints for economic growth.

First, a shortage of energy supplies – mainly oil – would cause significant economic turbulence. Second, economic progress, political reform and financial regulation may not be embraced by developing nations with the vehemence that developed nations would like. Unless some emerging states become genuine players in globalisation, they will not survive the upheaval of even minor financial and currency hiccups, and capital will relocate back to the safety of developed markets, further widening the gap, and providing fewer export opportunities for everyone. Third, population crises will crush growth. Europe and Japan, for example, require massive additional numbers of workers, while the Middle East, India, Pakistan and China will face the economic burdens of unemployment and housing shortages. Finally, the United States may fade under the pressure of its prodigious trade deficit, bringing demand in the global economy down with it.

The Technology Nexus

Few of us are in doubt that technology will play a pivotal role in our lives and in the future of sport. How technology plays a role in the future of the world must be considered a key uncertainty. We have already noted how technology may develop, but it is still unclear to what extent the developments in technology will either benefit or disadvantage the people of the world. We may draw several continua to illustrate the possibilities.

First, it is conceivable that technology will become more accessible and more integrated into the lives of people in disadvantaged and developing nations. Improvements in communications, manufacturing, distribution, education and medicine may flow more freely. On the other hand, the internal political wrangling present in many developing nations may discourage the accessibility of technology for the masses. Worse, technological improvements could be applied in nuclear, biological or conventional weaponry.

Second, new technology will emerge and information about its use may flow freely, facilitating the development of extraordinary processes to help humankind in all aspects of life, from the repair of spinal injuries incurred in sport, to improving manufacturing efficiencies. Technology will also play a major role in shaping the nature of entertainment in the future, which can potentially provide greater opportunities and cater for a wider range of interests than ever before.

The other side of this coin, however, is that fringe groups and national governments may lack a full awareness of the wider economic, political, social, environmental, legal, cultural and moral impacts of their activities utilising advanced technologies. While it has also been noted that the use of technology such as computer networks for operational necessities like running complex transportation systems may be labour saving and ensure greater safety, an overreliance on such technology may in fact be a massive vulnerability for technologically advanced countries which are already targets of technological sabotage.

The Cultural Nexus

In addition to the key uncertainties that the global economy and technology present, it is also necessary to acknowledge the impact that significant changes in global cultural patterns and identity formation may have on the rest of the world and, as we shall argue shortly, on the future of sport. We shall examine the possibilities by focusing on what we view as the critical regions of the world in that regard: the Middle East and Asia.

In some ways it goes without saying that sport is largely driven by the activities and practices of North America and Western Europe where most of the (hyper)developed corporate sport nations are located. For that very reason, these regions do not present particularly uncertain environments in which sport may develop. Instead, we are interested here in those that may take radically different paths in the future.

As we noted in the first chapter, the globalisation outcomes for the Middle East are likely to be more negative than positive. The abundance of energy resources makes the region less likely to change to accommodate a perceived injection of Western values. Nevertheless, the power of globalisation to facilitate change by promising opportunity and economic progress can be compelling. The question that we cannot answer is the degree to which the Middle East and other Islamic states will form economic partnerships either on the basis of opportunity and mutual gain, or alternatively on the basis of religion and ideology. The former outcome presents some significant opportunities in terms of the introduction of Westernised forms of sport, whereas the latter may lead to ongoing tension, conflict and possibly war.

The role that China plays over the next few decades will prove pivotal to the future of the world order. Unfortunately, this role is packed with uncertainties and 'unknowables'. On the one hand, China is working hard to complete economic reforms that will see it flourish as a member of the World Trade Organisation (WTO) but, on the other hand, political inflexibility and territorial ambitions make it an ongoing target for Western consternation. India's future similarly affects the future of the world. Unlike China, however, India's technologically driven economic growth almost assures her a place amongst the winners of globalisation.

However, India's nuclear tensions with Pakistan and a severe over-population problem could undermine the economic progress that could have been achieved.

These drivers of change examined in Chapter 1 culminate in the nexus of key uncertainties, channelling an effect upon the future of sport.

The Near Future: The Next Five Years

We shall introduce the next stages of global sport by commenting on those trends presently in sport that we are confident will persist irrespective of the outcome of global forces over the next few years. However, we acknowledge that the breadth of these characteristics of future sport may be confined to some select, developed regions of the world.

Technology will continue to become more integrated into our societies. Technology will also become more pervasive in every element in life, from sport equipment to toasters. This pervasive influence will exacerbate the segregative impact of technology. The division between those who have the economic and social advantages of high-end technology will increase and advance the capitalistic gap that plagues technologically under-developed nations. Although the integration of technology will enhance the base through which it is experienced, it will also have a separative influence. Individuals will have less need to venture beyond their domestic residences to experience almost all aspects of life as it can be delivered in the comfort of home, particularly if that location will be their office as well. Isolation will be an outcome of technological advancement, despite its ability to transgress communication barriers. In particular, technology will become progressively more interactive. Technology will place specta-tors game-side when we remain at home, allow us to select alternative endings to films, to relive and reinvent legends of sport to compete with modern teams, stepping inside player rooms as one of them, and ultimately playing the game with them and influencing team strategy and positioning. Advances in technology already allow budding film-makers to shoot and edit feature-length films using digital video equip-ment. It is only a matter of time before celluloid and light is replaced in mainstream cinema by ones and zeros. George Lucas has successfully employed the top end of the highly popular and accessible digital technology, which is making filmmaking accessible to the personal computer owner. He used the Sony digital HD (high definition) format, which completely removed the need to use film. Every single frame (of which 24 appear per second) of *Star Wars Episode II: Attack of the Clones* had some form of digital effect or animation added to it, an exercise that is expensive and time-consuming using film. Lucas has made it clear that he will never use film again. The ultimate goal for film producers is just around the corner: eliminating the actors. *Final Fantasy* was the first feature film to be produced entirely using a computer (actors were used only for voices). Just how far away are we from eliminating athletes in favour of programmed images?

The future of entertainment will be dictated by our own insatiable appetite for vicarious experience. Principally we will be provided with what vast media conglomerates believe we will consume repeatedly. Already, the capitalist world's media is predominantly controlled by a handful of immense companies and their subsidiaries. They own television networks, radio stations, newspapers, magazines, film production companies, animation houses, Internet firms, telephone companies and music producers and distributors. AOL Time Warner may turn out to be the archetypal media-entertainment firm of the next decade. The remarkable horizontal integration that characterised the 1980s and 1990s will be overshadowed by a sweeping vertical integration that began seriously only five years ago. As we argued earlier, media conglomerates have virtual monopolies in every system of information distribution and are seeking reliable and lucrative content to fuel it. As we have observed earlier, the technological development and adoption rates of broadband technology in particular, will determine the medium-term success of the current rulers of the world's media. However, one thing is certain, sport will provide this content admirably.

What will characterise the 2000s and who will own the factors of production? The answer is that it will be the same firms that own the mechanisms of distribution. Already media companies own professional sport clubs. The next step will be the ownership of leagues, or the creation of new, media-driven super leagues. Does that sound familiar? Feeder leagues and clubs will be developed to provide an ongoing pool of talent to drive the leagues.

Largely, entertainment will become further customised and personalised; each stream of sport will blend seamlessly with other entertainment options. Presently, if you are so inclined, you can manage or coach your favourite stars, both current and retired, in impressively animated computer games. Shortly, the characteristics and statistics of each player will be available for the computer to access which, in combination with the next generation of graphics and computer simulated intelligence, will allow us to construct our own teams and realistically play them off. Similarly, computer generated images will act out our own screenplays, both in sport and outside. We shall modify performances with direction, adapt sets, props and lighting with a click, and manipulate camera coverage with choices of every angle and composition imaginable. Some of us will share our opuses with others and the Internet will provide the testing ground. Do you want Keanu Reaves as the star, or what about Sean Connery at 35? No problem. They can be downloaded from their agents' sites, for a modest royalty of course. What about your dream to see Julia Roberts as Scarlett O'Hara, or Rowan Atkinson as Dirty Harry? Better still, why not star in the film yourself? After all, your own digitised image is far less costly. You can use the same image of yourself that plays alongside Pele, Batistuta and Matthews. Entertainment and sport have become irrevocably interwoven. The maxim that drives the industry will be that everyone has his or her own needs and each sport entertainment experience will be unique.

Of course, this customised, technologically integrated, globalised sport product is at the core of sport in the near future. The predomination of services will continue to expand as trade barriers are removed, chiefly through the political power exerted by multinationals. E-commerce is inculcated but unsatisfying. Instant transactions are the norm; products and services must be delivered immediately for instant gratification. The experience economy has been transcended by the interactive s-economy.

The development of global sport will be grounded more in economic evolution than in its popularity. One of the pivotal factors in this evolution will be the recognition by large sport-business firms that their interaction with other economic entities is forcing them to synthesise their operations with these entities at different levels of product delivery. In essence, they will become cognisant that they are evolving together, in cohesion, rather than independently.

In the 1980s when total quality management (TQM) principles were commonly employed, techniques such as supplier certification were embedded in the fabric of business practice. The premise behind supplier certification was that it is more expensive in both costs and quality to consistently do business with the cheapest bidder. Businesses had learned that when they constantly changed suppliers in order to obtain the least expensive supplies or business inputs, be they products or services, the quality was so varied that it inevitably cost them more to maintain quality output; so they formed strategic alliances with their suppliers, construct-ing formalised arrangements where quality and price were rigidly regulated.

However, gradually, communications and computer technology began to revolutionise business processes. Computer manufacturing will ultimately mean that quality deviations will be effectively eliminated, but advances in computer technology mean that any firm can cross traditional market boundaries: markets will become accessible to players who had never entered those markets before. Moreover, communications technology (allied with more efficient and rapid distribution methods) will destroy traditional geographical barriers. National economies will be transcended. The world will see true globalised economic interaction. This is particularly the case with sport, as the product is so easily transportable to anywhere in the world where the requisite technology and infrastructure is present.

Some sport organisations will resist this market expansion. They will attempt to restrict and regulate their sport's trade, intervening in attempts to control distribution and maintain national order. Ultimately, however, they will succeed only in disadvantaging their own situation. The inexorable breakthrough has already arrived in the form of the European Union. Recognising their vulnerability, Asian sport will begin to reduce sport trade barriers.

As regions and sport organisations clamour for alliances, not just within their local circumstances but also within a global economic entity, small sports will get crushed into even more parochial and marginalised recreational activities. Those remaining will have forged alliances to protect themselves, leaving only a handful of enterprises in each sport market segment. The added resource base of the well-positioned sport enterprises will lead to the development of the first mega-clubs.

Survival will necessitate commercial awareness. Mega-clubs will be owned or at least controlled by even larger, content-driven media conglomerates, which will in turn own the feeder clubs (or talent farms) that will provide player and revenue sources. The mega-clubs will operate independently, but will still operate at the discretion of the media money-brokers. In this sense, they can allow functional independence, but capitalise on structural interdependence.

For example, while club A may make a profit from supplying company B, and are both owned by a single corporation, the amount of profit will be determined by the corporation in an attempt to maximise earnings all round. Thus corporations will counter the effects of bureaucracy by allowing and encouraging independent management, but retaining a common strategic direction. This, of course, will be increasingly possible as a result of technological advancements.

People will always play sport or games, just as they did in ancient civilisations and just as they do today. Will sport grow? The answer is yes and no. Some sports will assume an ongoing, pervasive place in the social fabric of entertainment. They will grow because they were already popular, both from historical evolution and from their spectator-friendly nature. Pushed ruthlessly by the media, fewer and fewer sports will receive greater and greater coverage. Mega-clubs and leagues will emerge which will be owned or co-financed by the media conglomerates that market them so fiercely. They will stand as organisations that stimulate massive quantities of economic activity. They will be global in appeal and, at the very least, hemispherical in competition. Additional leagues will spring up focusing on the same few sports. Meanwhile, other professional leagues and clubs less favoured by the media will sink further into obscurity. Ironically, while more sports than ever will exist to cater for a diverse range of participation needs, from extreme sports to bocce, they will find it next to impossible to compete with sport's global monsters. To summarise, in the near future we can look forward to customised, interactive, technologised sport, inevitably limited to a small bundle of globalised, core sport products generating extraordinary amounts of economic activity. But what about the medium and long term?

The DreamSport Society: The Next 15 Years

The matrix contained in Table 8.1 summarises the direction sport is currently taking towards 'the next level', by linking elements of the Dream Society with fan types and showing how they interact through each of the three nexus variables. The outcomes are categories of what we have termed, with due credit to Rolf Jensen, *DreamSport Society*, the characteristics of which are discussed shortly. We shall show how each of these DreamSport Society constituents will provide opportunities and obstacles to sport enterprises. We should note before we proceed any further that this society would largely be confined to developed nations. A natural link with Table 7.1 may be observed.

We ended the last chapter convinced that consumers' needs are changing society toward the dream of consumption, based upon the fulfilment of emotional needs within an appropriate cultural context rather than material acquisition. But the Dream Society is only a polish to the lens through which we might scrutinise the motivations and behaviours of sports fans. The Stewart–Smith fan model we presented in Chapter 2 gives us a solid basis for demonstrating how the world of sport is likely to develop within the context of a society that increasingly demands emotional satisfaction as an outcome of sport consumption, but also faces a number of key uncertainties that will unquestionably affect the dynamics of the world order. Because it represents the next stage of the sport industry's evolution, it is worth a commentary on each.

Table 8.1 The next phase of sport business in the global marketplace

Dream Society	Fan Link	Economic Nexus	Technological Nexus	Cultural Nexus	DreamSport Society
Adventure	Theatregoer/Actor	Entertainment value	Interactive entertainment	Parochial entertainment	Sport Entertainment
Together	Champ Follower	'Catchment' size	Ubiquity and success of team/heroes	Confined heroes	Sport Fantasy
Care	Aficionado	Sports' intrinsic value	Game quality	Local sports	Sport Quality
Who Am I	Passionate Partisan	Strength of identity	Distribution of identity	Tribal identity	Sport Identity
Peace of Mind	Reclusive Partisan	Sporting moments	Access to 'bandwagon'	Traditional links	Sport Tradition
Convictions	Community Partisan	Exploitation and fairness	Choice	Community citizenship	Sport Conscience

Sport Entertainment

The desire to satisfy the emotional need for adventure, as we explained in the last chapter, can be seen in the escalation of activities such as bungee jumping and extreme sports. Important questions remain, however, as to the nature of the individual seeking this fulfilment and the impact of the nexus variables on its delivery.

In the first instance, the need for adventure is epitomised by the sport theatregoer who attends sporting contests with the express desire for entertainment and spectacle. The difference between the current theatre-goer and the theatregoer of the future is a reflection of a transition towards emotional expression from the platform of pure but segregated entertainment. Put another way, 'new' theatregoers care more about being entertained by satisfying their need for adventure than sitting on the sidelines and enjoying a pleasurable vicarious experience. Current sports fans can observe a sporting performance, but the degree to which they can satisfy an emotional need is limited by the natural boundaries of the mechanisms through which they are watching. This is not to say that theatregoers necessarily want to be *in* the game, but in order to realise their emotional peak they must have some influence *on* the game. As this is impossible in a practical sense, they instead require an interactive *presence* to best fill their emotional needs.

From an economic perspective, and further to our discussion in Chapter 5, the ability of sporting enterprises to manipulate their services from product units suitable for packaged consumption into customised experiences that meet emotional expectations is the critical success factor. The risk is that economic pressures will force intermediaries such as the media to continue to commodify and re-sell sport products, and in so doing remove the emotional elements until there is nothing left but a cold, contrived product shell that is lifeless and uninteresting rather like a can of beans or a bar of soap that will never stimulate radical emotional reactions in consumers the way that raw sport can. Sports fans such as theatregoers, fitting into this Sport Entertainment category of the Dream-Sport Society, will therefore be forced to make ongoing judgments about the entertainment value of sport within these changing parameters. If economic forces get out of hand, then inevitably disaffected theatregoers will seek alternative devices to satisfy their need for adventure and performance.

Alternatively, in the event that these economic factors do not force sport services to become faceless, mechanised products, the evolution of technology may provide greater opportunity for sports fans, and theatregoers in particular, to achieve an emotional connection with sport hitherto confined to players, coaches and a handful of live spectators. Interactivity is the key. Technology that facilitates a spectator's emotional connection to the sport product by engaging them in ways they have never experienced before will triumph, and will ultimately revolutionise sport delivery. We have talked about the various possibilities the Internet affords, along with the potential of digital broadcast technologies in Chapters 5 and 6.

The greatest challenge for sport enterprises will be in the provision of culturally satisfying emotional experiences to the adventurously-inclined theatregoer. In this sense, the new theatregoer will insist that sport is not only entertaining, but also fits their specific parochial circumstances. The value placed upon entertainment, interactive or not, will revolve around a culturally sensitive delivery; it will not be enough simply to show a great game. As we have shown in exploring the limited following of football (soccer) in countries such as the United States and Australia, the cultural disposition of the theatregoer is vastly – and dangerously – under-recognised. Similarly, the ability of theatrical 'sports' (such as professional wrestling) to thrive in places such as Asia and South America will be determined by its capacity to adjust its narrative to entice local audiences to become emotionally attached, and subsequently entertained.

Sport Fantasy

Achieving the emotional need which Jensen described as togetherness revolves around products that can bring consumers together. Naturally, most sport teams and some events capitalise on this emotional bond that sport can provide better than any other products, including beer, fast cars and film. At the heart of this emotional requirement is the desire for comradeship and direction. In other words, the interest in sport – whether conscious or not – is more about the other fans that sport attracts, rather than the game itself. This can be seen in participation-based events such as University Games, the Gay Games and the Masters Games. However, only a comparative minority of people seeking to fulfil this need for togetherness do so directly through involvement in sport. Most attempt to meet this need through 'champ-following', particularly in team sports. The new champ followers are different in that they select winning teams to support because they provide a convenient opportunity to experience the pleasure of togetherness that only success can deliver.

Champ followers, as we explained in Chapter 2, are principally motivated to watch sport because they have an interest in a specific team or club that is winning. This is, of course, the iceberg's tip, because their unseen motivation is more concerned with finding likeminded groups to share the experience and satisfy the emotional need to feel part of a winning community. To that end, champ followers rely on their loyalty to a successful team to ensure that they can predictably receive a dose of togetherness to reinforce their personal winning nature. The interesting fact is that these individuals are reluctant to watch sport by themselves. New champ followers will increasingly look for opportunities to share the emotional experience of sport consumption with other likeminded individuals and groups, to share around their winning affiliation and reinforce to themselves that the world is viewing them as a winner.

Through the economic slipstream, new champ followers may be delighted at the expansion of their team's recognition across the world. This means that they can find kindred spirits almost anywhere they travel who will instantly recognise that they are winners, just like them. On the other hand, this can leave champ followers cynical, and risks them diluting their sense of importance. Any economic stimulus that decreases the champ followers' expression of demonstrating themselves to be winners or, worse still, makes it more difficult to choose when the team is worth following, will damage their interest in sport consumption. Thus, the 'catchment' zone in which the champ follower becomes part of a group is all-important and highly sensitive. For example, merely sitting in a stadium with other sports fans is not enough. Champ followers must derive a sense of importance from belonging to the group; the others in the group must care about their presence and recognise them as winners, just like the team they are supporting. Channelling sport exclusively through pay-television is therefore a certain way to ensure that new champ followers will find it more difficult to access the groups they need in order to reach satisfaction. No one can envy their winning side or listen to their witticisms about other teams over lunch in the office if they have no audience. The economic environment must give the champ follower the opportunity to jump on the bandwagon in the first place, and then bask in the glory that team victory provides. If there is no opportunity to share this with other 'winners' then the attractiveness of sport consumption is diminished.

There is a similar danger in the introduction of new technologies. The sort of technology that the theatregoer might find irresistible might isolate champ followers and reduce their ability to achieve satisfaction. On the other hand, using technology to increase the ubiquity of a team or player will give champ followers a feeling that togetherness is never far away, and neither is recognition that their team, their players, their coach are winners, just as they are. In this way, the exchange about the team's performance with a co-worker at the coffee machine in the office provides a useful reminder to the new champ follower that winning is just around the corner, that the last failure was merely an anomaly. Inevitably, technology is the enemy of the champ follower as no team can always win, and technology ensures that no loss goes unnoticed. Eventually, the champ follower will find a new team, sport or hero that can deliver a winning feeling. That is why this category has been named Sport Fantasy: the fantasy is vicarious and is associated with finding a winning team with which to be linked. This public association will encourage feelings of comradeship amongst likeminded winners.

Like all categories, the boundaries are not necessarily concrete. The need for togetherness can be found in other fan types and new champ followers are not exclusively interested in meeting their emotional need for togetherness. However, the Sport Fantasy component of the DreamSport Society will be affected by cultural variables more severely than most other categories. The main issue is the nature of the champ to be followed. Strong cultural circumstances can ensure that the champ remains consistent with local cultural expectations. In contrast, for others with fewer cultural barriers, the return of Michael Jordan has been all that was needed for New Zealand basketball fans to renew a passionate interest in the National Basketball Association (NBA) and switch from Chicago to Washington.

Sport Quality

The Sport Quality segment of the DreamSport Society is a combination of the expression of care and the intrinsic enjoyment of the sport product being consumed. Sport organisations are full of opportunities for members and fans to demonstrate that they care. Volunteers are the backbone of club-based sport systems such as those in Europe and Australasia. The composition of the Sport Quality segment reflects a slightly new role for the sporting aficionado who has traditionally been interested in sport because it possesses the intrinsic aesthetics that they find alluring, or even addictive. In the DreamSport Society, new aficionados are no longer satisfied with their position as semi-detached sports lovers. The visual pleasure of watching a good game is not enough as other competing products offer more than quality skills on show, seeking to reach consumers on an emotional level. New aficionados want the quality sport experience to reach a deeper level, which allows them to fulfil their need to show they care intensely about their sport and the skill with which it is played. For athletes to appeal to this segment, they need to care as well. Care about the people and communities that allow them to reap the benefits of their superior athletic performances. The move towards athletes being viewed and positioned as 'good corporate citizens' is of particular interest to the celebrity marketing industry. Sport performers will only continue to earn their sometimes outrageous salaries if they show their fans they care about them. Sometimes this comes natural to athletes, for example, to tennis ace Patrick Rafter, who has set up his own charitable foundation, the Cherish the Children foundation, and is the patron of several others. Other athletes may need the assistance of their agents to select appropriate charities to support and donate parts of their earnings to, in order to convince the public that they do care about the communities that they benefit so much from.

From the Sport Quality perspective, the influence of the economy can be significant. Trends and pressures that affect the intrinsic quality of the sport itself will determine the commitment of the Sport Quality aficionado. For example, where economic imperatives drive the amount of money associated with sport and force the evolution of new 'elite of elite' leagues, and also foster the development of super-athletes to perform in these competitions, the Sport Quality segment will happily consume sport. However, where these pressures erode the quality of the game, or manipulate it to an extent that the pure element of the game is lost, then the segment will react unfavourably. This segment will make assessments about the value of the sport's quality, mediated only by their ability to fulfil their need to demonstrate that they care about this quality.

Technology may facilitate this expression of care, from interactive fora with players to talk-back radio. Some of the Sport Quality segment will be able to meet their needs through involvement in the grassroots of sport, by way of volunteer coaching or managing. In addition, technology may aid the quality of play in many sports. Biomechanical analysis, improved nutritional supplementation and for some, more effective drugs will help players reach the next level of performance. However, as always, technology may overwhelm some sports or curtail their aesthetics. Choosing camera angles and listening to sideline banter does not affect a sport's actual quality of performance.

Should culture play a strong role in a country's experience of sport, the Sport Quality segment may find that they can reach emotional fulfilment through involvement in local sports. They may be able to enjoy the sport's unique qualities which distinguish it from imported sports.

Sport Identity

Sport fans have a history of eliciting a sense of identity and meaning from their association with sport teams and clubs. The Sport Identity segment of the DreamSport Society combines the emotional need for identity, (which Jensen refers to as the 'who-am-I' need) with the strength of conviction held by the passionate partisan. The Sport Identity segment will seek the emotional satisfaction of a strong sense of belonging and identity, married to the unwavering loyalty of the passionate fan. At the superficial level the Sport Identity segment comprises focused sport watchers, keenly observant about the state of the game and their team, and compelled by the most trivial team-related information. However, at the deeper level, this segment is looking for self-definition. At this deeper level, that search is answered by a close affiliation with a team or club, where a personal identity can be moulded indistinguishably by a club or a supporter group. As a result, the Sport Identity group members define themselves in a way that is consistent with their association with a team of choice.

From an economic viewpoint, the Sport Identity consumers of the future are sensitive but worth a special effort. In order to meet their needs they are quite prepared to spend significant sums of money in pursuit of ongoing self-identification through the purchase of sports spectating services such as tickets and pay-television subscriptions, memorabilia, merchandise, endorsed products such as club credit cards or home loans, and product extensions such as junk food and beer. However, they can be easily alienated. Like any of the segments, economic forces that interfere with the identification process are harmful to this consumer. To that end, if economic pressures come between clubs and the Sport Identity consumers, and reduce their ability to derive the emotional satisfaction that comes with identification, then the sport industry will ultimately lose the economic benefits that this group delivers. For example, when fans are locked out of venues in favour of corporate ticket holders and hospitality services, there will be a distancing of fans from their beloved club, and a consequent weakening of their identity. This is why, of course, some 'hard-core' or passionate partisan sports fans feel so disillusioned when their players are transferred to another club or leave for more money. It also helps to explain why the collapse or merger of a club is so devastating; it is because the fan's personal identity, self-esteem, ego and psyche are mixed up in the fortunes of the club. That is why some fans say that if the club were to die, part of them would die as well. The interesting counterpoints to this 'negative' sort of commodification of sport are the opportunities that economic forces can stimulate. As identity is at the core for this fan segment, its ultimate form can arrive unexpectedly as a direct consequence of economic wealth creation. The number of professional sporting clubs that have 'gone public' in share flotation is growing. Although, in some cases, this move is a reflection of a club's ambition to milk as much money as it can from its assets, it can also offer a unique opportunity to the Sport Identity segment to genuinely own a part of their own identity, irrespective of the investment wisdom of such a purchase.

The future might bring some challenges to the Sport Identity segment via forces other than the pecuniary. Technological progress offers this segment a considerable benefit in terms of access to the beloved team and, as a result, additional chances to reinforce their character and 'top up' their emotional connection. The distribution of this character can also provide some grounds for satisfaction. It is a vicarious yet powerful fame in which fans may bask as their glorious club is beamed across the world. The dangers of technology are similar to those associated with economic influences. It is essential not to get between the Sport Identity segment and their bond with the sport or club. Technological developments can be perilous because they have the potential to compel interaction with the game by giving more choices to the viewer, or to separate the viewer from the game with endless and unemotional statistics, replays, camera angles and cheerleaders. The Sport Identity fans are not necessarily looking for a spectacle; they are seeking an experience that engages them in the reflection of self-recognition and renewal. Technology can polish that mirror.

Understandably, the cultural nexus has great authority in the identity-making process. Sport and clubs must align with the cultural values of fans in order to appeal to their sense of self-recognition. In other words, fans peer into the sport mirror in the hope of seeing themselves in a different form. Unlike a mirror in the fun park, this one yields a kinder reflection that takes into account the cultural characteristics held dear by the voyeur. Culturally 'rich' sports have the opportunity to cement a relationship with the Sport Identity segment because they can provide them with a unique sense of belonging that begins with a cultural pride, increases with a sport interest and peaks in a club affiliation.

Sport Tradition

The Sport Tradition segment is more nebulous than many of the others. The emotional need to be met is more complex in that it is difficult to define in terms of the tangible features of sport. We have discussed many needs which can be fulfilled through sport, but none is quite so tenuous as that associated with the 'peace of mind' which arrives through reminiscing about better times in the past. Of course, history is important to all sports fans, but especially the Sport Tradition segment, which combines the 'Peace of Mind' element of Jensen's Dream Society that focuses on the good feelings and the 'old-time' values that the consumption of some products can elicit with the reclusive partisan sport fan who will come back to fandom from the bench when the right set of circumstances seize their interests. The Sport Tradition segment is therefore sophisticated in the way they assess the value of sport watching. Their emotional interest is engaged when sport can offer them a chance to re-ignite past values, bask in a new winning streak that reminds them of the glory days, or inspire them with confidence and trust.

The quest to make money out of sport, including taking advantage of great historical events can provide some opportunities for the Sport Tradition segment both to spend their money and to relive past glory. The key to their emotional fulfilment lies in a sport or club's ability to satisfy that sense of 'specialness' that being 'on the bandwagon' can deliver. That is why they see the economic forces that lead to the corporatisation of sport as confusing. On the one hand, the corporatisation can disenfranchise the fan and take sport away from that special traditional base that is held so important. On the other hand, corporatisation (in the form of corporate hospitality, for example) can offer some of the special treatment that the Sport Tradition segment needs to satisfy their sense of personal service and value. However, most fans cannot afford the salubrious pleasures of corporate dining and instead lament the loss of the good old days when they could walk into the club bar or social club and everyone knew their name and was willing to have a drink and talk about that remarkable season some time last century. They now view much of sport as an exploitation of an amateur ideal, and return to the fold less often and with less fervour. The successful sport organisation of the future must be able to offer these fans a special reason to get involved again.

The rise in technological involvement in sports is generally unwelcome to the traditionalist seeking psychological comfort in their affiliation with a sport or club. Nevertheless, technology can sometimes remind them that the bandwagon has arrived without them realising it, and that they should remount. Again, the pervasiveness and penetration of technology in sport will be a deciding factor as regards the satisfaction of this segment. The Sport Tradition segment may, ironically, be re-introduced to the sport or club through technology, but may ultimately be unwilling to submit to technological innovations, rather like a grumpy grandparent who refuses to learn how to set the videocassette recorder. Technology and innovation can also deprive them of the personal touches that sport can provide, such as the suburban stadium that is replaced by the soulless but architecturally stunning, multi-purpose venue, or the old memorabilia-filled pub or bar that was sold to make way for 'yuppie' apartments.

Those sports or clubs that have the opportunity to capitalise upon the unusual features of their traditional culture without completely avoiding the juggernaut of economic 'progress' and technological integration will succeed in attracting fans. With some admittedly serious exceptions such as the wages strike, Major League Baseball in the USA has managed to continually attract reclusive partisans to the game, in the normal cycles in which they take intermittent interest. It is the sports and clubs that no longer have the ability to awaken the reclusive partisan which will struggle in the future. Unless they can find ways of assimilating the past values that the Sport Tradition segment of the future find irresistible into their activities, they will fail to keep them out of dormancy. In many ways, cultural pressures can give sports and clubs the motivation to do this by capitalising upon idiosyncratic traditional practices.

Sport Conscience

The final segment we are using to help focus on the future of sport has been named Sport Conscience. The name is a reflection of the emotional requirements of this group, as they are more interested in the broader picture than they are necessarily with sports or clubs themselves. The important element is a sincere desire that something worthwhile is accomplished which affects people at a greater level than merely the enjoyment of sport participation or spectatorship. There is a moral conviction at work. Allied to this there is a sense of community, which we have encapsulated into a new addition to the Stewart–Smith fan typology, and have named the community partisan. The community partisan is concerned with the needs of others in their association with sport. In particular, this fan attends sport to please others and to contribute to the community interest. These are the mothers and fathers who bring the half-time tea or oranges, provide the taxis and coach the team. These are also the individuals who turn up to the local game because the team 'needs the support', or because they view it as a manifestation of their community pride.

The combination of the community partisan and the need for some conviction to be realised can be seen in the Sport Conscience segment. Their principal emotional necessities revolve around feelings of moral righteousness, usually achieved through benefits to the community, or at least to people other than themselves. These people use sport in the way some people use charity, to alleviate guilt and to sustain a sense of personal rectitude. They will purchase only the shoes that were manufactured in 'appropriate' circumstances, consume healthy, organically grown foods and attend sporting contests and events that show themselves to be worthy community contributors.

Given these boundaries, the Sport Conscience segment shies away from any sport, event or club that has been corrupted by the evils of commercialism. They will not accept the exploitation of fans or participants. Instead they are attracted by events which bolster their sense of measure and justice. Events such as the Gay Games and the Masters Games, and sports with definitive moral philosophies about issues such as racism and gender inequality, are attractive to this segment irrespective of the Sport Conscience fan's sexuality, age or gender. Although generally suspicious of sponsors, they can at times view sponsorship in terms of favourable corporate citizenship, and are prepared to purchase products that are affiliated to 'appropriate' sports and activities. Thus the economic imperative can be overlooked when it is seen to work in favour of the 'little guy', instead of being used to pay those 'egotistical', overpromoted 'louts and bimbos' of professional sport.

The direction technology takes is less important to the Sport Conscience segment than how it is used: the operative word is choice. Where there remains choice, there is also the opportunity to support consciousness-raising activities and events, such as those promoting health awareness or those that are community based. Technology can raise awareness, but it can also feed the exploitation of sport for economic advantage.

The cultural nexus gives us a unique insight into the disposition of the Sport Conscience segment. As they are susceptible to community building activities and are seeking at the deeper level to support their need to make a moral statement, or at least take a moral position, they can become quite passionate about sport when it reflects these important issues. Sport that is inculcated with significant community and cultural meaning will automatically be more attractive to the Sport Conscience segment.

Sport Societies in the Global Marketplace

The previous section elaborated on the fan types introduced in Chapter 2 and employs Jensen's vision of the imminent marketplace designed to satisfy the emotional needs of its consumers. But we do not want to suggest that sport will rise to meet this new societal obligation and proceed no further, and neither would we wish to imply that the needs of some sport consumers are simpler, while others remain more sophisticated still. What we do want to reinforce is that presently society's dominant products and services, as Jensen suggests, are moving from a more materialistic focus to one that revolves around the satisfaction of emotional needs. From this basis we spent some time exploring the new segments that are emerging in the world of sport and the factors that influence them. This may be seen as the next stage of sport's evolution throughout the developed world. The strength of this perspective is that it helps us focus on the development of the sport product to meet the evolving needs of the sport's consumer. The problem, however, is that this only gives us a snapshot of the dominant shift, the slow advancement of 'progress'. It does not fully capture the capacity that sport has as a vehicle for fulfilling the needs of human beings, or the idiosyncrasies of certain groups of people when they employ sport in culturally unique and unexpected ways, and neither does it account for the characteristics of developing and underdeveloped regions.

The important realisation is that every sport and sport experience has the ability to meet a range of needs that can vary considerably between nations, groups and individuals. The fact that the global pressures are such that over the next decade or two we shall witness the shift towards the DreamSport Society (particularly in Westernised sport nations), while highly relevant, does not give us the full picture! The full picture encapsulates what sport has been in society and what it can become but, more importantly than that, it shows how sport can transcend the boundaries of the global marketplace and its dominant features. In other words, we are talking about a model that can be interpreted on two levels. At the first level, we must acknowledge that each category we will explore can be manifested during a sport experience. A sport participant or observer can experience the tribal elements right through to the spiritual during any interaction. This model, therefore, represents a continuum of sport experience. However, at the second level, we use the model to explain how a critical mass of certain experience expectations from sport can entrench a society within a particular element. It reflects the fact that sport can be one of the most powerful vehicles humans have ever created to satisfy their needs and achieve personal development. Table 8.2 provides such a holistic overview. (The contents of the matrix are discussed in the next section.)

The argument that we are forming revolves around the assumption that sport has the capacity, at least theoretically, to meet different needs at different levels for different people. This notion is consistent with the typology we presented earlier in this chapter that was primarily concerned with the next iteration of sport. Because we see the DreamSport Society as the next dominant stage of sport, we ventured into its nuances in some detail. However, now we move to a larger stage, further from the confines of time and trend.

Six sport societies are identified in Table 8.2: Tribal, Pleasure, Gratification, Dream, Imagination and Spiritual. The reader should quickly see that the Dream Society, or what we have extrapolated to form the DreamSport Society, sits on the fourth tier. Immediately below this is the Gratification Society. This position effectively represents the paradigm that is currently prevailing in Western nations. It is manifested by the attempt to accumulate material wealth or satisfy materially based desires. We live in the 'I want' society, and sport, like any other product, attempts to give us what we want before we run out of patience. To that end, the most important aspect of sport is that it captures consumers' attention. It is one thing having a high-quality sport product, but it is another thing to wrestle consumers' attention away from the instant gratification that so many competing products offer for long enough to show them that the sport is worth experiencing. Fans and participants are treated as little more than commodities or assets to be bought, sold, manipulated, exploited and sometimes rewarded. The major driver is therefore economic in nature. The expectation is that sport consumers need to be cajoled with promotional deals, mega-stars, cheerleaders and spectacle. After all, sport is not about the game, it is about 'me' and what I can get out of it. Sport in the Gratification Society is, in a word, a product.

We are in the grip of the Gratification Society, which has been spelt out in some detail during the course of this book, particularly in Chapter 4. Along with Jensen's ideas, we have predicted that society – and sport, of course – will gradually cultivate the desire for emotional satisfaction where the dominant level will be the DreamSport Society. If we were to take a step backwards for a moment, we might observe that humanity has evolved from the Pleasure and Tribal societies when it comes to the role of sport. As we detailed in Chapter 2, sport originated as a community activity that was designed to meet the practical need for the development of skills associated with hunting and fighting, as well as social, human

Table 8.2 Sport societies

Sport Society	Needs Satisfied	Sport Captures Your ...	Fans/Participants As ...	What Is Important	Major Driver	Sport Is ...
TRIBAL	Practical/Social	Community	Members	Involvement	Culture	Identification
PLEASURE	Physical	Body	Actors	Fun	Culture	Game
GRATIFICATION	Material	Attention	Commodities	Me	Economy	Product
DREAM	Emotional	Beliefs	Dreamers	Achievement	Technology	Satisfaction
IMAGINATION	Psychological	Psyche	Artists	Creativity	Technology	Inspiration
SPIRITUAL	Spiritual	Soul	Monks	Resolution	Culture	Meaning

interaction needs. At this time sport, or the equivalent informal games, were about community consolidation and involvement. Being involved as a member of the community was important because it defined members as part of a social system, however abstract and underdeveloped it might have been by modern standards. The parochial cultural standards of the time and of the group were unquestionably the primary mediators of physical activity.

The Pleasure Society developed concomitantly with the Tribal Society, but outlasted it to form the next dominant stage. Although society has grown out of this stage to a large extent, especially when it comes to global professional sports, the intrinsic pleasure that sport participation and viewing can provide is still pivotal to the lives of some individuals and communities. The need is essentially a physical one, where the individual behaves as an actor in the performance, driven by the sheer fun of playing what is not a product, but a game. Like the Tribal Society, the Pleasure Society is strongly affected by cultural norms, expectations and boundaries that collectively determine what individuals think is fun.

Jumping ahead in time to speculate about future societies, we can build on the Dream concept that begins with emotional realisation. Like the way that the Tribal and Pleasure societies evolved together, but with one eventually becoming more dominant than the other, the Dream and Imagination societies can be seen to overlap. The difference is that the Imagination Society is more concerned with the balance of the psyche rather than the actualisation of an emotional need. It is the difference between wanting to feel loved and being in a loving relationship; the difference between being a club member in order to feel a sense of belonging and knowing who you are in the first place. Sport in this society is a mechanism for individuals to explore themselves and their psyche. Sport provides a canvas upon which the imagination can paint a portrait. It encourages a sense of creativity and passion in the participation or following of sport, but not with blind loyalty, 'one-eyed' support or 'groupthink'. Sport becomes a device of inspiration where the individual or group can challenge their limitations, share growth experiences and find their place in the world. It can be another apparatus for psychological balance by helping consumers to seek meaning in personal experience and reflect upon their commitments, values and beliefs. Sporting participation or experience is akin to artistic or musical introspection. Technological innovation, through new avenues of experiencing and reflecting upon sport, may prove important in escalating consumer expectations from emotional fulfilment to psychological nourishment.

The pinnacle of sport's ability to fulfil the needs of human beings can be encapsulated in the Spiritual Society, which builds upon each of the previous levels to culminate in a society wherein sport can be a vehicle for the ultimate self-realisation. We are not referring to the religious fervour with which sport is worshipped, the genuflection that takes place before sport heroes, or even the stadium as the 'new' cathedral. The spiritual dimension is one that is manifested through the participation or experience of sport, like serious martial arts enthusiasts who claim that their activities are more art than sport, and that the philosophy behind the art is more important than its technical execution. The Spiritual Society is characterised by consumers who want products that will help them define not just who they are in terms of mind and body, but who they are beyond their mind and body, within the vast, esoteric universal order. The demand from consumers for this type of product can already be seen in the proliferation of spiritual self-help resources on the market, but the supply side is still firmly rooted in the Gratification Society which views the consumer's need for instant spiritual fulfilment as yet another opportunity to exploit for financial benefits. Nevertheless, although potentially decades away, the Spiritual Sport Society will recognise the need for sport to offer a meaning beyond the trivial and the tribal. Coming full circle, cultural forces offer some scope in leading society to this eventuality.

It is not so much that any level is eclipsed by the next, but rather that each level tends to subsume the previous and change the orientation. This is why we can still see the manifestation of the Tribal and Pleasure societies in our present mode of experiencing sport. In reading the descriptions of the sport societies, it should occur to the reader that some of the needs are repeated, at least in crude ways, within each of the DreamSport categories. That is because the varying nature of sports fans and participants that were linked with the model give each one a unique manifestation within the DreamSport Society. It is further reinforced that sport can appeal to the range of human needs, but is restricted by societal boundaries. For example, the need for identification can be seen in the DreamSport typology, which reflects a link to the past. However, the DreamSport Society does not contain enough consumers who are convinced that they can achieve spiritual development through involvement in sport. The link to the distant future is tenuous and yet to be embraced, whereas there will always be groups and individuals who have never developed from older dominant societal sport roles, or who want to return to them despite current trends. The ultimate test for sport organisations in the future will be their ability to offer as many levels as possible to their consumers.

Global Sport Scenarios: The Next 50 Years

We have argued that the drivers of change or globalisation will converge through the nexus of uncertainties that will determine the fate of the world and of sport. Our goal in this final section is to make some cautious and some radical predictions about the most likely scenarios for the future. We have named the four scenarios Virtuous, Vicious, Regional and Cultural sport globalisation. Table 8.3 summarises some of the characteristics of these alternative future sport scenarios, particularly as they apply to the societies just presented.

Virtuous sport globalisation

In this first scenario, the majority of the world benefits from the effects of globalisation. Information flows freely, technology is used to improve quality of life, and emerging nations gain opportunities to advance their economic status and political stability, control their populations and manage natural resources. Technological innovation is inexpensive and accessible, while conflict is minimal. Although this best-case scenario proposes a positive impact of globalisation, it is unreasonable to expect that all regions of the world will be victors. Even with technological options, economic opportunity and cultural liberalisation, it is almost impossible to conceive that there will not remain large populations in sub-Saharan Africa, the Middle East and Asia that suffer from marginalisation and rampant poverty.

Future sport will thrive in this scenario. Accessible technology will facilitate spectatorship and cultural liberalisation will open hitherto untapped markets to sporting products and services. Economic progress will drive sporting infrastructure development, and hallmark events will be attracted to new parts of the world. World and regional professional leagues will flourish. The sport sector will expand radically to meet the demands of huge entertainment-starved populations.

With the technological and economic nexus being kind to the world, encouraging progress, cooperation and innovation, the pathway opens for the DreamSport and even Imagination societies to take hold and flourish. If we dare to conceive that these societies become entrenched, it may be reasonable to hope that they may even provide a springboard into a Spiritual Sport Society. The winners of this form of globalisation will not only be the Western world as it desperately attempts to sink its teeth further into some of the emerging markets of the world, such as Asia, but

Table 8.3 Global sport scenarios

Scenario	Major Characteristics	Most Influential Nexus	Dominant Society	Winners (opportunities to...)	(Global) Sport is ...
Virtuous Sport Globalisation	Information flow, equality, balance, stability, innovation, sharing	Technology-Economy	Pleasure/Imagination with a touch of Spiritual	Most	Diverse
Vicious Sport Globalisation	Mass dominance, inequality, power and control with money, little cooperation	Economy-Technology	Gratification/Dream	Wealthy and dominant	Narrow and elite
Regional Sport Globalisation	Economic alliances formed for security and competitiveness	Economy	Gratification/Dream	(Those who can enter or form) new markets	Clustered
Cultural Sport Globalisation	Alliances based on ethnic, religious or ideological similarity	Culture	Tribal/Gratification	(Those who can provide or form) culturally aligned activities	Ethnic

also those developing regions which have yet to form the capability of exporting their sporting products. Nevertheless, the sport marketplace will continually expand. For some sports, leagues and clubs, the effects of this 'new' world order will mean unprecedented exposure and perhaps even popularity. The sport industry will be able to celebrate its diversity. We estimate that the chances of this scenario coming to fruition are about 5 per cent.

Vicious sport globalisation

Vicious globalisation assumes that the elite will survive and prosper, but the majority of the world's population, who of course reside in emerging nations, will fail to experience any of the benefits of their wealthy counterparts. These emerging nations will succumb to terrible resource scarcities arising from uncontrollable population explosions. Technology will not be accessible to emerging nations, and the little that is will be costly, outdated and misused. Economically, the world will be divided into distinct leaders (the 'haves') and the distinct followers (the 'have nots'), with little prospect of one becoming the other. Conflicts will escalate and wealthy nations will avoid involvement unless it affects their resources and interest, such as oil or strategic geography.

Future sport will continue to develop admirably in the handful of wealthy nations, but will degenerate and inexorably be extinguished in those countries whose economic progress has reversed into survival mode. Markets that presented wonderfully opportunistic possibilities (such as parts of Asia and the subcontinent) will retreat, hidden away and preoccupied with domestic concerns and uninterested in entertainment options and capital investment in sporting infrastructure.

The Gratification Society will live on for some time longer, punctuated by periodic shifts in the delivery mechanisms provided by technological innovation. It will, sooner or later, give way to the DreamSport Society, as a critical mass of consumers seek to extend their gratification to their emotional needs. The 'global' sport industry will largely be confined to North America and Europe. The largest sports will become larger, the largest companies will take stronger and stronger strangleholds over the sport product and all its peripherals. There will be opportunities of course, but they will mostly fall into the hands of those with the power and infrastructure to seize them. In short, this scenario is a current trend projection. We believe the likely chance of its arrival is about 60 per cent.

Regional sport globalisation

In this scenario, in response to the pressures of globalisation, geographic regions will band together to form vast economic alliances that will improve their market power and collective bargaining. The EU, NAFTA and ASEAN style agreements will prove the blueprint for these regional arrangements, although they will advance in strength. Motivated by a resistance to a US-driven world economy and the recognition that on their own they cannot combat the power of the global leaders, the newer alliances will gradually become the more powerful global constituents. In the medium term, the European Union will significantly overtake the United States in economic influence. However, over time, with the advantages of technology and human resources, an Indian–Asian economic cluster will form including the new powerhouse economies of China and India, and will become the new world leaders. Economic integration and regional collaboration (and, in some cases, governance) will assist in eradicating the potential for major conflict in Asia, North America and Europe. Such cooperation will also naturally lead to the formation of regional sporting alliances and competitions, and eventually the development of interregional competition. Information and technology-sharing amongst regions will, for some countries, advance their performance in international sport rapidly.

While the potential for cooperation amongst Asia, North America and Europe is strong in this scenario, it is difficult to envisage a united, cooperative and competitive South America, Africa, Middle East or Eastern Europe. These regions are likely to be the losers in a globalisation scenario that continues to encourage regional development in order to compete with Western Europe and the United States. Thus, again, the economic nexus will deliver a sour taste of progress to parts of the world unable to play a part in a solid regional alliance. Sport will remain clustered within regions in this scenario, but will still have the potential to play a strong part in the emergence of the Dream Society. Sport organisations that have the capacity to hurdle these regional barriers and penetrate other markets will be rewarded. The progress of soccer in North America and the National Football League (NFL) and NBA in Europe will be measures of success. Many of the features of Vicious Sport Globalisation will also be found in this scenario, but will be confined to the boundaries of economic and technological zones of participation and spectating. We consider the likelihood of this alternative becoming the dominant scenario around 25 per cent.

Cultural sport globalisation

Instead of regional affiliation, cultural globalisation assumes that alliances will be constructed on the basis of ethnic, religious or ideological similarity, and may therefore cross vast territory without capitalising upon more local economic opportunities. The most likely scenario suggests that Western (largely Christian) nations will band together in trade, technology-sharing and military cooperation against Muslim and Hindu alliances. This cultural globalisation will be inefficient. Countries such as Australia and New Zealand will overlook the opportunities of trading with Asian nations in favour of Western European or North American associations. Similarly, the Middle East may prove uncooperative in sharing energy reserves and suffer the consequences in slow technological development. The potential for international conflict will loom larger than it has since the Cold War. China and India, both with nuclear capabilities, will largely go their own way, forming tentative trade affiliations when required. A number of emerging nations will suffer from severe internal crises, but will resist the intervention of Western nations that will be keen to install culturally friendly governments.

While this scenario again constricts the flow of sport into the world, probably limiting professional sport to Western nations, it does not exclude the possibility that sport will develop in culturally appropriate ways in the other cultures. This does not preclude the establishment of professional sport, but it does suggest that sport will remain subordinate to cultural and religious activities and values. In some parts of the world, sport will revert to its tribal beginnings, to serve community purposes, bolster ideological values and marshal political inspiration. The opportunities will revolve around the ability to provide culturally acceptable activities and sports. Although considerably escalated in likelihood as a consequence of the September 11 terrorist attacks, we believe the chances of this alternative are slim at around 10 per cent.

Final Comments

As with all human experience, we may have to travel to places far away, in order to realise how good it is to come home. After all, home is where the heart lies, where we are loved, where we love to be, and where we may gather around the safety of the fire to tell stories. Our prehistoric tribal ancestors were forced to be in touch with nature and were closer to our quintessential origins than any other human beings throughout our short, shared history. It may still take some time, even with the benefits of hindsight and advanced knowledge, to realise that third millennium *homo sapiens* have to come full circle in order to return to awaken an awareness in their own being. Our progression towards the Spiritual Sport Society may be one of the most important homecomings of humanity. The final model, presented in Figure 8.1, summarises the arguments we have put throughout this book that may play a part in this homecoming.

The trouble with any scenario is that it assumes a clean separation of possibilities. This is, of course, not always the way life turns out. For example, even within a Virtuous scenario there are always going to be losers, always another side of the coin. We must, ultimately, recognise that no scenario will dominate completely.

The purpose of this book, however, has been to establish the range of plausible alternatives that may emerge from the nexus. We have suggested that the economic, technological and cultural nexus' will determine our ride into the next incarnation of sport. Most likely, we will continue down the current path, as we described in Chapter 4, eventually culminating for the developed world in the DreamSport Society we explained earlier in this chapter. However, if technology abbreviates the gap between the sporting 'haves' and 'have nots', then the world of sport might play a pivotal role in the evolution of the Imagination Society. A pessimistic view of the role of the economy would lead us to believe that the world, and sport, will become more clustered and regionalised. If the cultural nexus fails to produce the increasingly liberalised values that the Virtuous scenario requires, then sport may find itself caught inside cultural boundaries.

You can be fooled into thinking that sport is cemented in the Gratification level, gradually emerging from the economic shadows to help people realise their emotional dreams, and that the world of sport is less about those bold enough to roll the dice, and more about those who own the dice. But the truth is that people will always seek to fulfil their deepest needs. Irrespective of the direction in which the mega multinational corporations push the humble sport consumer, the successful sport enterprise, now and in the future, will recognise that its duty is not to deliver what corporations tell us we cannot live without, but to use sport as a vehicle to help its consumers to achieve self-realisation and to decide for themselves what they really live for.

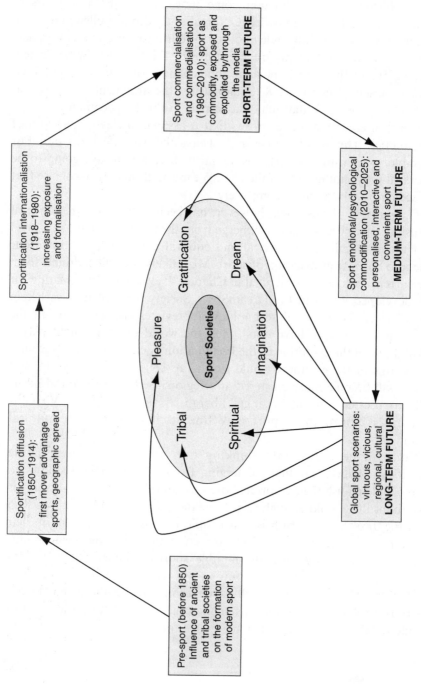

Sportification internationalistion (1918–1980): increasing exposure and formalisation

Sport commmercialisation and commedialisation (1980–2010): sport as commodity, exposed and exploited by/through the media **SHORT-TERM FUTURE**

Sportification diffusion (1850–1914): first mover advantage sports, geographic spread

Sport emotional/psychological commodification (2010–2025): personalised, interactive and convenient sport **MEDIUM-TERM FUTURE**

Sport Societies

Gratification

Dream

Pleasure

Imagination

Tribal

Spiritual

Pre-sport (before 1850) Influence of ancient and tribal societies on the formation of modern sport

Global sport scenarios: virtuous, vicious, regional, cultural **LONG-TERM FUTURE**

Figure 8.1 Sport in full circle

Brilliant Orange Finally Go all the Way!

Amsterdam, 10 July 2038. Celebrations are under way in Amsterdam where a whole nation indulges in the 'Orange Eleven's' victory in the World Cup final against Cameroon. In a capacity filled Manage-to-Manage Dome, 100,000 on-site spectators and 6 billion people worldwide celebrated a three-hour entertainment extravaganza culminating in a World Cup final that will be remembered for its brilliant soccer and mind-boggling drama.

First Time Ever Sell-out of Virtual Stadium

Pre-match entertainment started off in spectacular fashion with holo-grammatic appearances by Elvis Presley, Marilyn Monroe and Frank Sinatra, complemented by a live appearance of the Rolling Clones. Presley and Monroe performed the World Cup hymn, Sinatra treated the crowd to some classics from the last century and the Clones performed three songs from their first album, before they took the honours of kicking off the World Cup final.

The Dutch turned around what proved to be a high-scoring and equal contest throughout the four quarters of the match during extended play, when the score was still level at 4–4. Twenty minutes into extra time, after both teams were forced to take six players off the pitch (one player every three minutes) and goals were increased in height by 20 centimetres, cloned veteran striker Hans Westerbeek scored the golden goal. Wester-beek II was the first person in the world to be genetically modified with the help of 'top striker' DNA. Former Dutch great Marco van Basten donated his superior genetic material through FIFA's soccer development foundation, for a modest fee of course.

Nationality gene chip measurements indicate that 88.02 per cent of all Dutch in the world witnessed this moment live, 3.02 per cent on free to air television in the continent of Africa, 1.90 per cent on pay television, 23.12 per cent on the mobile Internet, 0.1 per cent on-site (predominantly backpackers who were willing to cope with the inconvenience of actually attending the event live at no cost) and a staggering 59.52 per cent virtually live, having bought tickets in the virtual Manage-to-Manage Dome. The Quantum Entanglement technology that was trialled first at the 2006 Commonwealth Games in Melbourne, Australia, has become so popular that the virtual Manage-to-Manage Dome was sold out for the first time in the history of digital virtual stadia. The technology has become so sophisticated that it only takes a contact lens-based microchip, with a wireless link to a MoGMeD (Mobile Global Media Device) to be transported to the stadium and interact with those who also subscribed to the match. So many people (3.2 billion worldwide) wanted to log on to the server powered through the international Duff beer space station that memory capacity to interact as a live spectator in the Dome ran out. The newly introduced violence protection chip was reported to work very well, with only minor clashes reported among non-football interested cyber-space fringes. Given the effectiveness of the violence protection chip, denying access to the stadium by any spectator who is genetically predisposed to cyber violence, the virtual police had little trouble containing the culprits.

Your Preferred City's Perfect Show

Long gone are the days of Sydney 2000, when Australia's time zone impacted on the ability of Olympic Games organisers to broadcast the top events into the world's major television markets' prime time slot. As widely reported, AOL Time Disney Corp, in an effort to control their exclusive rights to sport broadcasting, financed the development of the recently launched sun reflection shields that regulate the earth's atmosphere, climate and day/night cycle. Since then time zones have been abandoned in order to accommodate the complete standardisation and globalisation of the world economy. This, of course, has also led to all people on the globe being able to interact and be entertained independent of regional time differences or climatological uncertainty.

With the World Cup organised for the first time in one city, rather than a country, using only four stadia to schedule 64 games, yourcitytovisit.dig has signalled a new era of sport spectatorship. Matches were all scheduled during 'old economy' prime time and the selection of starting line-up of eleven players was based on spectator choice, validated by nationality gene chip statistics. Organisers in England performed well in their efforts to fill the stadia in order to create the 'old time' atmosphere for the players on the pitch. Local school children and a multitude of sport history tourists, who revelled in the opportunity to experience how sports spectatorship must have been ten years ago, attended most matches.

Since Canada is a particularly attractive tourist location for people of Dutch descent, Toronto was given the honour of hosting the final in the Dutch version of the virtual spectator programme. For Australians, however, London was the most popular location for the final. Ironically, this coincided with the actual location of the event. yourcitytovisit.dig, the broadband site that manages city marketing programmes for the top 100 cities in the world, indicated that to host the actual event at a location with perfect infrastructure (England) has worked well for them. A smoothly organised event ensures that all cities which host the World Cup final will benefit from the positive exposure they get from the event.

World Sport is World Politics

Following the Prince of Orange's decision to stay on as an IOC member when he was crowned King of the Netherlands in 2007, the politics of sport have become the forum of the politics of the world. With another eleven Heads of State appointed as IOC members since 2007, four of whom also occupy executive positions on the FIFA board, the most powerful sport organisations in the world have also become the informal boardrooms of world politics. Both FIFA and the IOC have what was lacking at headquarters of the now defunct United Nations in New York: products that unify the world, and resources that allow them to communicate with the world. Football, in that regard, has developed to become the planet's most comprehensive form of popular culture, a language that is spoken and understood by 97.89 per cent of the world's population. Microsplit, the offshoot of one of the biggest software companies of the previous century, has developed a translation package that allows people universally to understand each other by simply using football lingo. The lingual conversion sensor that drives the package transforms the football talk into the receiver's language.

For the Good of the Game, For the Better for All of Us

Holland's victory on the football field propels them to the top of the FIFA rankings, closely followed by the Australian and Chinese sides.

These rankings are one of the most important means of measuring a nation's narcissistic standing in the world, given its constituting statistics of the Global digital marketing index (country ranking), the Olympic medal tally adjusted by GDP, indexed performance in international football as a function of talent (DNA) development funding and player trade turnover. Although the Netherlands have consistently featured in the top ten of this ranking, given their leading position in the Global digital marketing index since 1999 and consistent Olympic performance since the 1996 Atlanta Games, their national coach, Dennis Bergkamp, knew that only a World Cup victory would be sufficient to wrestle the top spot from Australia. Even stratospheric supersonic travel has not convinced Bergkamp of the safety of air travel, which is why he chose to coach his team from the virtual bench. Virtual coaching facilities have been powered throughout the tournament through three separate servers, avoiding peak time viewer congestion with two servers as backup facilities in case of a breakdown. However, the FIFA top spot does not really matter to anybody since economic equalisation will ensure that the success of one nation will be used to the advantage of others that need extra support. Nations are also strictly abiding by the global GDP cap, and the draft for national leaders has ensured that the Third World countries of the last century have used their first-round picks sensibly and are well on their way to achieve GDPs that are equal to those of the former economic leaders of the world.

Football is now the only global religion and has also grown into the world's biggest industry, followed by space tourism and birth control pharmaceuticals. We are lucky that football as a unifying activity and platform for spiritual regeneration has also ensured that, finally, even the most powerful have understood that everything in life that matters is about teamwork. Because all of us can now be the best players, the stars of yesteryear cannot demand the bulk of the resources any more. And with the World Cup final alone making 77 billion Universals (€160 billion in the old European currency), football money is now used to feed the stabilising world population and is even funding part of the settlement of Mars. 'For the good of the game' has turned out for the better for all of us.

If you have any commentary, insights, remarks, opinions or queries in regard to this book, please let us know. Our contact details are listed below.

Hans Westerbeek and Aaron Smith
Manage to Manage
PO Box 74
Burwood, 3125, Victoria
Melbourne
Australia
www.manage-to-manage.com

westerbeek@manage-to-manage.com
smith@manage-to-manage.com

Index